Stuck in the Story
No More

Stuck in the Story No More

Breaking Down the Defenses
That Define You and Bind You

Dr. Nicki J. Monti

WALLA PRESS

BEVERLY HILLS, CALIFORNIA

Address inquiries to:
Dr. Nicki J. Monti
269 South Beverly Drive, Suite 430
Beverly Hills, CA 90212

Published by Walla Press
Beverly Hills, CA 90212
Call toll-free: 1-877-NOT-STUK

www.stucknomore.com

ISBN 0-9723004-5-7

Cover and interior artwork by Russell Naftal
Back-cover photograph by Linda Vanoff

First Printing: August 2002
Second Printing: January 2003

Printed in the United States of America

For my beloved Konrad

Who is constantly evolving as a husband

Who is amazingly relentless as a partner

Who is unfailingly persistent as an emotional and intellectual provocateur

Who is passionate as an advocate for me (and us)

Whose encyclopedic mind makes him a brilliant teacher

and

Whose huge heart makes him an extraordinary friend and enduring partner

Acknowledgments

First, I thank John Niendorff, the incredible word warrior, who was as much a writing instructor as he was my editor throughout this book project. He is the sculptor who molded this clay into comprehensible shape.

All along the path of my life, I have had astonishing mentors. From the start there was the late Basil Burwell, my first important teacher, who guided me sure-footedly over the rocky terrain of my childhood. My second important teacher was my profound friend Bodhi, who, over two decades ago, introduced me to a deeper version of spiritual exploration. Though Bodhi's body has passed, I feel as if he guides me still.

Among the living teachers, I thankfully acknowledge Nancy Steiny, M.F.C.T., whose constant, gentle insight and sly humor helped me grow up (in my life and in my work). I also gratefully acknowledge, above all other teachers, the brilliant, wondrous, and challenging W. Brugh Joy, M.D., whose perspectives entirely changed my personal and professional view of the way we human beings work, inside and out, and whose teaching style required new levels of emotional integrity from me.

For the constant professional and personal faith they have shown in my work, I thank my God Daughter, Elizabeth Shara; Cameron Thor and Alice Carter, William and Kazuko Hefner; Carmine and Bill Hogan; and Lee Garlington.

I wholeheartedly thank Margaret Cho for writing a generous Foreword. Her professional success is a wonderful example of how great creative work can (and does!) flow out of an individual's difficult personal history.

A particular thanks to Russell Naftal, whose ability to turn our cartoon brainstorms into charming visuals both delighted and surprised me.

A hats off to my glorious team: Hutt Bush, Donna Carsten, and Nina Knepper. All of them have valiantly contributed in pushing this book project forward.

A special thanks goes to Bill W., whose perspectives infuse and inform my life.

Also, I salute the greatest of teachers: my mother and my two fathers.

Finally, I would have no book at all without the countless clients who, over many years and on a daily basis, have trusted me to assist them with the deepest concerns of their lives. They have elaborated my understanding and opened my heart. Many were brave, others were hesitant; some screamed, others joked; some resisted, others persisted. Each one added to my understanding and appreciation of how we each can walk the often perilous but ultimately rewarding road of emotional recovery.

Contents

Foreword by Margaret Cho xi

Onward: Why Should You Listen to *Me?* xiii

Defending Your Life: *Recognizing those defenses that protect and sustain the basic belief system that keeps us stuck in our original story* 1

1. **The Nature of Defenses**: *Understanding what defenses are, where defenses come from, why defenses work, and when defenses work* 17

2. **Beware of Falling Rocks**: A Healing Alert
   Do & Don't guidelines for healthy communication 33

3. **Defense Profiles**: *A detailed exploration of forty-one fundamental defenses* 45

Hit (Connection) Defenses

ANGER—feelings of hostility 65

CONTEMPT FOR OTHERS—despising, negative, disdainful feelings toward other people 72

BLAME—feeling and believing that someone else is at fault 75

SPILLING—constant (often inappropriate) talking 79

GOSSIP—talking to someone about someone else who is not present 82

HUMOR—comical (sometimes inappropriate) self-expression 85

DEPENDENCE—excessive reliance on others 90

CODEPENDENCE—excessive reliance on people or things to define your self-worth 96

THERAPIZING—excessive (often unrequested) advice-giving 101

CONTROL—exercising a regulating or directing influence 105

CRITICISM—constantly finding fault 109

PROJECTION—using other people as a screen for unconscious thoughts and feelings 115

JUDGMENT—opinions that tend to be moral, critical, or righteous 122

COMPARING—measuring the way you feel against the way others appear 125

ANALYZING—intellectual examination that discounts emotional or intuitive factors 129

MASKING—saying one thing while feeling or thinking another 133

Run (Disconnection) Defenses

SHAME—your all-pervasive sense of basic defectiveness 139

SELF-CONTEMPT—using excessive expressions of self-disdain 145

FEAR—persistent feelings of eminent (emotional or physical) danger 149

VICTIM—feeling cheated, fooled, abused, or ignored by people and/or circumstances 156

WITHDRAWAL—emotional and even physical retreat 161

DEPRESSION—feelings of emotional, mental, and/or physical paralysis 165

TERMINAL UNIQUENESS—feelings of being completely different from other people 170

SPIRITUALITY—the use of excessive religious or spiritual referencing 174

CHAOS—vast, disordered confusion 180

COMPULSIVITY—impulsive, repetitious, self-defeating behavior 183

COUNTER-DEPENDENCE—stubborn self-reliance 187

PROCRASTINATION—putting things off until the last minute 190

WITHHOLDING—holding back emotionally and/or physically 194

PHYSICAL ILLNESS—constant, nagging, repetitive experiences of body problems 197

DISSOCIATION—emotional separation from everything and everyone 202

PARANOIA—assuming that people and/or circumstances are against you 208

GUILT—thinking you have done a bad thing 212

CONFUSION—emotional and/or intellectual ambivalence and disorder 216

INTELLECTUALIZATION—excessive analyzing, pondering, mapping, exploring, investigating . . 219

DENIAL—refusing to accept (an obvious) truth 222

SKEPTICISM—excessive, pervasive negativity and doubt 225

OBSESSION—repetitive focus on an idea, feeling, person, or thing 228

SELF-ABSORPTION—excessive self-centeredness 232

FANTASY—preoccupation with illusory notions 237

PERFECTIONISM—insisting upon *excessively* high standards 241

4. **Yesterday's Tales**: *Stories that platform our lives* 247

5. **A New View**: *The tale yet to be told* 273

   Appendix: *Fifteen steps in defense busting* 279

Foreword

When you work with Dr. Nicki, expect nothing less than a complete transformation.

I walked into her office, what now seems like a hundred years ago, in a state of utter depression. The darkness would not lift no matter what I did. After a short period of sobriety, I was a compulsive overeater, a shopping addict, a sexaholic, and a drama queen. Not only that, I thought that since I didn't use drugs or alcohol, I had it all under control.

I was angry at the whole world, taking it out not only on myself but also on my long-suffering boyfriend. Lashing out at him for virtually no reason at all, I was a nightmare to be with. I realized I needed help. It wasn't that I cared about our relationship all that much; it was the magnitude of my rage that terrified me.

Why was I so unhappy? Why did I hate my body? Why did I loathe and despise men? No longer able to deny my feelings, I realized I had to face my troubles head-on. I went to Dr. Nicki, not knowing what to expect. I had been in therapy before, and it made me hate myself even more. Just listening to myself whining to a stranger was the last thing that would help me—or so I thought.

Nicki looked less like a doctor and more like a fairy godmother. Here was this green eyed, red-hot mama draped in black and ivory silk, jangly with expensive bracelets, with a fiery shock of auburn hair framing a calm and serenely beautiful face, ready to hear all the pain of the world with her bejeweled ears. I thought, "Oh, good. Auntie Mame has finally gotten her therapy license."

I sank in her rose damask couch and told her that when my boyfriend held me in his arms, I wanted to punch him in the face. I told her a little about my history, my story that I was stuck in, the neglect and violence I had experienced that never failed to get a reaction from even the most hardened listeners.

Dr. Nicki wasn't buying it. She fixed me in her gaze and proceeded to "unzip" me. That is the only way I can describe it. She told me that I wasn't thin because I didn't want to be, that I wasn't satisfied in my relationship because I didn't want to be, that I wasn't happy because I didn't want to be. I was so angry, I wanted to leave right then and there, but I didn't. I stayed—because I knew somewhere deep inside that she was right. And what she said after that changed everything about the way I had viewed life up until then. What she told me is in this book.

I worked with Dr. Nicki individually and also in her classes, in which we used the exercises that are outlined in *Stuck in the Story*. My defenses: anger, contempt for others, codependence, compulsivity, and many, many more were sticky to work through. I am eternally grateful, not only to the good doctor, but also to the students who walked alongside me from the deep darkness into the light. A few of them became the best friends I have ever had.

I have experienced quite a metamorphosis (incidentally, the title of Nicki's final, and most advanced course). I am at peace. I have a body I love to be in. I am more successful in my career than I ever dreamed I would be. I laugh and cry all the time because life is so beautiful. Most important, I am happy. Truly, madly, blissfully, gratefully happy.

Dr. Nicki J. Monti saved my life, and she continues to save the lives of countless others on a daily basis. She is not just a therapist. She is healer, teacher, lama, shaman, friend, artist, mystic, mirror, mother, scholar, superhero, diplomat, comedienne author, genius, goddess—in one very fashionable package. I am so glad that her teachings are now available to those who are not able to work with her personally, that her ideas are out there, healing the world.

Be glad you have found this book. I am so glad for you. Let Dr. Nicki be your guide for the most exciting journey of all. The one that leads you to yourself.

— MARGARET CHO

Onward

WHY SHOULD YOU LISTEN TO *ME?*

To my readers—

It's funny to hear myself described as the fantastic Margaret Cho describes me. Funny and jaw-dropping at the same time. Sure, for a long time I've thought of myself as outside the mainstream! Yes, I may be a little flamboyant. And indeed I have often been described as an in-your-face therapist—a description that makes me proud, since directness and truth-telling are two of my basic professional tools. However, when I hear some of her extravagant praise, though I'm grateful for her generous assessment, I also tend to wheeze and cough with embarrassment.

Who am I really? I am a woman who, for much of her life, dragged herself over the narrow, perilous road that winds along the cliff's edge and who, most likely due to God's good grace, was spared a deadly fall off into the adjacent abyss—spared long enough at least to learn a little something along the way.

What I've learned is this: none of us needs to (or should) feel defeated by the experiences of our lives. Everything that happens gives *to* us more than it takes *from* us—if we know how to take what is given. I've also learned—and this is fundamental to all I now believe and teach—that everything we do, from start to finish, is about *relationship*—the relationships we have with ourselves and the relationship we have to others. How we play out those relationships decides how great our life *feels* from moment to moment, from day to day, and from decade to decade.

For a long time, I didn't know life might be offering me anything. I did all I could to prove true my worst ideas about myself. That included interlacing my life for years with the compulsive use of drugs, alcohol, food, over-spending, and men of every imaginable type—all with a desperation that oozed out of my every pore like sweat on a hot summer day. For many of those same years I tried also to find relief through spirituality, sensuality, and workaholism. But nothing, and I mean nothing, quieted the screaming inside me.

Finally, when nothing else seemed to work and I was at my wits' end, I thought I'd try sobriety. The year was 1982. That's when a new life began for me.

But beginnings are rough, and now I truly had to *feel* my life. I certainly did not like what I started feeling, yet there really was no way out of the feelings. Once I'd collapsed that damn protective wall, everything started pouring out! Open the way for one emotion and, like young children at recess, they all start racing onto the playground, screaming for attention. Or just plain screaming.

At first, everything came out mostly in the form of anger. The rage in me found its way free. Rage toward anyone, at any place, about whatever might be in front of me. I became a crusty thing, draped in a heavy, scratchy, unpleasant overcoat of protective energy. No one could get in. No one. Still, at the same time, my great hunger for love and attention, my need to make up for what I felt I'd never received, overtook me. Yet I had to find a way to stop the flood of vitriol. I had to find a way to open my heart.

In my life to that point, I'd worked for other people in dozens of different jobs and owned several businesses. None of this work had ever truly scratched my itchy itch. Then, I got a bright idea for a new business. I recognized that this idea would clearly fare better if I had some additional degrees behind my name. My young goddaughter wisely reasoned that a psychology degree would best serve me in my efforts. Seemed like a good idea! After all, I could run some more by getting really busy. So I ran again. This time back to school. "Keep moving, keep moving. Don't feel, don't feel. I'm too afraid to love. Too afraid. Maybe later," I thought. By September 1983, I had secured a training internship at the prestigious Southern California Counseling Center—a wonderful teaching environment for therapists.

It was my birthday.

I was doing what is called an "intake session"—in which I conducted preliminary interviews with clients to determine who might be the best kind of therapist for them to see. I was sitting there observing how, because I was still so green as a therapist-in-training, I really had very little idea of what I was doing. Suddenly a wild recognition made its way into my thoughts. It was this: "For the first time—the very first time in my whole life—I *know* I am in the *right* place at the *right* time." I took a deep breath as a sweet wave of gratitude washed over me. I felt as if, finally, I had come home.

That day in 1983 truly was a birth-day for me—a realization that my life had simply been waiting for me to find it—to find it, accept it, and embrace it. Since then, I've never looked back.

Of course, I am and always will be a work in progress. Still it's fair to say that little by little, over the years—through amazing teachers, a self-help program, and my own relentless pursuit of truth—I have fundamentally healed the gaping wounds that once had driven me to destructive actions and interactions.

At one memorable juncture, when I realized that healing *had* occurred and I felt really good, I asked myself *how* I'd done all of the things I'd done. You, my readers, are certainly familiar with that kind of question: you've walked far along a certain path and all at once, in a startling moment, you realize that you're not sure if you remember where you started!

Well, I didn't want to forget. Further, I wanted to remember the features of that path in sharp detail—so I could present them clearly and concisely to others, offering an understanding of the same awakening I had myself enjoyed. That, in turn, meant writing it all down.

Among the key aspects I wanted to present was and is my certainty that everything we do, from start to finish, is about *relationship*—the relationship we have with ourselves and the relationship we have to others. How we play out those relationship structures decides how great our life *feels* from moment to moment, from day to day, and from decade to decade.

This book—the result of my recognition and my remembering—is about the defenses that run us and ruin us, that hold us back from having the lives we dream of having. Above all else, it presents the good news that by acquiring the tools to understand the ways in which defenses direct or interrupt our lives, we can really, truly, actually, finally help ourselves to be Stuck in the Story No More!

Love,

Nicki

DEFENDING YOUR LIFE

From the beginning

When I was seven, my mother sent me to boarding school in Ojai, a small, rural town in Southern California. At that time, and in fact for all the years of my childhood, Mother traveled the country selling advertising. At first she traveled alone and later with the man who eventually became my adopting father. On vacations or in the summer, I flew from school to wherever they were working. Mom and I would stay in motels or even sometimes apartments. I never knew anyone in these towns and was always very, very lonely.

I am thinking now of the early days. My first year away from home—when it was just Mom and me. I must have been seven. It was vacation time and I flew in from school to . . . somewhere. We were staying in one of the hundreds of motels that mark the years of my childhood. We had one small but nice room with two double beds, across from which sat a light wooden dresser with a television on top.

Now, when I was a kid, I was scared of everything . . . of thunder, of lightning, of noises, of monsters hiding in open closets, of the dark and, of course, of being alone.

My mother, on the other hand, was seldom alone. No matter where we traveled, it seemed, she managed to find men. That night as I watched Mom dress for her date, I got real, real scared. I cannot remember what frightened me. I tried to be grown-up. I tried and tried but just couldn't stand it. I did not want to be alone. Could not be alone. Would not be alone.

I started asking Mother not to leave. She kept dressing. As I became more and more insistent that she stay, I suspect she began to get frustrated. I suppose she told me not to be silly—that I should act like a big girl. But I did not feel big. I felt seven.

Soon I was pleading and begging—begging her to stay. I am certain she was angry. I do not remember what she said. I only remember a stark, unrelenting terror ripping at me. I cried and cried. I could not stop.

My mother got madder and madder. Finally, she took her nylon-bristled hair brush and began spanking me really hard. I remember the sting of the bristles. I screamed and wept. She spanked and spanked. But still I begged her to stay. *Don't leave me alone! Don't leave me! Don't leave!*

I thought I would die.

My mother finished spanking me, told me to turn off the TV in an hour, and left.

I do not remember what really happened after she left, but in my mind's eye I see that little seven-year-old, her hazel eyes red and huge with fear, her tiny face streamed with beggar's tears. I imagine that child lying on the bed feeling the darkness close around her like a vampire's cape. I imagine her wondering what happened . . . why she was spanked. I hear the child say, "I'm sorry Mommy . . . I'm sorry . . . ."

As I scroll through this memory, I see the picture dissolve like the ending of a film.

After that night, the lights went out . . . for a long, long time.

———··✄··———

This, a typical childhood experience for me, only reinforced the suspicions and suppositions that were quickly becoming an integral part of my basic belief system—the belief system from which I would operate for many years. Already in my young life, I had come to *expect* to be lonely and unloved. Now I began also to assume that no one could or would respond to my cries of pain. Better to keep that pain to myself. When I was sad, therefore, I hid my tears. No one would hear me pleading anyway.

I already knew I was not my mother's first priority—and I came now to believe that I did not *deserve* to be her first priority, therefore I began to work on developing independence and self-sufficiency. I learned to live with loneliness and to expect loneliness. It was obvious, after all, that I was unworthy of attention.

I would spend many of the years that followed waiting alone in the dark, leading my life day after day, year after year, as if the tales that had been told were carved in stone. This was my story . . . and I was stuck with it.

Stories as patterns

Each of you, everyone who is reading this book, has stories like this, some more difficult, some less difficult—stories that describe you and your life. They are tales of horror, tales of woe, remembrances of neglect, or incidents filled with fear. They are old, shabby stories, so often told or thought of that they are worn through. They are the stone-carved stories in which you, the storyteller, are stuck.

There are many different ways we can deal with our own remembrances. Some of us *refuse to let go* of our more horrible recollections—and instead we flail around in them, regaling anyone who will listen. Some of us *refuse to acknowledge* that there even *were* any childhood difficulties—telling tales of a perfect life with perfect parents. And still others of us remember the early woes, but *dismiss their importance*—acting as if their effect dissolved upon impact, leaving no residue. But however we choose to deal with these stories, the fact remains: they did happen and they are still locked in our memory.

Now if each of us had only one or two riveting experiences of horror—one or two stunning, life-changing, negative past events—perhaps we could easily get over them and move on with our lives. In fact, that's what often happens. A difficult or even terrible thing occurs, we handle it in some fashion, then go on living. Only in highly charged, devastating cases (such as sudden and permanent physical injury, the unexpected death of a loved one, or the birth of a physically or mentally impaired sibling) are individual events—regardless of how startling or painful—impactful enough by themselves to *create* the (destructive) thoughts and feelings that can continue for the rest of our lives.

Rather, what usually happens is that each separate experience of trauma—of neglect, abandonment, or ridicule, for instance—is really a reflection of an overall *pattern* of similar events, a pattern that is reinforced over time by many comparable experiences.

Think about it. Does it make sense that the woman who was willing to leave a young child alone in a strange room in a strange city did such a thing only once? Not really. This behavior most likely *exemplified* her parenting style. It suggests, therefore, that she made similar decisions

Repeated events create the patterns that describe our lives

again and again. That kind of constant *repetition*—even if it's slightly modified now and then—is what eventually establishes *our story*.

After that story is established, it is held in place by the system of defenses we have carefully constructed. To live fully, however, we need to get through—in fact, we need to *bust* through—those defenses. Thus, to augment the defense-busting theme of this book, I have weaved fifteen major defense-busting *steps* into the pages that follow. All are related directly to the text nearby, and you can start using each of them immediately. We begin with:

Step 1 in defense busting:
Identify the childhood patterns that still color your life.

Defense mechanisms

For many of us, childhood included nearly intolerable growing pains, as often we were dubbed too sensitive, too demanding, too quiet, too noisy, too slow, too quick, or simply too much. In response, like a stone rolling down a mossy hill, we began to cover ourselves in stories about our horrible world and our horrible selves. Those stories, repeated frequently enough, soon became our "truths": *Everything is all my fault. A cruel life is my lot. I don't deserve much. Everyone in the world is untrustworthy and selfish. No one really cares about me.* And they also increased our pain—pain we needed to keep at bay, no matter what.

In response, we began developing powerful inner mechanisms called *defenses*. They were our shield and our sword—protecting us from the monsters in the closet and the terrors in our heart. At first, these mechanisms—to which we later gave such names as *Withdrawal* or *Perfectionism* or *Anger* or *Compulsivity*—had the desired effects. They made life tolerable and created the illusion that we felt comfortable. Eventually, though, that self-protection turned into self-confinement and the result turned out to be that we had become stuck.

At that point, we started having all kinds of problems, because our defenses began intruding upon our ability to succeed (with relationships, money, friends, career). The worse we felt inside, the worse we felt in the world. Our so-called protectors, then, started draining us of energy and robbing us of glee. The worse we felt in the world, the worse we felt inside.

If you're reading this book because you feel trapped the way I felt trapped, you are caught in a dizzying maze of assumptions. These assumptions support the story you've constructed about yourself and your life. You are convinced and convincing about these assumptions. The more you repeat them, the more you believe them. The more you believe them, the more you must defend against them. By now, your defenses (beliefs, postures, thinking, behaviors) have become the glue that keeps your story lines in place. You're stuck like a fly to flypaper.

This book is about those sticky defenses—where they come from, how you can identify them, and also how you can begin to tear yourself free. You will do this by coming to recognize how and when to rightly use your defenses. In other words, the defenses that have grown ferocious and come to run your life must now be tamed, being transformed thereby from a vicious enemy into an accommodating ally.

How we develop

Two fundamentally different explanations can be cited to explain how we develop psychologically. They are, essentially, current versions of the old nature-nurture debate: we are *born* as who we are, or we *become* who we are, or something in between. For me, the "in-between" or "mixture" approach holds the most truth. That is, I believe the events in our lives have had an obvious and undoubted effect on us, but I also believe *they reflect and elaborate tendencies present within us from birth.* Those tendencies and the reactions dictated by those tendencies will have as many repercussions as do the events. Some people, for example, are born with a fundamentally aggressive personality, while others tend (naturally) to hold back. Some individuals are inherently thought-full and others are feeling-full; some people are more artistic, some more mechanical, and on and on. Each of these personality "types" is likely to respond differently to similar circumstances.

From the time we were three or four year old, these essential characteristics began to surface. Some of us moved spontaneously to leadership while others followed. Some exhibited an easy independence and others couldn't wait to share and move toward *inter*dependence. Whether we ran away or fought back, spoke up or shut down, involved ourselves or hid out, what we did was a product not only of what we had experienced and been taught, but also of our nature. Because we are, then, a *combination of nature <u>and</u> nurture*, the direction of our lives, I believe, is not determined *solely* by *what* happens to us or even by *how many times it happens*, but rather by the effects of what happens on the potential already present within us that is waiting to be triggered by external events. Even with a highly charged, devastating circumstance of abuse, neglect, or other trauma, our unique, inborn (or natural) responses to what occurs will likely determine as much about the after-effects of the circumstance as will the details of the circumstances itself.

Our life's direction is primarily determined by the way external events trigger our natural potential

Step 2 in defense busting:
Recognize and appreciate your own particular, natural style.

Thus, we have developed a story about ourselves that is based to a significant degree on how our essential natural (inner) self responds to

*Our story
takes shape
when
nature
meets
nurture*

the various (outer) influences and experiences of life. These outer influences and experiences include: (a) general social attitudes and the way they are reflected in our particular community and in our lives (these attitudes involve such matters as race, gender, ethnicity, physical appearance, and intelligence); (b) the quality and kind of education we receive; (c) our birth order and family size (are you the oldest, middle, or youngest, and how big is your family?); and (d) our peer-member influences (friends, classmates, even casual acquaintances). For a few of you, this story forecasts a happy, successful life. But for many others, it leaves you thinking of yourself as flawed and damaged—and you feel stuck in that damage.

What lies beneath

The worst part of being stuck is that we start to believe the way life is right now is the way it must always be. We get this idea because when we look at the unpleasant and unfulfilling aspects of our lives, we feel powerless over them and mystified as to why they occur the way they do. We have *no idea at all* how the particular situations and people in our lives came to be there. It all feels beyond us.

Well, I believe it is not beyond us—it is, in fact, a part *of* us.

You are probably quite certain that you're being guided through daily life by an intentional mind—a mind reacting as it must to circumstances and to people. This so-called intentional mind is usually described as being *conscious*. I believe, however, that we are actually seldom directed by a conscious mind, but are more often guided by what is called the *un*conscious—a crusty, deep-dish pie of ingredients that include myths, distortions, and long-ago-established defenses. And worse still, this unconscious driver—who most often bases new direction on old history—has come to the ludicrous (and currently irrelevant) decision that we're better off *with* our problems (of relationship, finances, career, friendship) than without them. Change, the unconscious mind thinks, is too difficult, forbidding, or dangerous! It turns out, then, that *critically influential <u>unconscious</u> reasoning* is what leads to much of the trouble in our day-to-day life.

What this means is that problematic circumstances and difficult people come into our lives mostly as a result of our own choices. But because the reasoning that brings them into our lives is *unconscious,* we don't *know* we're the ones who are doing what's being done. We have no idea that we are in charge of what's happening. So we do not know we're following our own directions when this unconscious reasoning tells us to *expect to be hurt*, and we therefore place ourselves in hurtful situations; or when this unconscious reasoning insists that we must *expect to fail*, and we then sabotage our lives; or when this relentless unconscious reasoning directs us to *expect to be alone*, and we seek out the kinds of people who reinforce our loneliness.

Spotting your unconscious intentions

If these intentions are hidden, how can you identify them? It's simpler than you think! To make this identification, merely look at your life—at the way it works in terms of what is and what is not happening to you. In other words, the evidence of our intentions will be seen in the realities of the life we lead. Initially this may seem like trying to identify a fast-moving bird, but eventually it will be like spotting an elephant in Times Square.

Appreciating two important ideas will facilitate your spotting these unconscious intentions.

The evidence of our intention is to be seen in the realities of our life

☀

Idea #1: We have what we want. What we don't have, we don't want. To really embrace this startling notion, you need to examine your yearnings in a new way. Do you think you want a mate but still don't have one? Then stop saying you want a relationship, and (to the contrary) consider that you don't have one because unconsciously you don't *want* one—perhaps because you think (unconsciously) that having a relationship will limit you or damage you. If you have no friends, consider that you have no friends for some "good" though presently unconscious reason, and start to figure out what that reason might be. If you're troubled about being broke all the time, consider that your struggle over money is a response to some unconscious process that leads you to thrive on money-worries or poverty. A well-known proverb declares that "the road to hell is paved with good intentions." Perhaps instead we should say that the road to hell is paved with unconscious intentions—of all kinds.

Your first response to such a notion is likely to be disbelief. Feeling blamed for your own difficulties, you might proclaim, "I don't want these problems. They're not my fault—what are you talking about?" But this thinking does not fix blame, either on you or on others! Rather, it asks you to stake a claim on the truth. Here's the good news—if what you have is, on some level, what you intend to have, then by truly changing your intention, you can actually change what you have, and thereby change the course of your life!

Step 3 in defense busting:

Understand that what you have is what you (unconsciously) want.

·☼·

Idea #2: All behavior has a payoff. We can recognize the payoffs of our attitudes and behaviors most easily by noticing the *effects* of those attitudes and behaviors on our lives. For instance, let's say your fear is that you will always be alone. You try not to talk much about it, thinking your belief is a secret, but what is likely is that even your unspoken attitudes and actions—which may subtly be revealed through hesitation (looking, for instance, like shyness), impatience (looking, for instance, like desperation), or extreme criticism (looking, for instance, like a tendency to be rejecting)—register on the people with whom you come in contact. Those people, then, will (unconsciously or consciously) react to these attitudes and beliefs, and before you know it, you will have successfully achieved the very thing you *say* you least want—aloneness. Of course, you may achieve this aloneness even more directly, by simply choosing not to seek the company or friendship of others. Regardless, as an individual who makes this choice, you surely have a list of "good" reasons for doing so—you're too busy, everyone else is too busy, no one likes you, you don't know where or how to meet people, you're too shy, and on and on. Whatever the reasons, the effect is the same: you're lonely. This is an example of the way we are *driven by our inner decision-maker*.

We are driven through life by an unconscious decision-maker

Step 4 in defense busting:
Realize that *all* behavior has a payoff.

After your first glance at the more obvious payoffs ("I believe I will always be alone; I find reasons and ways to reject partnership; I am therefore alone"), you will want to dig a little deeper into the underlying beliefs that support your behavior. Even loneliness, for instance, has its payoffs. To name but a few: your loneliness proves Dad was right when he said no one could love you; loneliness keeps you from having to face the pain of another loss (after all, you can't lose what you never had); remaining lonely prevents you from having to confront the responsibilities associated with relationships.

DADDY'S GOODBYE

Talking about Dad, I remember it as though it were yesterday. I was around four. We stood on the back porch, Daddy and I. Daddy was a handsome man: dark wavy hair, dimples, and sparkling hazel eyes. He had a mustache that tickled my cheeks when he hugged me, and he had marks on his face from long-ago chicken pox. Daddy was a handsome man.

He told me he was going away for a little while. He held me and said he would be back. He said he would write.

I sobbed in Daddy's arms, begging him not to go. "You won't come back, you won't come back," I choked.

"Yes, baby, I will. I promise. I'll be back."

I stood there on the porch long after he left. Waiting. Sobbing. And as I knew, Daddy—after going off to have a new life that did not include me—never came back.

Forty years passed before I recognized my father's leave-taking as *the very moment* I decided that, for me, abandonment was inevitable and would always occur. That means the frightened seven-year-old with Mom in the lonely motel room had already been well-schooled in the matter, which may be why that child's fear was so enormous.

Early on, then, I began (unconsciously) acting and feeling in accord with my most pain-filled beliefs—responding to the majority of circumstances not as newly-encountered (even sometimes benign) experiences, but rather, as if they were actual reenactments of the original "traumatic" event. Have you, perhaps, done the same?

To defend against the pain of this abandonment expectation, and in accord with my nature, I chose a strong, "independent" stance for myself. Like the previous generations in my family, I would be a bread-winning, career-oriented superwoman.

For years I answered this unconscious call. *People cannot not be trusted*, I told myself. *Especially men. Yes, men cannot be trusted. Everyone's out for themselves!* I told myself. Mother felt this way, Grandmother felt this way, and I felt this way. ***I would never be safe.***

Feeling safe

Wait a minute. How did safety get into this story? Well, it turns out that safety—which goes hand-in-glove with trust—is one of the first bridges to collapse under the weight of our stories. Because our parents (and sometimes other family members, peer-members, or teachers) taught us various facts when we were children about whether we could or should feel safe, we often act *now* as if we are still those children— with no more resources, no more ability to cope, than we had then.

Please do not mistake what I'm saying here. Risk *is* real at particular times and places. For instance, walking in certain neighborhoods at night is not safe. Nor is meeting in person and alone with every Internet connection we make. Those are matters of good sense in the face of genuinely threatening or potentially threatening situations. However, the safety issue to which I refer here is not so much about what others *actually* do, as it is about what we perceive they *might* do. Thus, our feeling of threat can be present no matter how benign the circumstances or non-threatening the individuals around us may be. The question therefore becomes: how vulnerable are you willing to get in the face of your fearful feelings?

The idea that our sense of safety is based on what other people do is a misconception. In fact, our emotional and psychological safety mostly have very little to do with others. Rather, safety is primarily a matter of how we feel inside about *ourselves.* In other words, your hesitation to expose yourself emotionally is actually about your inability (or perceived inability) to withstand other people's responses to you. This doesn't mean you simply "need time" before you can feel safe with others. Nor does it mean you are just responding reasonably to the fact that the world really isn't a safe place! Instead, it turns out that your insecurity is based on a fear that you will, in some way, crumble in the face of others' responses to you. Can you count on yourself to survive how they might feel or what they might say? Are you up to handling the challenge of disappointing others when you tell your truth or show them who you are, warts and all? Can you withstand seeing the evidence of your own imperfection reflected in their eyes?

Fear stimulates insecurity

Insecurity expects betrayal

To go forward into a healthy life, you must recognize that you've had years of practice making your own decisions, and now you can use your power as a resourceful individual to make *better* decisions and have a more fulfilling life.

Step 5 in defense busting:
Realize that feeling safe is an inside job.

As you can see, we often take the specific concerns and beliefs that have been inspired by particular events (*"I will be abandoned and am not safe"*) and apply those concerns in a general way to our lives. Once we have become aware that hidden dynamics exist, sought to associate the symptoms with the unseen causes, and then worked to bring those causes to awareness, we need to establish *new* attitudes and take *new* actions. These new attitudes and actions will allow us to feel safe as we create and venture out into a different kind of life.

A terrific personal example of how we impose old ideas on new, unrelated circumstances is evidenced in the following story—a recent tale about another leave-taking.

Establish new attitudes

Take new actions

MY HUSBAND'S GOODBYE

My husband Konrad was leaving for an exploratory trip to New Guinea. The trip had been a gift to him from me, though it was not a journey on which I would join him.

I wanted to be excited for him. After all, this was the excursion of a lifetime and my own idea. However, as the day of his departure approached, I became more and more agitated. Despite all of my efforts, this agitation flourished and I became obviously and visibly irritable. Konrad was distraught. This was certainly not the sendoff for which he had hoped.

Just before he was to leave, we were in our living room talking— once again about my lamentable attitude, my aggravated mood.

At one point I found myself snuggled onto his lap. I was feeling smaller and smaller. As he held me, I began to sob. The tears flooded out unabated. It was a child's cry. Then I heard myself say, "I know it's stupid, but I just feel you're never coming back . . . never coming back."

At that moment, as I sat on my husband's lap, the memory of my father's "abandonment" came before me with intense clarity. I saw how even at that moment, forty years later, I was assuming that my husband would do to me what my father had done. This was one of those reenactment-of-the-original-trauma moments! Obviously what I needed to recognize was that *my husband is _not_ my father*. As the truth of this recognition slowly dawned on me, my anxiety lifted.

Unfortunately, this initial realization was not enough to prevent the (later) recurrence of my defensive behavior. Like most people, understanding—even startling, sudden, revolutionary understanding—is just the beginning, an announcement of what needs attention. Eventually I had to dive deep down into myself—into the dank pool where slime-covered old ideas live—and wait to slither on to (unrelated) current circumstances. Wait to erode the potential joy offered by today's experiences.

Step 6 in defense busting:

Notice the way yesterday's ideas are affecting today's happiness.

I began to reassess prior relationships. Doing this forced me to acknowledge how often I had sought untrustworthy and undependable men, men who would meet my grim expectations (as I no doubt met theirs), men who would confirm my sad story. And now, when I came across men who were *reliable*, I denied their reliability and vilified them anyway. I was empowered by recognizing this strategy, for it allowed me to realize how much authority I could have, both over my choices and also over my *responses* to those choices. To you, the readers of this book, I offer the same authority.

CHAPTER 1

THE NATURE OF DEFENSES

Home again

When I was thirty-one years old, I decided the time had come to reconnect with the biological father who left when I was four—the one who said he'd come back and never did. After tracking him down, I spent several days with him at his home in Florida. While I was there, he excused much about himself and apologized for little. At one point he told me the following tale in a self-satisfied way—as if to say he was a wonderful parent, and I would certainly have been much better off if he'd stayed.

My father's story was as follows: "You were around two or three years old. Your grandparents had given you this big life-size doll. You loved that doll and dragged her everywhere with you. You played with the doll, ate with the doll—even slept with the doll.

"One day you ran out into the street without looking—as children tend to do. I wanted you to know how dangerous that was. So I took

17

your doll and, as you watched, put it in the driveway, got in my car, and ran back and forth over it until it broke into a million pieces."

Then he concluded proudly, "You never again ran into the street!"

Although I did not remember this incident, I was moved by hearing it, picturing the little girl's response to her father's "teaching." *Don't trust anyone* is the first thought I imagined having had. The second was, *the people who are supposed to protect you will only hurt you.*

Again, however briefly he had been involved with my life, my biological father had an effect that was (unconsciously) deadly and long-lasting. But I'd gone so far underground emotionally that I hadn't realized it. I'd blocked out most early memories—including that dramatic doll-smashing.

In any event, those blocking defenses probably helped . . . at first. But as I came into young adulthood, my *involuntary* habit of emotional retreat—my *forgetting* horrid things that were said and done to me—became a crippling feature of my personality. Relationships failed. Long-term, worthwhile connections were nonexistent, and therefore I lived lonely inside myself. Of course, to look at me one might not have known it. People seemed to think I had it together. But what it looked like was not what it felt like. I had successfully followed the family rules. I trusted no one and expected betrayal by everyone.

The problems

Defenses promote as many problems as they alleviate

It does not take long to realize that defenses (like my stonewalling others and refusing to depend on anyone outside myself) *promote* as many problems as they *alleviate*. The question quickly becomes: How can mechanisms intended to protect and serve turn out to cause such problems? There are four reasons and ways:

First: defenses eventually *take over our lives.* Over time we lose control of how and when our defenses become active. Then they start popping up spontaneously, like uninvited guests, and we are no longer in charge of our own conduct. Instead, we must watch helplessly as our defenses twist our occasional, cute little barbed bursts of wittiness into constant sarcasm, or turn our charming ways of quietly observing situations from afar into humiliating shyness.

Second: defenses *reinforce stuckness*. Defenses imbue us with a certain manner. The process works this way. We begin with an impersonal fact: "Daddy left and never came back." We follow that with a (usually erroneous) personal interpretation, such as, "He left because I'm unlovable." That interpretation is succeeded by a line of thinking guaranteed to attach us to our original painful story: "I have been abandoned because I am unlovable and I will always be abandoned by everyone, because I will always be unlovable." Since we thus know ourselves to be unlovable, in addition to defensively holding ourselves away from others in general, we create a defensive double-check to make sure no one can get close enough to see our unlovable self. To do this, we adopt a certain "stay away from me" *manner*. We might become strident, sullen, or reluctant, or display other evidence of unpleasantness or unavailability—whatever best reflects our natural proclivities. However we decide to be, the result is the same. We end up reinforcing what we believe to be true—that "no one can love me because I am unlovable." And the evidence is all around.

Third: defenses *pass on the pain*. When we react defensively we impact others, often in negative ways. We already know how quickly someone else's bad day can become our bad day. So consider it in reverse. Imagine the potential influence of your own erratic emotional temperature on others—how your uncontained chaotic behavior might affect your coworkers, how contempt might impact the mood of the friends you deal with every day, or how emotional inconsistency might disconcert your family.

Defenses—

* Take over our life
* Reinforce stuckness
* Pass on the pain
* Require huge amounts of energy

Fourth: defenses *require huge amounts of energy*. Focusing on protection is draining and leaves little energy for productive living. Even the most zestful human being has limitations with regard to expenditures of energy and power, and when those expenditures are concentrated on self-protection through defense, the possibility of vigorous activity in other areas (such as creativity, building healthy relationships, and passionate support for a career) is restricted.

We start out by building a fortress wall around our property to protect ourselves from home invasion, theft, unwanted visitors, and curious onlookers. At first this wall does the trick—it guards us well. But over the years, we find that we are slowly, almost imperceptibly, *imprisoned* by the very wall we built to serve us. We have forgotten how to open the gate and allow access—even when doing so is desirable. The hinges have rusted in place; the bolt is permanently locked.

But how did this happen? To answer that question, we must first understand *what* defenses are, *where* defenses come from, *why* defenses work, *how* defenses work, and *when* defenses work.

What are defenses?

A defense is first and foremost a psychological mechanism of *self-protection*. What we are so ferociously protecting ourselves from turns out in almost all cases to be *fear*—an enormous inner fear of facing the hurts and heartbreaks of life; fear of facing the ravages of our own devastating memories; fear of various foes (actual or perceived); fear of other people (whether or not those people are really fear-provoking); fear of our own desires; fear of our own vulnerable feelings; fear of the unknown; and even fear of fear itself. We are afraid of these things because we anticipate that they will be—psychologically (inwardly) and/or physically (outwardly)—traumatic, disruptive, or undermining. In other words, we are afraid of the world both inside *and* around us.

Actually, if you were to look carefully, you would see that in the scheme of things, fear is simply one more hue in the rainbow of feelings. But for some reason, this particular feeling is usually elevated above all others—as if it must be kowtowed to, revered, even worshiped. We will pause all action in the face of our fear. Stop all gladness and faith. Shut down all hope.

Often, then—too often—fear drags us to the cliff's edge and demands that we peer into the breach. *Anticipate great sorrow and loss*, it whispers or screams. *Anticipate total destruction*. Why do we give it such power? Why?

Whatever the reason may be, the fear requires that we ferociously defend ourselves against the terrible possibility that our "self" will somehow be compromised, diminished, or destroyed. (Some people reduce this even more finely to the fear, on some level or another, of death itself.) This defensive determination is usually expressed in one of two ways:

❖ *Hesitation to step forward toward <u>people</u>.* This is revealed in such (often unconscious) beliefs as: I am afraid to be intimate, connected, visible, expressive, vulnerable, truthful, feeling-full, or dependent, because when people *find out* how defective I really am, they will abandon me, and the loneliness, blame, criticism, rejection, condemnation, or censure that follow will destroy me.

❖ *Hesitation to step forward toward <u>accomplishment</u>.* This is revealed in such (often unconscious) beliefs as: I am afraid of success, personal power, the unknown, and change, because I am sure to be disappointed and to disappoint others—and the pain that follows will be absolutely intolerable and will destroy me.

Fear
is just
a feeling
and
very often is:

False
Evidence
Appearing
Real

Where do defenses come from?

Defenses, as we have seen, are *self-created*. Initially, these creations are deliberately established to ward off the battalion of fears just mentioned, the fears by which we feel assaulted. Unfortunately, in what seems like merely a breath's time, we get so accustomed to the presence of these soldiers and to the form they take that our self-image becomes rooted in them (at least partially). We are the defenses and the defenses are us!

Soon thereafter, probably because of overwhelm or perhaps even as a deeper form of defense, we intentionally forget why, in the first place, we picked a particular way of thinking, feeling, or acting. In fact, we actually forget that we are defending ourselves with these ways and means *at all*.

This deliberate forgetting—sometimes called *repression*—hides from our own view the whole defensive structure, the mechanics behind it, and even, to some extent, the reasons the structure originally came into being. Repression, then, acts like a thick, dark tarp laid over a wood frame—the initial intention is to keep out the elements. The effect is total, dank darkness. Still, this dark tarp serves several important functions in our lives:

❖ It guarantees that we will not stumble onto the truth about our defenses and perhaps take steps to diminish or even dismantle them.

❖ It completely protects us from any contact at all with the pain that inspired the defenses. (Unconsciously, you probably regard that pain as too profoundly dangerous to be confronted. You don't even want to *know* about it, much less *feel* any of it.)

❖ It speeds up our implementation of the defense process by eliminating any hesitation we might have to protect ourselves. (When you feel threatened, you must take protective action *now*. You do so *automatically*.)

Defenses
are
self-created

❖ It keeps us from feeling impossibly split, from being aware that the face we present to the world is a distortion, a lie, an image invented by us. If we were consciously aware of this profound inner division between the real self and the manufactured self, we might be paralyzed with shame and confusion. Better to keep the whole messy business out of sight—repressed, out of the mind's eye.

Why defenses work

Defenses *originally* worked because we wanted them to work, created them to work, and supported them to keep working. At first they made us feel more in charge or safer and less afraid. Now these defensive mechanisms are stronger than we are—we, the very persons who initiated them. We have become more their slave than their master. But the great news is that in spite of appearances to the contrary, our defenses still have only the power we give them! The exercises in this book (as well as those offered in the companion workbook) make it possible for you to take that power back.

How defenses work

Our particular defensive patterns began during a specific period of time in response to distinct circumstances—circumstances we continue to remember as "our story."

The more we unthinkingly use those particular defensive patterns, the more we reinforce both our need for those patterns and our belief in the continued power of the situation that led us to initiate the defenses in the first place. Eventually, every single time we (even unconsciously) *perceive* a situation to be similar to the situation we encountered in our original story, we respond by employing the defense we have come to count on. *This automatically reinforces the difficulty as it was originally perceived.*

Defenses
reinforce
our
original
pain

Step 7 in defense busting:
Realize that the *defense itself* is not the actual problem. The actual problem is that you have made an *inner connection* between the defense and the pain-filled fears that originally called the defense into play.

As we have seen, at the time you created it, the defense was a good idea. In fact, the defense itself continues to be useful in some ways—when it's used with awareness. Even (defensive) fear is good, for instance, when it guides you to hesitate before jumping off of a cliff into a canyon. Fear only becomes a burden when it prevents you from ever going near enough to that cliff to view the beauty of the canyon. In your daily life, when your fear stops you from driving a car, trying to get a new job even though you hate your present job, or risking the pleasures of love, it's a burden that needs to be overcome.

When defenses work

Defenses work everywhere, all the time

Defenses work everywhere, all the time. They were originally meant to spare us from the sometimes extraordinary stress of two situations—threatening *home-life* experiences (such as the strain of mother/father/sibling relationships, the way those relationships were expressed in the household, our own perceptions of powerlessness, and feelings of not-enoughness) and threatening *peer-life* experiences (how we fit in with others, including such issues as popularity and body image).

Certainly we continue to be challenged and therefore stressed throughout our lives. And though the content or landscape of the stressful experience may shift, the defenses we established early on continue to act as vigilant, well-trained guards, fighting off potential discomfort. Eventually, however, when we are stuck in the story no more, we will realize that the discomfort we've been defending against is far less difficult than the protected life we have created.

The three kinships

The bottom line is this: you are stuck spinning your wheels in the muddy trench of your personal history. How this stuckness appears in your life will be most easily recognized through an examination of *your relationship to yourself* and *your relationship to others*. This approach may seem so obvious as to be trivial—until it is placed in a particular innovative context.

After years of clinical work with a variety of clients, I have come to agree with those researchers and theoreticians who announce that surprisingly enough, life in its entirety involves only three relationship *templates*:

❖ The relationship we have with our *father*,

❖ the relationship we have with our *mother*, and

❖ the relationship we have with the *child* we once were (the so-called "inner child," a designation now so overworked and wrongly applied that it has come to mean everything and nothing at the same time; we will later understand that "child" with much greater precision).

To clarify and assist in your understanding this "three kinships" idea, I offer, in addition to stories from my own life, accounts of the childhood experiences of others. These stories (always announced by the "story-book" icon) are followed by glances at the present, dealing with what I have noticed are the five most common areas of trouble (the ones that most often move people to seek change): *abandonment, punishment,*

The five
most common
trouble spots:

✳ Abandonment
✳ Punishment
✳ Body-image
    shame
✳ Sex
✳ Relationships

body-image shame, sex, and *relationship.** (You will find specific additional information about these areas in "Yesterday's Tales," starting on page 247.) Told to me by clients, those tales were cited as causes, justifications, and explanations for current difficulties. They were expressed in various ways, sometimes furiously, sometimes with quiet resolve. Often they were told as meaningless anecdotes, and even in some cases as stand-up comedy. I present these stories essentially as they were reported to me (with names changed and identifying details appropriately altered), offering them as emotional touchstones and hoping they may stimulate revelations related to your own sticking points. We'll begin with the story of Betty.

BETTY & THE MOTHER KINSHIP
Punishment
The Silent Treatment

The usual fight broke out. I was about ten years old. It was summer. My mom was angry at me and yelled. I talked back to her. She got the silver yardstick out from the kitchen to hit me. I ran real fast into the bathroom, which was the only room with a lock on the door. She pounded and yelled at me to open the door. I was terrified, screaming and crying. In that evil tone of hers, she said, "You just wait till I get in there." I sat on the bathroom floor and watched myself cry in the mirror and noticed all the pain in my face. I was scared to death. I knew if I opened the door I would get hit. But I would have to come out sometime!

---

* You can get right to work on challenging your defenses. Consider two questions: What story do you tell most often? What area of your life does that story appear to affect most?

The next thing I knew, Mom had gotten a screwdriver and was taking the doorknob off—yelling and warning me what was to come. I had no way out. I screamed "NO!" I cried. I said, "I'm sorry, I'm sorry." I tried to get out the window but couldn't fit. So I watched and screamed as the doorknob came off.

Of course, Mom hit me very hard, and then what followed were the usual few days when she would not talk to me at all. At those times, she would not even look at me. I had nobody when she was mad that way. I was trapped in the house and not able to go anywhere. It felt like I was being locked in a dungeon.

Today, fifty-three-year-old Betty still finds speaking her mind or establishing good boundaries almost impossible. This means she seldom gets her needs met. Her unconscious driving ideas are: "I must not talk back or speak up. If I do, people will either be really mean to me or will ignore me altogether. Either way, I'll die."

Betty still remembers how mean and rejecting her mother was and behaves in her life today as if everyone she meets is going to treat her the same way. Of course, because of her silence no one really knows what Betty needs or thinks. Therefore, those around her constantly fail (from her perspective) to give her the attention that might make her feel appreciated or important. So, in the final analysis, she is herself creating the experience she's supposedly trying most to avoid.*

---

* Now that you've read Betty's story, start wondering about your own unconscious driving ideas. How might these ideas be promoting the very things you think you most want to avoid?

Step 8 in defense busting:

Uncover the basic *stories* in which you are stuck. To do this, look at your relationship with your father, with your mother, and with yourself as a child.

House of mirrors

Our present-day world reflects our history

The "three kinships" notion is provocative and demanding. It suggests that the people we choose to be around—the boss we work for, the partner we marry, and the friends we accumulate—*all* present us with characteristics, contradictions, and conflicts that closely imitate the formative relationships of our early life. It means that when you become the rescuer of your partner, you are actually (even if unconsciously) rescuing either poor beleaguered Dad, battered misunderstood Mom, or your own neglected, abandoned child-self. It suggests, via example after example from everyday experience, that throughout your life, as you continue choosing friends, mates, and employers, you are unconsciously but accurately re-membering (reassembling) your original mother-father-child relationships. It further suggests that these three relationships—whether they were wonderfully supportive and caring or wildly dysfunctional—have been the source and model for *all of your relationships, past and present.* This viewpoint even goes so far as to suggest, for instance, that in cases of early desertion or death, the absent parent can stimulate within you a fantasy relationship (with the nonpresent person) that can result in your conducting a lifetime search for the *perfect* parent, which often militates against successful relationship by setting you up to seek the impossible.

The world, then, becomes a house of mirrors, reflecting back to us our own history and the way that history lives inside of us. And this remarkable overall fact follows, as night follows day: unless we do something to change things, these three kinships will define *our future relationships* as well.

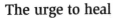

Although you may at first not recognize how the people in your life today are like those of yesteryear, be patient. Learning to spot the resemblance is easy, and once you know where in the valley to stand, the ancient echo from those distant mountains can be clearly heard.

The *great* news is that you *can* substantially change your relationship to these three kinships—until finally you are stuck in the story no more!

The urge to heal

If you assume for a moment that you are recapitulating early (perhaps dysfunctional) relationships, the question becomes: Why would you *do* such a thing? Why on Earth would you repeat over and over again what did not work in the first place? Some authorities say you are simply reproducing what you have been taught; others speculate that you just don't know you deserve better and are therefore unable to seek anything better. While both of these inclinations may influence your behavior somewhat, I hold a slightly more optimistic view of apparently self-damaging choices. I think you have a *natural urge* to heal what has been harmed—and since you could not fix your life "back then" (when you were little), you try doing it today (in adulthood) by recreating the same circumstances that existed all those years ago and seeking this time to fix things.

Is that possible? Can you heal yesterday's problem relationships through the relationships of today? I think the answer is a definite yes and no. What I have observed is that the restorative effects of being loved, respected, attended to, included, listened to, and seen *now,* if you do not also *directly attend to* early woundings, are usually minimal. The result of ignoring the past is a nagging (often indefinable) discontent

You have
a natural
urge
to heal

Achieve
real
and
lasting
happiness today
by rigorously
facing
yesterday

with the present. Even if that present *appears* generally terrific, you're often left feeling this: "My life is fine. I'm just not fine in my life."

The point is: working *only* on your present-day happiness can provide limited relief for the fundamental discomfort you feel in your own skin. For a truly expansive, fulfilling life, it is necessary to look back—to reveal where and how the patterns began. Otherwise, you are newly decorating a termite-ridden house.

In summary: understand that defenses are initiated to protect us from the uncomfortable feelings that accompany difficult circumstances. Those circumstances may involve the natural bumps of growing up, such as establishing your territory in the family and finding out what you do well; or, among your peers, figuring out who you are and how you fit in. Defenses like that are usually reasonable—and can even be essential to your well-being, as in *Withdrawing* to your room to figure things out when life gets too rough at home or *Masking* at school to feel more a part of everything. However, when the circumstances inspiring your protective defenses are extreme (molestation or violence; insistent, demeaning ridicule; or emotional and/or literal abandonment), you tend to go further—not establishing mere defenses but setting up intricately woven defensive *patterns* as well. Then, pretty quickly, these patterns begin working to attach your defenses to the circumstance of the stories that inspired them. At that juncture, the defense is the seductive and sometimes deadly spider; the pattern is the web she weaves; and you are the captured fly.

Finally, the initiating tale and your defensive response to that tale work so closely together that every time you think you are running across a similar circumstance, you summon familiar defensive help. At some point, as with the chicken and the egg, you have difficulty identifying what came first—the story or the defense.

Circumstances
set up the
defensive patterns

The defensive
patterns
attach you
to your
"stuckness" stories

Luckily, what you must do to get unstuck is not difficult to identify. Through my own personal struggles and in my years of practice as a teacher/therapist, I have developed a five-stage program of identification and solution that offers freedom from the limitations of defenses and from the stories that hold defenses in place. I explain it fully in the pages that follow. Please note, however, that the point of making the identifications I present in this book is *not* that you should begin using them to label yourself or others. Not only does labeling encourage a lack of the rich, profound thinking that leads to true change (since mere identification is equated with useful self-knowledge and further exploration tends too easily to be curtailed), but labeling can also easily then become just another defense ("I'm *codependent*," "Dad's *alcoholic*," "Mother's *narcissistic*"). Used this way, labeling limits rather than elaborates understanding, becoming an easy way to avoid real connection with others and deeper levels of work with yourself. That being said, begin now to follow the program, so you may be Stuck in Your Story No More!

Standing firmly
on each
healing stage,
one level at a time,
will eventually
allow you to
build a
strong platform
for your life

THE FIVE STAGES

STAGE 5
Incorporate new responses
and **choices** into your life.

STAGE 4
Acknowledge your feeling, doing, and thinking
contributions to your own circumstances.

STAGE 3
Appreciate the value of those **patterns**.

STAGE 2
Notice exactly how you have created
duplications of these patterns in your life.

STAGE 1
Recognize the patterns that were established in and by childhood.

CHAPTER 2

BEWARE OF FALLING ROCKS:
A Healing Alert

One weekend a number of years ago, I left my home in Los Angeles to attend the National Conference on Codependency in Phoenix, Arizona. Konrad decided to surprise me by taking advantage of my four-day absence to move the two enormous floor-to-ceiling bookcases from our spare bedroom to a more desirable spot in the hallway. After taking down the hundreds of books, he moved and painted the bookcases, returned the books to the shelves, and then repainted the now-empty bedroom. On top of all this, he orchestrated the installation of track lighting above the newly positioned shelves.

I spoke to Konrad a number of times that weekend by phone, and never did he give the slightest hint of the surprise that awaited me. From the time he got home after dropping me off at the airport to the moment he left to pick me up, he worked feverishly, day and night. He also brought in various helpers in different shifts. As I was later to realize, his exhilaration and anticipation as I walked in the door were very high.

I looked up, saw the work he'd done, and was indeed surprised. In a reaction with a length that could probably have been measured in milliseconds, I expressed my pleasure, saying something like, "Wow, look what you did." Then almost immediately, looking up to the ceiling, I followed with, "Oh, I see a couple of holes around the track lighting. Guess you didn't finish."

The minute the words left my lips, I reached to pull them back in. It was as if I had been momentarily possessed by my critical stepfather—the man who brought me up after my biological father's goodbye. I was appalled at what I had said. But not any more so than my tired, stunned husband! Konrad's face was ashen. He was deflated and defeated.

While my response to his efforts could have been regarded as nothing more than thoughtlessness or even a result of my being exhausted after an intense weekend of study, the fact is that I was displaying a defensive behavioral pattern—for in that moment, I wasn't concerned with *him*. I was only concerned with *me* and with having been let down one more time by a man who, after all, hadn't done his work perfectly. By focusing more on what was slightly wrong than on what was hugely right, I displayed the twin defenses of *Perfectionism* and *Criticism*.

———··✦··———

Before the bookcase incident, I'd already begun to realize how I frequently turned to those defenses in my daily life. Now, in light of this incident, I started reviewing my past relationships.

As I ruminated, I remembered the way I had insisted and believed that what I wanted, needed, longed for, drooled over, searched after, and sacrificed for was a loving, honest, intimate, committed relationship. I had professed to want a love that would last a lifetime, a partner I could count on, a commitment I could cherish. This, I (unconsciously) thought, would let me give up the idea that I deserved to be thrown away, and I could thereby end my lifelong loneliness. I thought my problem was that I wasn't able to find men willing to be as intimate as I was willing to be. In other words, I thought the problem was *them*.

I was wrong. I found this out when I met Konrad. From the moment we joined together, this man's love for me never wavered. He was available, intimate, and steadfast in his appreciation of me. Eventually, his unswerving passion forced me to realize that *my own* terror of intimacy is what had all the while prevented me from healthy partnering. I was shocked! The problem, in actuality, was never them. *It was me.* Of course, there is the fact that I had often chosen unreliable, damaged relationship partners (and friends, also) to reinforce my negative assumptions, but the doubt and resistance themselves began with me.

Your partner is not your parent

Well, I'm here to tell you that this is the truth for everyone. Whatever the challenge is, it begins with you. The other people in your life merely reflect (or exaggerate) that challenge. Remember the house-of-mirrors idea? Its truth constitutes both the good news and the bad news. The bad news is: the major responsibility for whether a relationship works or doesn't work falls upon us as individuals. Who do we choose? Do we choose wisely? Do we insist on refusing the genuine love that's sometimes offered? The good news is: the major responsibility for whether a relationship works or doesn't work falls upon us as individuals. We have the opportunity to choose wisely and then to accept the genuine love that is sometimes offered.

It took a long while, however, for me to arrive at these conclusions. At first, I simply continued my habitual pattern. I had (unconsciously) thought marriage to a man who really, obviously loved me would fix everything. It didn't. Instead, my fears seemed to grow. I ran like hell, keeping my husband at bay by using my most well-developed defenses: Anger, Criticism, Control, Spilling, Analyzing, Judging, Compulsivity, and Counter-dependence. (All of which, along with many more, will soon be examined and explained.) By artfully using those defenses, I managed to keep one foot out the door. I constantly wondered: *Should I stay or go?* That question took up so much space inside me that no room was left for real, sustained intimacy.

But luckily I was eventually worn down by my own inner conflict. At that point I awakened rudely to the understanding that enough was enough. Finally, *I just didn't want my fear to control me anymore.* I wanted so badly to rid myself of the inner turmoil that I was willing to fight back against the story in which I felt stuck.

Fight
the fear
that controls
your life

That fighting back required immediate *behavioral change . . .* and the sooner the better. I needed to start that change before I felt like it. Even before I completely understood it. I began making the change by replacing old defensive impulses with specific new behaviors (see *The 14 Solutions* in the *Stuck No More Companion Workbook*). Unlike what I had done in prior relationships, I kept to myself the constant critical voice that yapped annoyingly in my head like a frantic dog during a furious storm. And I did not run away. Slowly and increasingly, I allowed myself to trust and rely on my husband's powerful love. I exposed my need to him. Much of the time I was feeling my way through the dark—all the while meditating, writing, praying, crying, struggling with my fears, telling my emotional truths, and controlling my vicious tongue. Above all, I needed *constantly* to remind myself that because the terror had nothing to do with the man, the man could do nothing to soothe the terror. This would have to be an inside job.

Healthy communication

I had known for years about the critical voices that lived in my head—the ones that yammered: "You don't do enough. You don't do anything well-enough. No one will ever really love you." What I hadn't realized was that when those vicious voices finished with me, they went searching for other prey, like the long tongue of an anteater snapping out to swallow up its victims. In this way, I was able to suck others into my story—to make certain we were all stuck together.

If I was going to save myself from myself, I needed information—about how to spot my own defensiveness and about how to communicate my real and appropriate concerns as those concerns arose. I needed to figure out what triggered my huge, overblown reactions and learn how to turn those excessive reactions into reasonable, reliable responses. I needed to discover how to yank myself free from my historical story so I could live boldly and realistically in my current life story.

Of course, everyone experiences various forms of this excessive reactivity—reactions far too big for the circumstances to which they appear to be attached. Hopefully, however, you are able to see that these ways of dealing with circumstances—which can easily be described as battleship-in-a-bathtub reactions—are too much for too little. Healing the hurts of our history inevitably includes altering these kinds of behaviors—learning to *respond* rather than to *react*. Thus, feeling better about ourselves will be, in part, exemplified in terms of our *communication with others*—how we express ourselves to them and how we deal with what they are expressing to us.

The question thus arises: How do we communicate our thoughts and our feelings in healthy, hearable ways? How do we take care of ourselves while being truly intimate (speaking from a place of emotional integrity) with others? This book, especially in combination with the companion workbook, intends to lead you to both fundamental answers

Learn
to respond
rather
than
to react

The bigger
the reaction,
the older
the source

and to long-term solutions. Eventually, diligence, as always, will be the key to change. For now, I suggest you merely glide through the text, scooping up tidbits along the way with the sincere intention of digging deeper later.

Healthy communication has four primary components:

1. When we are communicating in a healthy way, we *avoid excessive reactivity*. A few examples of excessive reactivity are:

✿ you're accused of wrongdoing, and your response is fury;

✿ someone ignores you, and instead of asking directly what the problem is or ignoring the presumed offense, you make a desperate play for attention, as if getting that attention is essential to your life;

✿ another driver on the highway cuts you off, and you want to ram his car;

✿ a friend forgets to call to see how your family dinner party went and you're ready to dump the relationship;

✿ your partner does something hurtful and you stop talking to her or him for three days.

Excessive reactions are most likely rooted in old (childhood) stories. In fact, *all* excessive reactivity indicates our stuckness in personal historical events. When we overlay those old responses onto our new circumstances, we are fighting the wrong fight with the wrong person at the wrong time. The result is that we find ourselves drifting from one senseless argument to another, never feeling quite satisfied that our point is being made or that our needs are being recognized.

The fact is, the bigger your reactions, the more ancient is the material that's inspiring those reactions. If you really want a more satisfying life (and more fulfilling relationships), you need to be brave enough to seek answers within yourself.

First, look back in time. Delve into the aspects of your personal history that continue to inspire your reactivity. Discover what ignites

The four elements in <u>healthy communication</u>:

✳ Avoid excessive reactivity

✳ Speak clearly

✳ Speak up

✳ Try connecting instead of rejecting

your anger, stabs at your grief, plunges you into disappointment, stimulates your anxiety.

Second, learn to recognize how current-life concerns look and feel, and also to differentiate them from the *old, long-held ideas, resentments, and fears* that are masquerading as current-life issues.

The idea of being free from excess reactivity can easily be misunderstood. I am not recommending a life dully experienced, where little affects you and you look more robotic than human. No. The only thing I'm suggesting here is that in *all* cases, your present-day (passionate, authentic) responses should more precisely fit the time and the crime!

Step 9 in defense busting:
Realize: the bigger your reaction, the older the memory inspiring that reaction.

DEEP
SUFFOCATING LOVE

DEEPER
FATHER CRUELTY

DEEPEST
MOTHER NEGLECT

2. When we are communicating in a healthy way, we *speak clearly and without irrelevancies.* Over-explaining, trying to be convincing, and using too much corroborating evidence all indicate that you think your own opinions are not good enough. Speak your truth without elaborate explanation.

3. When we are communicating in a healthy way, we *behave* with directness. Unspoken feelings tend to show up as bad behavior (attack, rejection, withdrawal). Instead of remaining silent or acting inappropriately, try saying things like: "I'm really angry at you," "I feel terrible when you ignore my requests," or "I need to be alone." *Containing* bad behavior introduces the possibility of intimacy.

4. When we are communicating in a healthy way, our intention is *to connect.* If you want to connect effectively, you need to be clear about what you're trying to say and find out if listeners understand what you're saying.

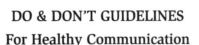

DO & DON'T GUIDELINES
For Healthy Communication

In order to communicate in healthy ways, there are specific things we can do and things we can avoid doing. Here are some of the most effective. Pick out two or three of the *Do* and *Don't* guidelines and see how they work for you in your real daily life. Keep what you like and leave the rest, but always remember: different results will require different procedures.

Do

① **Be certain you're saying what you mean to say.** Figure out what you're feeling, then think before you speak.

② **Stay present.** Stop your mind from wandering off. Pay attention to the person in front of you and to your own internal responses.

③ **Really *listen* to what other people are saying.** Sincere interest fosters intimacy. Find out who other people are. Ask questions and volunteer emotional identifications. Share pertinent experiences from your own life.

④ **Talk about *your* feelings instead of talking about other people's behavior.** Focus on your own reactions, not on what another person *did to you.*

⑤ **Hold consistent boundaries.** Boundaries are the limits that keep you feeling safe. An absence of good boundaries puts both you and others at risk. Be clear about your boundaries. Know when to say yes and how to say no.

⑥ **Apologize immediately when you are wrong, and do so without excuse.** It's tempting to blame your behavior on others—to assume you are responding a particular way because you were provoked to respond that way. The truth is that you and only you are responsible for the way you react—even if the other person's behavior is reprehensible or aggravating (if someone combatively cuts you off on the freeway, you don't have the right to shoot the person). When you're out of line, admit it readily and without explanation.

Don't

① **Don't expect yourself or others to be perfect.** Perfectionism is a setup for abuse, because it creates impossibly high standards. Expecting other people to be perfect guarantees disappointment; expecting yourself to be perfect guarantees self-contempt.

② **Don't compare yourself to others.** First, things rarely are the way they seem to be, which means that making so-called reality-based comparisons often fails. For instance: *She's thinner and richer than me and therefore happier with herself and her life.* Clearly what we have here is *apparent* information, not necessarily *accurate* information. Also, any kind of comparing robs you of intimacy, because it either sets you above or below others. Feeling connected to someone you're looking down on or up at is hard—you're too busy either bemoaning your fate (inferiority keeps you a victim) or protecting yourself (superiority keeps you contemptuous).

③ **Even if you feel self-contemptuous, you don't need to keep announcing it.** When you hesitate to celebrate yourself, the world hesitates to celebrate you. If you keep telling people you're worthless, eventually they'll agree.

④ **Don't share *everything* you think.** It's a misconception to think that being honest means presenting an unedited monologue. Before rushing to share an insight you haven't taken the time to evaluate thoughtfully, pause to examine what you are going to say and what your true intention is.

⑤ **Don't offer unsolicited fixing, advice, or commentary on people's problems.** Although you may have the very best intentions, offering this kind of "help" is separating at best and intrusive at worst.

⑥ **Don't justify your position.** The more you feel the need to defend yourself, the more likely you are to suspect you're wrong. When there's a problem or a conflict, instead of explaining, complaining, convincing, or analyzing in an attempt to support your viewpoint or to change others, figure out what *you're* doing to make that problem worse.

⑦ **Don't make proclamations.** Proclamations usually involve the words "ever," "never," and "always." When you announce your future behavior ("I never have sex on the first date—don't ask," or "I'm completely off sugar—don't ever offer it to me"), you're attempting to get other people to maintain your boundaries for you, so you don't need to say an uncomfortable "No!" at the appropriate time. Proclamations indicate an underlying doubt, announce an inevitable inconsistency, and invite contradiction.

⑧ **Don't blame yourself or other people.** Instead of beating yourself up or pointing a finger at someone else, explore the idea that placing blame on anyone—yourself or others—is actually your attempt to avoid some other, underlying feeling (like shame, for instance), that seems unbearable to you. Instead of blaming anyone, identify this "other" feeling. Then consider a valuable exercise: sit down and write about the feeling. This kind of writing is best done in a stream-of-consciousness fashion, when you let the words flow forth freely without evaluating them or trying to determine whether they are grammatical or would make sense to or be approved by anyone else. Try not to judge what comes forward. Simply witness it.

——··✄··——

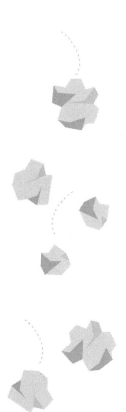

On the roads that wind among the hills of Southern California, I have been fascinated to notice occasional signs that read "Beware of Falling Rocks." I've never quite understood what this notification intends. At the point we encounter these signs, we are usually *already* on the dangerous stretch of highway—often overlooking a ravine. I wonder: What are we supposed to do now? Drive with our head out the window, as if to spot flying rocks? Should we creep along so we can stop suddenly in case a giant boulder plunges toward us, or should we speed up to get through the area as quickly as possible?

Of course, what I do is what most people do—drive at my normal pace, aware of potential danger but not allowing that danger to impede or significantly affect my progress.

As you move into this book and begin to recognize the nature, tone, and effects of your defenses, you are likely to find yourself dealing with the psychological equivalent of a falling-rock alert. This alert can (happily) take the form of excitement or curiosity, but it can also (unhappily) create a sense of alarm—producing hesitation, sadness, and/ or fear. I encourage you to move forward even in the face of such signs, finding the pace that suits your personal journey.

ANGER   DEPRESSION   FEAR   SHAME

CHAPTER 3

DEFENSE PROFILES

Hit or Run—you decide

In order to break free from our old, undermining ways, we need to begin recognizing the defenses that glue us to our sticky story. For the sake of clarity, I have split the defenses into two major categories: **Hit** and **Run**. Although to paint the picture and make a point I often describe these two classifications in extreme ways, please always keep in mind that defenses (appropriately used) are usually more divine than deadly, and therefore the aim of the work described in this book is NOT to rid ourselves of these lifelong companions or even to change the defenses themselves. Rather, the aim is to change *the way we deal with our defenses.*

All right—that being said, let us begin with the first major category: *Hit*. Hitters tend to be assertive types of individuals. This assertiveness, in its benign form, might mean you could be described as outwardly-oriented and proactive. Unrefined (or untransformed), however, Hitters

are often seen as bulldozers (behaviorally, emotionally, physically, or even intellectually). Actually, though, if we could look beneath the surface, we might be surprised to find that for Hitters, *connection* is, more often than not, the (unconscious) goal. What we really want most is *inter*action. Unfortunately, the hitting methods frequently leave much to be desired, for they involve plowing through the world in a way that often earns more enmity than love.

Our second major category is *Run*. Runners are likely to appear somewhat passive, and tend toward reserve. This often (mistakenly) gives them the air of being easygoing individuals with low-maintenance personas. If this describes you, others around you assume that you're mostly unaffected by the people and circumstances you encounter. You're seen as a person who simply goes with the flow, but your so-called even temperature is really just a device for maintaining emotional and physical distance from others. You maintain this distance **not** because you're unaffected by what's happening, but more truly because you're so *extremely* affected by your surroundings. The vulnerability arising from this exquisite sensitivity has thrown you head first into fear. In other words, you've simply been scared into your reluctance, inactivity, and silence! To handle this inner onslaught of fear, you create the (unconscious) emotional goal of *disconnection*. You bob, weave, hide, and flee the scene. Anything to prevent the hurt you are certain will come through actual contact. Unfortunately, your methods also leave much to be desired, for as you skulk through the world, all too often you experience more loneliness than safety.

Hitters want to connect

Runners want to escape

Personal relationships offer helpful examples of ways in which these two categories operate, since couples are frequently on opposite sides of the defense fence (examples: one is extremely social and gregarious while the other is a quiet homebody; or one is a go-go-go type while the other procrastinates and gets little done). In fact, the general belief is that opposites attract, but a more accurate statement would be that individuals carrying opposite *characteristics* attract. The hand finds its glove.

Recently, a fine example of this opposite-characteristic theory walked into my office. Joe and Freida came in to "fix" their failing marriage. When the time came to discuss in detail the difficulties of their relationship, Frieda spoke minimally and with little clarity, only barely managing to say out loud how unappreciated she felt. Obviously, she was depressed. In addition, Frieda seemed confused and kept referring to her husband in the third person, as if he were not there in the room with us—which was, as it turned out, precisely how she experienced him in their relationship. Meanwhile, Joe fumed and sputtered, lashing out contemptuously with palpable anger. He *hit*, she *ran*.

What Freida and Joe needed to do is similar to what we all must do to approach change: (1) *identify* our feelings and concerns, (2) *recognize* the ways those feelings and concerns are (or are not) being communicated, and (3) *find* new ways to communicate.

Healthy communication introduces us to new information that can prepare us for necessary change. Suddenly we realize that our boss is contemptuous, that our close friend's emotional suffering calls for compassion, or that we need to wake up to what's going on in our relationship.

For better relationships:

* Identify your feelings

* See how you are (or are not) speaking up

* Find new ways of getting heard

HIT & RUN QUESTIONNAIRE

Identifying your own primary defensive mode—that is, the category into which your defenses most often fall—will allow you to understand the changes you must make in order to free yourself from the story in which you are stuck.

Keep in mind as you do this, however, that most of us do not express ourselves *exclusively* in only one way (either hit or run). Thus, although you're likely to find yourself falling mostly into one or the other category, occasional crossovers will certainly be found, where one kind of defense easily leads to another (or even includes another). This categorization, then, is meant to light your pathway, not to narrow your view.

Answering the following questions will help you figure out whether you are primarily a hitter or a runner. It's a wonderful way to begin personalizing the concepts in this book. Don't over-think when you're answering, though. Simply mark your first responses and move on.

1. When I am in a new circumstance, I am most likely to:
   a. Talk more.
   b. Focus on what the other person is thinking.
   c. Get quiet. ▾
   d. Feel unable to organize my thoughts.

2. If someone hurts my feelings, I usually:
   ⦿ a. Remember and list to myself previous, similar hurts.
   b. Explain to the person what he or she is doing wrong.
   c. Assume I caused the problem.
   d. Let it slide.

3. When things do not turn out the way I hoped, I usually:
   a. Get mad.
   b. Joke about them.
   c. Ignore them.
   ⦿ d. Worry or sulk.

4. When I have a project, I usually:

    a. Feel like I can never do it well enough.

    b. Organize a team.

    c. Do it all by myself.

    d. Leave it until the last moment.

5. When I am under extreme stress, I usually:

    a. Figure out the best way to handle things.

    b. Imagine how other people feel in the same circumstances.

    c. Get overwhelmed.

    d. Try even harder to make things turn out just right.

If you answered with a or b in three out of five cases, your defenses are primarily of the *hit* variety. If you answered with c or d, you lean toward using *run* defenses.

FEELING–DOING–THINKING QUESTIONNAIRE

You are beginning to think of yourself primarily as a hitter or a runner. That's the stroke that outlines the profile. Now you can fill in the facial features. You will do this by examining the ways in which you initiate and sustain your most-often-used defenses. That is, what are the eyes through which you see the world? What are the lips through which you speak and the ears through which you hear? To define these features, you will ask yourself: *Do I operate primarily through feelings, behaviors or thoughts?*

If *feeling* is your primary mode, your first response to perceived provocation—either from others or even from your own memories—is (generally) emotional. You are, then, the kind of person who expresses and/or experiences feelings often and easily.

Perhaps, on the other hand, *behavior* is the newspaper through which you report your responses to the (inside/outside) world. You're on a doing track and action is your pathway.

The third defense expression style is *thinking*. In this case, your responses come across primarily via mental pictures, concepts, thoughts, and through your words.

As we've already noted, environment is only one determining factor where our personal style is concerned. Nature will also greatly impact that style. This is one reason why different children bought up in approximately the same way in the same family will have very different ways of behaving, thinking, and/or feeling toward the world around them. The idea at this point, though, is *not* to focus on *why* you are who you are, *but* rather on *how* you are who you are.

The following series of questions will help you understand whether you are primarily a feeler, a doer, or a thinker. Again, answer off the top of your head. Don't over-think it.

1. When I am caught in a conflict, I usually:
   a. Get really mad at whoever is causing the problem.
   b. Feel overwhelmed and try to stay quiet until the conflict stops.
   c. Try to lighten up the situation with humor.
   d. Step aside and watch from afar.
   e. Figure out what caused the problem.
   f. Wonder if it's all my fault.

2. When other people ignore me, I:

   a. Feel bad and remember that people are mostly selfish.

   b. Start feeling like there's something wrong with me.

   c. Start trying to figure out what's wrong with them.

   d. Say nothing.

   e. First imagine they hate me, then wonder *why* they hate me.

   f. Go over and over what I might have done to alienate them.

3. When I'm having a bad day, I:

   a. Recognize who or what has put me in this bad mood.

   b. Become afraid that my life will always feel this bad.

   c. Try to get myself and the people around me really organized.

   d. Notice that I am starting to get sick.

   e. Think about the way my life compares to other people's lives.

   f. Start doubting all the choices I've made in my life.

Do you—

* Feel it?
* Analyze it?
  or
* Do something
  about it?

4. When I'm in an uncomfortable circumstance, I:

   a. Begin to notice what's wrong with other people nearby.

   b. Feel shy, as though I have no way of fitting in.

   c. Get really talkative.

   d. Avoid whatever is making me uncomfortable by doing something else.

   e. Act as if everything's fine.

   f. Start thinking about something more pleasant than the circumstances I'm in.

   If you answered yes to a or b in three out of four cases, your defenses most likely operate primarily through *feeling*s. If you answered yes to c or d, you operate mostly through *doing*. And if you answered yes to e or f, you mostly employ *thinking* defenses.

Another good way to figure yourself out is to notice which *verbs* you most often use in your sentences. Do you say, "I feel sad about my loss," or "I think we should investigate the circumstances of his leaving," or "Go find him!" In other words, do you *feel* it, *analyze* it, or *do* something about it? (Remember, these are not rigid categories, but merely pointers and generalities.)

Feature this

This is a good time to combine the results of the Hit-and-Run Questionnaire with the results of the Feeling-Doing-Thinking Questionnaire. Subsequently, you will be able to quickly and efficiently locate the set of Defense Profiles (starting on page 65) that's most likely to apply to you personally (or you might check the contents page to view the full list). You can use these profiles for many purposes, one of which will surely be to gain a greater understanding of yourself and of the people who are a significant part of your life.

Once you have identified your major defense stance (hit or run) and your primary defense mode (thinking, doing, or feeling) and you have located the set of associated Defense Profiles, you can carefully examine each profile in that set to see if you recognize anything about yourself there. (It's a sort of game and ought to be fun.) If you don't or can't identify or connect with anything in those profiles, that's probably either because the self-reporting you did when you answered the initial establishing tests wasn't accurate (perhaps you described yourself idealistically rather than realistically) or because you're denying that the defenses to which you've been led by the logic of your self-reporting is valid! In either case, stop judging yourself or the defense. Review—and try again.

Name it
then
claim it

Hit and Run defense list

Here is a quick-glance reference list of the individual defenses and their categories (each is described and defined in detail later in this chapter). As you examine it, you may at first be tempted to cringe at some defense categories, and to refuse even to acknowledge the potential (healthy) usefulness of others. But it's <u>essential</u> to remember this: *all defenses are valuable and effective*—that is, when they are used **conscientiously** and **consciously**. So don't set your sights on completely ridding yourself of the defenses (which is impossible to do anyway). Rather, aim to gain authority over the habitual patterns you have established around those (often invaluable) feelings, thoughts, and behaviors. Excess and unconsciousness ought be your key concerns!

In addition, please note that not everything listed below may appear at first to be a defense. Keep in mind, though, that *any* feeling, way of thinking, or behavior can be defensive when it's used excessively and when its (unconscious) aim is *self-protection*.*

The defense itself is not the problem

Aim to gain authority

Step 10 in defense busting:

Dig deep. Figure out which defenses you use most, recognize the origin of the defenses, and notice how they are now appearing in your life.

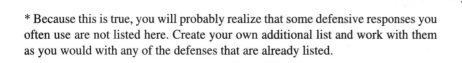

* Because this is true, you will probably realize that some defensive responses you often use are not listed here. Create your own additional list and work with them as you would with any of the defenses that are already listed.

HIT DEFENSES

Feeling defenses produce *connection* through emotion
Doing defenses produce *connection* through action
Thinking defenses produce *connection* through reason
(Individual Defense Profiles are on page number shown in brackets.)

DEFENSE AND DESCRIPTION	TYPE
ANGER—Protecting yourself with feelings of hostility [65].	FEELING
CONTEMPT FOR OTHERS—Protecting yourself with despising, negative, disdainful feelings toward other people [72].	FEELING
BLAME—Protecting yourself by feeling and believing that someone else is at fault [75].	FEELING
SPILLING—Protecting yourself with constant (often inappropriate) talking [79].	DOING
GOSSIP—Protecting yourself by talking to someone about someone else who is not present [82].	DOING
HUMOR—Protecting yourself with comical (sometimes inappropriate) self-expression [85].	DOING
DEPENDENCE—Protecting yourself through excessive reliance on others [90].	DOING
CODEPENDENCE—Protecting yourself through excessive reliance on people or things to define your self-worth [96].	DOING
THERAPIZING—Protecting yourself through excessive (often unrequested) advice-giving [101].	DOING
CONTROL—Protecting yourself by exercising a regulating or directing influence [105].	DOING
CRITICISM—Protecting yourself by constantly finding fault [109].	DOING
PROJECTION—Protecting yourself by using other people as a screen for unconscious thoughts and feelings [115].	THINKING

JUDGMENT—Protecting yourself with opinions that tend to be moral, critical, or righteous [122].	THINKING
COMPARING—Protecting yourself by measuring the way you feel against the way others appear [125].	THINKING
ANALYZING—Protecting yourself through intellectual examination that discounts emotional or intuitive factors [129].	THINKING
MASKING—Protecting yourself by saying one thing while feeling or thinking another [133].	THINKING

RUN DEFENSES

Feeling defenses produce *disconnection* through emotion
Doing defenses produce *disconnection* through action
Thinking defenses produce *disconnection* through reason
(Individual Defense Profiles are on page number shown in brackets.)

DEFENSE AND DESCRIPTION	TYPE
SHAME—Protecting yourself through your all-pervasive sense of basic defectiveness [139].	FEELING
SELF-CONTEMPT—Protecting yourself by using excessive expressions of self-disdain [145].	FEELING
FEAR—Protecting yourself through persistent feelings of eminent (emotional or physical) danger [149].	FEELING
VICTIM—Protecting yourself by focusing on feeling cheated, fooled, abused, or ignored by people and/or circumstances [156].	FEELING
WITHDRAWAL—Protecting yourself through emotional and even physical retreat [161].	FEELING
DEPRESSION—Protecting yourself through feelings of emotional, mental, and/or physical paralysis [165].	FEELING

TERMINAL UNIQUENESS—Protecting yourself through your feelings of being completely different from other people and through your ideas that you are therefore misperceived by them [170].	FEELING
SPIRITUALITY—Protecting yourself through the use of excessive religious or spiritual referencing [174].	FEELING
CHAOS—Protecting yourself through vast, disordered confusion [180].	DOING
COMPULSIVITY—Protecting yourself through impulsive, repetitious, self-defeating behavior [183].	DOING
COUNTER-DEPENDENCE—Protecting yourself through stubborn self-reliance [187].	DOING
PROCRASTINATION—Protecting yourself by putting things off until the last minute [190].	DOING
WITHHOLDING—Protecting yourself by holding back emotionally and/or physically [194].	DOING
PHYSICAL ILLNESS—Protecting yourself through constant, nagging, repetitive experiences of body problems [197].	DOING
DISSOCIATION—Protecting yourself through an emotional separation from everything and everyone—including separation from your own physical self [202].	DOING
PARANOIA—Protecting yourself by assuming that people and/or circumstances are against you [208].	THINKING
GUILT—Protecting yourself by thinking you have done a bad thing [212].	THINKING
CONFUSION—Protecting yourself through emotional and/or intellectual ambivalence and disorder [216].	THINKING
INTELLECTUALIZATION—Protecting yourself through excessive analyzing, pondering, mapping, exploring, and investigating [219].	THINKING

DENIAL—Protecting yourself by refusing to accept (an obvious) truth [222].	THINKING
SKEPTICISM—Protecting yourself through excessive, pervasive negativity and doubt [225].	THINKING
OBSESSION—Protecting yourself through repetitive focus on an idea, feeling, person, or thing—a focus that most often overrides all other thinking [228].	THINKING
SELF-ABSORPTION—Protecting yourself through excessive self-centeredness [232].	THINKING
FANTASY—Protecting yourself through a preoccupation with illusory notions [237].	THINKING
PERFECTIONISM—Protecting yourself by insisting upon excessively high standards [241].	THINKING

Breaking free

Our patterns of defensive thinking, feeling, and doing have long outlasted and outdistanced their original intentions. This fact reminds me of the story about how a circus elephant is trained. As a baby, the elephant is attached to a big stake with a heavy chain. At first the elephant struggles to break free, but the stake and chain keep her in place. As the elephant grows she soon outweighs her restraints. Yet the trainers never need to exchange them for stronger chains because, as things turn out, the elephant does not even *consider*, despite having grown so large, that she could easily tug free. Attempting to do so never occurs to her. She remains bound—not in truth, but solely by her own remembrance and by *her consequent lack of effort* to break the chains that bind her.

Similarly, we seem to get "attached" to particular notions about who we are and must be, whether or not those notions are accurate. Mostly these are ideas left over from when we were small. Then we grow up—

and throughout our lives we take great (unconscious) care to reinforce those initial ideas—binding ourselves to them through self-defeating behavior.

This first became obvious to me as I began facilitating workshops and ongoing seminars, and immediately noticed that the participants who most strongly reported feeling "unheard" and "unseen" in their everyday lives typically spoke very little during the workshops, apparently aiming to do everything they could to disappear into the background. The people who declared that they felt separated from others and routinely said "all I want is love" went to great lengths to alienate their fellow group members. And those who appeared most afraid of being left out were the very ones who refused to join in. Thus, for the workshop participants, the *ideas* they declared they had about themselves were the training stakes. However, their current *behavior* is what actually kept them chained down.

Robert, a dear, struggling client of mine, put it another way. Our working hypothesis was initially that through sexual, financial, and eating compulsivities, he'd chained himself to the notion that *something was wrong with him* and that *he deserved* his father's *abandonment*. (Dad left the family when Robert was born.) Robert's behavioral chains included the facts that his only sexual experiences were quick, unsatisfying one-night stands, that he was always broke, and that he was extremely overweight—all of which led him to feel worth-less and unlovable. Over time, however, Robert began objecting to the idea of being attached to old ideas, insisting that the word "attachment" was not strong enough—that it sounded tentative. *His* stuckness, he offered, felt more like being in "a big bear suit with a zipper." It felt like *an identity he had put on*, an outfit he had stepped into and zipped all the way up! He explained that his outfit then became the skin that totally and completely protected him from *any kind* of exposure. "It made me look bigger than

We reinforce our negativity through our own self-defeating behavior

I felt," he said, "and it made me seem more dangerous than I knew I really was. It camouflaged me completely and became my secure hiding place."

Step 11 in defense busting:

Are you chained to old ideas? Wrapped up in false self-concepts? Discover the specific ways you keep yourself attached to the past.

FACE YOUR DEFENSES

KARLA & THE CHILD KINSHIP
Relationship
A l o n e   i n   t h e   D a r k

I am six years old. I am alone in the dark, sitting on a bed in my aunt's house. I can hear the family—the many relatives—in the rest of the house. I feel there is no place for me with them, no place where I belong. Everyone else is together, talking and laughing, and I am here alone in the dark.

I am hiding but I want to be found. I want someone to rescue me and to include me. I do not want to be outside alone. I sit and wait and listen. Then my mother finds me. She says: "There you are. Why are you sitting here in the dark?" But she does not wait for my answer. I have no answer.

She does not wait for my answer because she would not know what to do. She has no time for me or for my answer. She has other things and other people she must attend to. Dad's the same way. Never any time for me. Today is like most days. Everyone is always too busy to pay attention to me, so I stay alone.

Karla, with her small, little-girl voice, appears even at 35-years-old to be young and childlike. Both at home as a wife and mother, and at her job as a secretary in the health-care field, she displays a reticence. This (*runner*) reticence, which is clearly a part of her nature,* leads coworkers and even friends and family to assume she is bothered by very little and that she is well-satisfied with her life. This is far from true.

Unfortunately, Karla still hesitates to set boundaries or to ask for her needs to be met. This leaves her feeling as she did in her childhood—like an invisible outsider who doesn't belong. Her unconscious driving ideas are, "I am alone. People do not understand. No one really wants to listen. I'll always live in the dark."

Karla's defenses of Shame and Withdrawal (profiled on pages 139 and 161) sustain and exaggerate her feelings of loneliness and her sense of alienation. Most often she feels like a little girl no one is paying attention to. Karla stays chained to her story through those defenses. How do *you* do it?

To change
your defensive
ways:

* understand <u>why</u>
  you do things

* figure out <u>how</u> you
  do things

To create a clear, comprehensible picture of our own defensive ways and means, we need to understand *what motivates our feeling, thinking, and doing* and *what particular defenses we have used in response to these motivations.* When we know *why* we do things and *how* we do things, we can make real changes.

* A natural *hitter* with Karla's same experiences might have tried to make up for the separations of the past by becoming an outrageously aggressive chatterbox or by becoming extremely social.

As you turn to the following forty-one defense profiles, I suggest that you first read through them all quickly. This general reading is likely to illuminate not only your own defenses but also the defenses of people who are important in your life. You will probably quickly recognize the ones most pertinent to you. You may also find yourself noticing certain behaviors or attitudes in yourself and in others that you would not previously have considered defensive.

To look fully at your particular "feeling," "thinking," and/or "doing" defenses, you will be specifically guided by the Defense Profile format to take the following important actions:

❖ **Identify** your defenses.

❖ Recognize the **personal impact** each of your defenses has on you—how it affects your experience of life and of the people in your life.

❖ Notice the **outer appearance** of your defenses—what they look like "on" you when they are seen by others. This will include *Signals* (your attitude or tone) and *Story Lines* (the things you say, whether out loud or in your head), since what you say and how you say it can announce the defense you're using.

❖ Discuss your **unconscious intention**—the fear or concern your defenses are trying to protect you against.

❖ Note the **community dynamics** associated with each defense— the ways in which your external community reflects and sometimes reinforces particular defenses.

❖ Realize your **personal sacrifices**—what you've had to give up to maintain your defenses. And then . . .

❖ Acknowledge the **resources** (skills) associated with each defense—the (often significant) abilities you have developed while practicing the art of that particular defense.

Finally, while you are drawing your Defense Profile, remind yourself that all of the thinking, feeling, and doing characteristics discussed here are only problems when, as defenses, they have more power over you than you have over them!

JAMES & THE FATHER KINSHIP
Punishment
The Swim Class

I am twelve. It's Saturday and something's up. When I come downstairs to see my father, he is talking to my mom about what he is going to do that day. Without acknowledging my presence, but knowing I am there, he mentions he has some particular thing he wants to do with me at the pool we go to on summer days. He never goes to the pool with us, and at the moment I feel special, but I know I must not get too hopeful, for Dad often speaks of plans that never materialize.

Dad takes me and my two brothers to the pool early. He is now excited. He wants to see me swim—he wants to coach me. This has never happened before!

I go to the other end of the racing lanes. Dad begins yelling across the pool, "As fast as you can!" I feel on the spot, but since I am faster than anyone my age at the pool, I figure this will be great. I rip across the pool and fling myself onto the deck, ready for praise and recognition.

My father is looking at me with a puzzled, disdainful expression. He says: "You can do better than that. I thought you said you were fast. That's not fast. That's terrible. Do it again. You're not trying. Do it again, right now." I think he must be right. He is Dad.

I go to the other side. I will show him. I dive in and beat the water to a froth, crossing the distance in what must be the world-record time for twelve-year-olds. Before my head clears the water he is saying: "That's terrible! You can't swim. You swim like a girl. You're not trying. Anyone could beat you. Your little eight-year-old brother could beat you." He shouts to my brother to get in the pool. He is really loud. The other people at the pool are pretending not to see what is happening.

My brother and I stand ready to race. I am twice my brother's size and weight. We hit the water. I cross in a flurry of arms, legs, and stolen breaths. I get to the other side and vault out onto the deck. My brother is only halfway across. My father ignores me. He is clapping and shouting encouragement to my little brother. I stand in silence.

Dad says to me, "You should have beaten your brother by twice that much. I am ashamed of you. Go practice. I don't want to see you for the rest of the day." Then he lifts my wet brother into his arms and says, "Come on, son. Want a Popsicle?"

They leave me standing there. I start walking, pretending to be unaffected. I am numb all over.

Today, James is a 45-year-old man whose rage toward other people is only exceeded by his self-contempt. James finds himself incapable of sustaining a trusting, healthy, primary relationship, because he constantly expects to be disappointed and criticized. Through excessive caretaking, he tries to control what relationship partners think of him—but this caretaking only ends up making him resentful. Much of the time he is quite certain other people dislike him. Actually, he simply dislikes himself. His unconscious driving ideas are: "I'll never be good enough. I can't trust anyone. Everyone's out for themselves."

In fact, neither James (an angry *hitter*) nor Karla (a withholding *runner*) need *give up* their defenses. Rather, they must gain authority over them. James, then, would employ (and contain) his fury—letting it provide him with information about *real* inequities, while Karla would allow her reticence to give her the time to figure out how and when to speak up on important points. And, of course, she would actually *do* the speaking out indicated.

Karla and James also offer examples of the way feeling, doing, and thinking responses will, at times, occur nearly simultaneously, and you are likely to make easy crossovers from *hit* to *run* and back again. Karla's defensive Shame (*feeling*), for instance, with regard to what she sees as her basic unacceptability often initiates her defense of Withdrawal (*doing*), while James's defensively Projecting (*thinking*) that no one believes he can do anything right is often the inspiration for his defense of Anger (*feeling*).

Frog-day nights

Have you heard the story of how to cook a frog so the poor thing doesn't even know what's happening? If you put a frog in a frying pan full of cold water and slowly turn the heat up, the frog's body temperature rises to match the heat of the water, but in such small increments that the frog will be dead before even realizing the water's hot!

It's just like this with our defenses. The degree and intensity with which we use them rises so slowly over the years that, unwittingly, we simply accommodate the change until—we're cooked! Turning down the heat through what I call "Defense Work" sometimes even feels at first as though we've jumped out of the frying pan and into the fire, since our growing awareness begins to turn up our own emotional heat. You may therefore find yourself feeling out of control (as in crying when you might previously have remained stoic, speaking up when you would usually be silent, or staying quiet when you would ordinarily be aggressive). But you should realize that the discomfort associated with your new behaviors is a *temporary* condition, and the knowledge that makes you uncomfortable at first, eventually becomes the power that saves you. Be brave then—and take the leap!

Also, as you trace your way through *all* the defenses we'll examine, please remember that the mere existence of *any* particular feeling, behavior, or thought is never the point. In fact, the mere presence of such a feeling, behavior, or thought will not automatically suggest that you have this quality or characteristic as a defense. Rather, what you'll want to watch out for is the **volume** with which these feelings, behaviors, or thoughts exist within you and the (excessive) ways they appear in your life.

THE HIT DEFENSES

The hit defenses:
CONNECTION THROUGH FEELING

The defense of ANGER
Protecting yourself with feelings of hostility.

ANGER

Personal impact

Anger has a huge range, feeling inside like anything from an indignant *how-dare-they* whisper to a roaring, five-alarm scream. But whether we silently stew or furiously spew, we would probably describe ourselves as *provoked*. That is, we think other people are to blame for our sore feelings. But an important part of changing requires a new perspective on how we assign this responsibility, for others may provoke us, but only *we* are in charge of our responses to that provocation.

Outer appearance

To appreciate the depth and scope of this defense, it's certainly helpful to keep in mind that anger is often more subtle than obvious. For instance, so-called teasing, when it has an edge or when it intentionally strikes a particularly personal cord, can mask seething anger. Other examples of more subtle versions of anger include *indignation, sulking, constant lateness* (which, in psychology, is classic for having anger as its source), and *forgetfulness*.

Swearing is another form of anger you may easily overlook. This particular method of expression is most often used to protect feelings of vulnerability that seem intolerable. Truly, swearing ought not to be ignored, for all too frequently it is a prelude to violence.

A great deal of the time, however, anger is less than subtle and can be most easily spotted by the way it bursts onto the scene. Notice the (many) times when you or those around you blow their stack, get hot under the collar, or hit the roof. Here Marty tells us about his early experiences of being raised by people who were dominated by the more obvious version of this defense.

MARTY & THE FATHER-MOTHER KINSHIP
Abandonment
Fight Nights

I am around nine years old. Dad is in one room while Mother sews in the kitchen. They are fighting, screaming back and forth. My father yells, "You fat-ass." And my mother screams back, "You stupid wop!" I am torn between them—hurting for them . . . wanting them to stop.

"Please stop," I think desperately. I am so sad for them both.

The next thing I remember is being with my eleven-year-old brother in our parents' bedroom. Mom and Dad are screaming that they are going to leave each other. I am dying inside. "No, no, don't leave!" They hurl more words back and forth as my dad pushes my mom onto the bed. My brother jumps on Dad's back. Again, I am torn. "Don't hurt my dad," I silently cry. "Dad, stop hurting my mom," I plead wordlessly. "Just stop . . . please stop."

Today, life is challenging for Marty, who is now fifty years old and still hesitates to put himself and his own needs in the forefront. (Meanwhile, his brother still tends to jump into the middle of things, fight for his own viewpoint, and demand new outcomes.) Marty continues to have difficulty being direct and clearly speaking his mind. When it comes to relationship, he feels torn, and though he appears to want a happy, successful partnership, he always manages to find something wrong with whomever he dates—something disappointing enough to make him give up sooner or later. When he does give up, he usually blames the other person. Inevitably, then, he feels powerless to change the outcome. (After all, how can he change what he was not in charge of in the first place?) Subsequently (and over and over again) he feels alone, unloved . . . and, of course, angry about his situation. His unconscious driving ideas are: "Life is pain. I can't win. No one's to be trusted."

The look, feel, and sound of anger

In the main section of this book, with each Defense Profile, you will find a two-column grid offering examples of certain possible (defense-inspired) behaviors. These behaviors **Signal** the defense with which you're involved and are a way for you to catch yourself in the act of being defensive. They also include the **Story Lines** that present examples of things you might say to yourself or others when you're caught up in a particular defense. These (internally felt or outwardly spoken) statements give you the right, or so you think, to behave defensively. I offer them here as yet another way you can spot your own defensive ways and means.

The possibilities shown in the Signals and Story Lines grids are certainly not meant to be comprehensive, since the variations are literally endless. Rather, each is presented with the principal intention of stimulating your thinking through diverse examples. At the end of each grid, therefore, you will find two blank spaces, where you may begin to fill in your own personal favorite Signals and Story Lines—whether those favorites are what you yourself feel and say or they are what you observe as you pay attention to people around you (who are, of course, involved in their own defenses!).

If you were to drop your Story Lines all the way down to the bottom of the (unconsciousness) pool, you'd be likely to find the driving ideas that propel your life. These (mostly unrecognized) driving ideas are your general **themes**. Each person has three or four such themes that he or she tends to apply to all circumstances. Overall, you will be wise to start listening hard inside yourself so you can identify your own personal themes. But for now, simply see if you can find yourself in the list of specific defenses noted below.

Start listening for the themes that drive your life

SIGNALS	STORY LINES
Anger can cause you to be . . .	**To feel the internal effects of anger, try reading the following words with sharpness and force. You may say things like:**
Vengeful:	"When I'm rich and successful, I'll show them a thing or two."
Resentful:	"The only people who make it in this business are the ones who kiss ass!"

Righteously indignant:	"How dare you say such a thing!"
Bitter:	"No one ever pays attention to me."
Sarcastic:	"Oh yeah! I'm *sure* you didn't mean to hurt me!"
Easily outraged:	"I can't believe the waiter is completely ignoring me! What an idiot!"
Sulky:	"Oh, everything stinks. I hate the stupid holidays—they're all so damn commercial anyhow!"
Provocative:	"Ah, is the poor little baby offended?"
Retaliatory (real or fantasized):	"I can't believe that jerk cut me off! I'd like to pull him out of his car and break his jaw!"
Your signals:	**Your Story Lines;**

The following two Signals and their accompanying Story Lines are frequently mistaken for Run defenses, but their true source is most often unexpressed hostility.

Forgetful:	"I completely forgot our date! Sorry."
Chronically late:	"I've really been under the gun lately—don't take it personally."

Unconscious intention

Occasionally, our anger is precisely appropriate to the circumstances we are facing, as perhaps when a stranger assaults us for no apparent reason. But more often, our angry expression is a secondary reaction, covering some even more awful feeling. In fact, peel away this protective layer called anger and we're likely to see either grief or fear—two emotions that threaten to make us feel terribly vulnerable. Our unconscious, then, may choose to defend through an anger that appears to have more authority and to be more powerful than those "weaker" (grief/fear) feelings.

Community dynamics

Today's society is increasingly angry. The evidence of this furious world can be seen in children killing children, violence abounding in the streets, home invasions, and even in a relatively new category of psychological disorder called *road rage* (the hostility you feel while driving). Everywhere, this explosive atmosphere threatens to blow up or boil over. Clearly, the most striking recent example is the World Trade Center attack of 9/11/2001, which, as we followed it step by gruesome step through the media, heightened in a rare way our collective awareness of the effects of extreme rage.

Engage
rather
than
enrage

Relate
rather
than
infuriate

But aggression has long been operating in our society. It weaves itself into every aspect and angle of our lives. Our fashion even reflects it (consider the ever-popular, hard-edged, silver-studded, leather look), music makes anthems of it (listen to rap music and heavy metal), and the media tout it (examine tabloid print journalism and television exposés).

Actually, by comparison to society at large, individuals often hardly seem angry at all . . . but of course individuals are, because individuals *are* society! That's why, if this society-wide epidemic is to abate or be resolved, the resolution must certainly begin with individuals, and that means you and me. We must have the courage to engage rather than enrage, to relate rather than infuriate. To do this, we need to get a handle on our defenses.

Personal sacrifice

As we previously discussed, anger is most often a brace against the dreaded vulnerability to which we feel exposed whenever our own fear or grief arises. You've been long hoping that if only you could override those uncomfortable feelings they would go away, or at least be unobtrusive enough that you could ignore them. But exactly the opposite happens, for as it turns out, avoidance only emboldens unconfronted feelings! Which means they actually *gain* power! How does this happen?

Imagine you are walking down the street with a screaming child tugging constantly on your arm. The more you ignore the child, the louder the screams get. Now picture what happens if you stop, bend down, and directly address the frantic youngster. Often the child will begin to explain or point out the problem and request a solution. ("My foot hurts, Mommy!") This gives you an opportunity to correct the situation.

What we face we grace

Vulnerability is like this. *Facing* it often gives you a better chance of relieving and containing the screaming—both in your head and in your life. So *face* your vulnerabilities and give yourself a fighting chance to heal! As many wise teachers have said—what we resist persists, while what we face we grace.

Avoidance stokes the fire of your pain

Resource acquired

Every feeling, behavior, or thought, when (unconsciously) wielded as a defense, can be both draining and undermining. However, those very same feelings, behaviors, and thoughts, when approached with some semblance of consciousness, offer amazing empowerment. Anger, for instance, a passionate response, is an explosive energy that can be rechanneled in order to inspire love, evoke great artistry, or move a person into devoted public service.

The defense of CONTEMPT FOR OTHERS
*Protecting yourself with despising, negative,
disdainful feelings toward other people.*

Personal impact

Contempt is a dark, dominating wall of negativity behind which we stand alone. It separates us from other people, who can sense it and are repelled by it. The more contempt we feel, the more others stay away. The more they stay away, the more contempt we find ourselves feeling for them. After a while, the wall becomes a permanent structure, more of a trap than a protection.

Outer appearance

When we're contemptuous, we often seem arrogant, self-righteous, and snide. We act as if we're above it all—strident, aggressive, haughty. We may even try to get others to join us in our Contempt through gossip, cutting humor, criticism, or controlling behavior.

Contempt traps and isolates us

SIGNALS	STORY LINES
Contempt for others can cause you to be . . .	**To feel the internal effects of contempt, try reading following words with a sneer. You may say things like:**
Scornful:	"What a fool that Randolph is!"
Critical:	"Every time I turn around you're making another mistake!"
Mocking:	"She's fat as a cow."

Self-righteous:	"Ignore their complaints and be smart—follow my lead. Remember: nice guys finish last."
Derisive:	"He can't chew gum and walk at the same time!"
Gossipy:	"I've never thought his ideas were worth a dime."
Prejudiced:	"Women just can't do this job!"
Judgmental:	"Hey, I'd rather be alone . . . I certainly wouldn't want any of the relationships I see!"
Arrogant:	"Look, this is the way the game is played, so if you can't stand the heat, get out of the kitchen!"
Cutting:	"If you want to know how it's *really* supposed to be done, do feel free to ask!"
__Your__ Signals:	__Your__ Story Lines:

Unconscious intention

Unconsciously, we're likely to be *condemning ourselves* with the very disregard and mockery we dispense to others—believing, though not realizing it, that *we* deserve disdain, ridicule, and criticism. We look down upon others, therefore, in an attempt to feel better about ourselves and as a distraction from our own *self*-loathing. This *never* works. In fact, our contempt for others only reinforces our self-loathing (see Self-Contempt, p. 145).

We sneer at others to avoid ourselves

Community dynamics

These days, the public complaint department is wide open. Radio and television talk-show hosts shout out divisive diatribes, indicting anyone who doesn't agree with them. Their vitriol *reflects* collectively what seems to be a growing personal taste for blood.

There are groups specializing in contempt (the Ku Klux Klan, which has contempt for many religions and especially for African Americans; the Aryan Brotherhood, which has contempt for Jews; the Red Brigade, which has contempt for democracy; and Al Queda, which has contempt for Western civilization). There are leaders who have historically promoted contempt on a collective level (Adolph Hitler and Joseph Stalin are good examples, and more recently Osama bin Laden). Actually any organized religion that promotes the idea that *its* way is the *only* way encourages among its members Contempt for Others. And bigotry itself, howsoever individually or collectively promoted, is a process of looking down on others in order to raise oneself up.

Personal sacrifice

Contempt for others is a disconnector—one that inevitably leaves you feeling more isolated than ever. Since what you offer (and therefore feel) is disapproval instead of affection, contention instead of consideration, and bitterness instead of benevolence, that's usually what you get back.

Resource acquired

Like so many aggressive defenses, contempt disciplines you and teaches you discernment. Your constant assessment of what's despicable in others has developed in you an ability to recognize problematic people when you see them.

HIT DEFENSES: CONNECTION THROUGH FEELING

The defense of BLAME

*Protecting yourself by feeling and believing
that someone else is at fault.*

Personal impact

Blame is a grim-visaged little varmint that whines and complains its way through our brain. It blurs our vision of our own life while simultaneously distorting our understanding of other people and of circumstances. At first, our blaming ways seem to puff us up with righteousness, but eventually our habit of reproach and recrimination simply leaves us feeling bitter, hopeless, and disempowered.

Outer appearance

Sometimes our complaints are even well-founded, but this is nearly irrelevant, for while our blame may include accuracies, it harms more than it helps, at the very least creating a blindness in us about our participation in the problem at hand. Blame is easy to spot. Look for complaining, resentment, finger-pointing, exaggeration, fault-finding, whining, passing-the-buck, and excuse-making.

Every time we point the bony finger of blame outward, three fingers point right back at us

SIGNALS	STORY LINES
Blame can cause you to be . . .	To feel the internal effects of blame, try reading the following words with a pout and a whine. You may say things like:
Pouting:	"I never get what I need because everything is always about what *she* needs!"
Self-righteous:	"Hey, leave me alone—I'm doing the best I can."

Victimized:	"No matter how hard I try, I just can't seem to get a decent break! I can't take it anymore."
Resentful:	"Hey, it's easy for you. You get to go to work. I'm stuck with the kids all day and when you come home you don't even help."
Indignant:	"Okay, so you're right!" I shouted. "So what? You're the one who started it!"
Exaggerating:	"My sister-in-law is ruining my life with her insane demands."
Condemning:	"What an ungrateful child . . . I worked like a dog to give her everything and all she does is complain about how I wasn't there for her!"
Finger-pointing:	"It's my mother's fault I'm so disorganized. She was too strict and I had to rebel."
Excusing:	"Sorry I'm late again. I tried to leave early but people simply wouldn't stop calling me."
Whining:	"I just don't have the strength to fight back when he's mean."
Your Signals:	**Your Story Lines:**

Unconscious intention

A blame defense reflects one of three blind stances: The first and probably the most common stance is our belief that *other people really are the problem.* As part of this idea, we see ourselves as having no authority over the way our life unfolds. The second stance is that we see ourselves as *truly incapable* of creating and having a healthy, fulfilling life. But rather than admitting the depth and scope of this feeling of incapacity, we blame others for our unfortunate state. (This feeling of incapacity is usually rooted in childhood experiences and reinforced by current behavior.) The third stance is one in which we think we're actually at fault for *everything* bad that happens to *anyone*. In this case, our blaming is an effort to shift focus. Maybe—we (unconsciously) think—they won't notice that *we're* really the central problem. This is an oddly self-centered perspective, that has the impact of making us feel important.

Community dynamics

In the early 1990s, society seemed to go through a phase in which nearly *everything* became excusable because "someone else was to blame." If a horrific event occurred, we looked first at the perpetrator's childhood for the reason (the Menendez boys killed their parents *because* of childhood trauma) and then at the *victim's* behavior (Lorena Bobbitt cut off the penis of her husband, John Wayne Bobbitt, *because* he abused her). When even more stunning events occurred (like the Littleton, Colorado, school massacre or the September 11, 2001, attacks), we, as a community, started desperately scrambling to figure out who was to blame—looking at parents, video games, drugs, guns, music, movies, and the media in general, for instance. Everywhere but at those who actually committed the atrocities. Certainly our wanting to put these events in a meaningful context is understandable, but we must be careful of sacrificing the first and most basic truth—that each of us is responsible for the actions we take.

Happily, general societal support for the blame game seemed in the latter part of the 1990s to abate. However, I suspect that, as individuals, we will always struggle against our tendencies to blame others for our difficulties. And our communities will continue to reflect this struggle,

The three blind "blame" mice:

* We <u>really</u> believe everyone else is the problem

* We <u>pretend</u> to believe everyone else is the problem (because we hate ourselves)

* We truly believe <u>everything</u> <u>everywhere</u> is all <u>our</u> fault

It's always
tempting
to
play
the
blame
game

easing the way for us to nurture a general feeling that we can or should blame horrific world events, modern technology, personal childhood trauma, and/or the media for our daily ills.

Personal sacrifice

When you blame other people for your problems, you give up any real power you might have over your own thinking, feeling, and behaving. This leads to a sense of impotence, which often reveals itself as an undermining of personal goals and a sabotaging of relationships.

Resource acquired

While blaming, you have learned to recognize the ways in which other people contribute to your problems. This eventually helps you understand which part of the difficulty is unquestionably yours and which part is genuinely theirs!

The hit defenses:
CONNECTION THROUGH DOING

Doing—the heart and soul of the "hit" defenses—results in (sometimes deleterious, sometimes helpful) action-taking tendencies. Though taking action can feel good and even lead to positive results, you must remember to stay aware of how you're <u>driven</u> to action as opposed to being led to <u>choose</u> action.

The first three defenses listed here (Spilling, Gossip, and Humor) tend to help you masquerade as social and connected. But in actuality, the noisy, sometimes funny mask you wear simply serves to disconnect and alienate you from others.

HIT DEFENSES: CONNECTION THROUGH DOING

The defense of SPILLING

Protecting yourself with constant (often inappropriate) talking.

Personal impact

As spillers, we're busy bees who drone on and on, often buzzing loudly and boldly. We hardly pause to hear others, and instead proceed self-centeredly with little consciousness of the impact we're making on our listeners. Our flamboyant disclosures actually announce (while at the same time exaggerating) our terrible sense of separation. That sense of separation is confusing to us, since we're convinced that conversation is connection. In a way, then, our frantic tale-spinning creates a kind of noisy, aggressive (and for us, quite mystifying) isolation.

Outer appearance

Recently in a supermarket, I heard a woman at the next checkout stand loudly proclaiming to the clerk that she was experiencing fear with regard to her upcoming mammogram—considering the fact that cancer ran in her family. After all, her sister had already lost a breast, she trumpeted resoundingly. Perhaps the grocery clerk was a close personal friend (doubtful!), but I know that the others of us within earshot were not. Sadly enough, what this woman was actually broadcasting was her excruciating loneliness—a loneliness for which we, the listeners, might have had compassion if only we had been allowed the space to feel and express that compassion.

To recognize spilling, look for run-on sentences, intrusiveness, breathlessness, self-centeredness, lack of focus, and lack of awareness with regard to impact on others and to the appropriateness of sharing particular content given the circumstances.

SIGNALS	STORY LINES
Spilling can cause you to be . . .	**To feel the internal effects of spilling, try reading the following words rapidly and breathlessly. You may say things like:**
Garrulous:	(to waitress/stranger:) "Thanks sooo much. I'm really glad to get this salad. I thought I'd never eat again after this morning. I had such a bad stomach ache. I guess it all started with that phone call from my mom. . . ."
Trying to convince:	"No matter what you believe, I tried to do the right thing here. I really opened up and made every effort. But you never seem to believe me when I say I tried!"
Anxious about not being heard:	"How many times do I have to say this for you to really hear me? Over and over again, I've tried to get you to understand, but you don't . . . you won't!"
Repetitious:	"Will you be able to come on Friday? It's very important to me, so if you can't show up I need to know. Everyone will be there and it will look pretty strange if I'm alone, so what do you say? I guess I'll just figure something out if you can't make it, but I really need to know."
Uncensored:	"Nancy always had it rough—how about her weird sex thing with that neighbor! Oh . . . you didn't know about that?"
Your Signals:	**Your Story Lines:**

Unconscious intention

Inside our wall of noise lives a terrified individual who's afraid of feelings. "I speak so I will not feel," we might say if we were conscious of what's going on inside of us. These feelings of which we are so afraid probably began in childhood as emotions we originally rejected because they felt overwhelming or even dangerous. And they still do. Our frenetic way of avoiding the stabbing silence that threatens to reignite these old feelings is endless noise.

We speak
so
we
will not
feel

Community dynamics

You might just as well call this the media/talk show syndrome, since "toxic" spilling has almost become a societal art form. Now little is left to the imagination or kept sacred. We talk about others (gossip—which equals spilling the beans) or we talk about ourselves (confession—which equals spilling our guts). Privacy is at a premium, and public expressions of personal information are commonplace.

Spilling misdirects us. If we're encouraged to tell everything to everyone all the time, eventually we lose track both of what's valuable to share and what's at the heart of our sharing. At that point, we start considering *any* talking as communication and *any* disclosure as intimacy. This thought-less chatter is more dangerous to our individual and collective psyches than might be evident at first glance. It's as if we're encouraged to engage in emotional promiscuity without being warned about taking the appropriate precautions to protect ourselves from (unknown) future damage. In this case, the potential damage is that our increasing loss of privacy and of the boundaries that secure it add to our general sense of living in a chaotic, unsafe world, which in turn undermines our optimism. The only mystery left seems to be how we will reestablish boundaries in this age of information gone amuck.

Personal sacrifice

Spilling tends more to alienate than to engage, thereby becoming a defense that robs the user of honest, intimate connections with others.

Resource acquired

Spilling teaches you to speak up. Once you know what you *really* want to say, this will be helpful knowledge to have!

HIT DEFENSES: CONNECTION THROUGH DOING

The defense of GOSSIP

Protecting yourself by talking to someone about someone else who is not present.

Personal impact

Gossip is fun, sometimes spicy, once in a while generous, but often merely mean-spirited. It is a common pastime for many and an occasional indulgence for some. The problem is that revealing personal information or intimate details about other people, though sometimes tempting, often leaves us feeling covert, collusive, disparaging, or ridiculing. We know we're going too far—crossing a boundary into private territory—but we do it anyway.

On occasion, gossiping allows us to feel superior to the person we're talking about and, at the same time, to feel intimate with our gossip partners. So this focus gives us a fraudulent sense of relationship—because in talking *about* others, we feel as if we are somehow *with* others. In that way, we get to pretend to have intimacy without actually risking intimacy. Still, gossiping can leave us feeling anxious, since it seldom scratches the real desire-to-communicate itch and instead leaves us wanting either something more or something different.

Outer appearance

Gossip can be overtly judgmental or it can be hidden in apparent good humor ("Her nose looks so much better than it did before her surgery"). We can gossip in person, by phone, in print, or by e-mail and

Gossip allows the pretense of pseudo-intimacy without the risk of real intimacy

the Internet. At worst, gossips are often referred to as rumor-mongers or tattletales. At best, they're referred to as information sources or even valued intermediaries.

SIGNALS	STORY LINES
Gossiping can cause you to be . . .	**To feel the internal effects of gossiping, try reading the following words in a conspiratorial tone. You may say things like:**
Flattering:	"Marsha looks wonderful doesn't she! Did you know she had a facelift?"
Telling secrets:	"James is leaving. He hasn't told anyone else yet so don't say anything."
Critical:	"She'll walk over anyone to get where she's going. And she's not even talented."
Judgmental:	"Everyone says Joe's a slimeball. I've heard all kinds of stuff about him, and you know how it is: where there's smoke, there's fire!"
Vindictive:	"Hey, I couldn't care less about making it with Donna— she's screwed everyone in town anyway!"
Comparing:	"I don't expect to meet anyone at my ripe old age of forty-five. Anyway, the reasonably decent guys like Frank are all dating women half their age . . . and half their IQ if Samantha's any example!"
Passing information:	"He said he never said that."
Ridiculing:	"Did you see that outfit? She looks like the side of a barn!"

<u>Your</u> Signals:	<u>Your</u> Story Lines:

*Gossip
is the
fool's gold
of
communication—
we think
we're sharing
but we're
really not!*

Unconscious intention

Gossip as a defense has two unconscious aims. The first aim is to *connect with others.* But gossip is the fool's gold of communication—it may look like it's worth something but it has little real value. The second aim is *to make us feel better about ourselves.* We (incorrectly) imagine we can accomplish this by undermining or demeaning other people.

Community dynamics

Gossiping is a popular sport, to the degree that many people seem to confuse gossip with real communication and even with news reporting. There are gossip columns, gossip columnists, gossip segments on television, office gossips, family gossips, neighborhood gossips, and more. This habit begins early on in the family, where talking about other family members and neighbors, too, is a common pastime. Then later, after this fundamental family training, we go on to gossip about the world around us—about the famous, the infamous, and the barely-known. There seem to be no depths to which we hesitate to plunge. We talk about people's sexuality (outing is a good example), about their psychology (noting, for instance, their drug and alcohol history), about their family problems (revealing sordid details), and about their social standing (reporting their financial status and going into their homes to see how they live). Perhaps we use gossip defensively to guard against a sense of our own dull inadequacies. In that instance, a vicarious life, we suppose, is better than living a non-life. The consequence is that these forms of gossip, which stimulate, alarm, revile, and intrigue us, will continue as long as we endorse them.

Personal sacrifice

Gossiping marks you as untrustworthy. (After all, if you'll tell Marie's secret to me, why wouldn't you tell my secret to Marie?) Acquaintances, therefore, and even friends are likely to keep their most precious sharing for more honorable ears, which means you often forfeit exactly what (you think) you're seeking: true connection.

Gossip forfeits true connection

Resource acquired

Gossip teaches you to be an accomplished storyteller. Once you learn to share your opinions, values, and ideas with more discernment and integrity, you can give up gossip for real intimacy—which includes entertaining communication.

HIT DEFENSES: CONNECTION THROUGH DOING

The defense of HUMOR

*Protecting yourself with comical
(sometimes inappropriate) self-expression.*

Personal impact

Genuine humor often feels like a sudden, welcome rainstorm on a sticky day—startling us, enchanting us, and enlivening us. However, what takes a delightful remark, gesture, or even attitude and makes it defensive is one or both of two ingredients.

The first ingredient to look for if you want to determine whether humor is defensive is *Context*—which is the "where and when" of it. So, when humor is employed as a device to deflect a poignant or serious moment, or when it is used to interrupt a connection rather than to further the intimacy that could come from the connection, it is most often defensive. Examples include: someone compliments you on your

Whether or not humor is defensive depends on:

* *Context:
where and when
we use it*

* *Content:
what we say
and
how we say it*

appearance or accomplishment and you respond with a quip instead of a thank you; you're in a serious setting such as an important business meeting or even a religious ceremony where other people are contributing their best, most heartfelt ideas and you come forward with a distracting (humorous) comment; you're with a good friend who is clearly distraught, even crying, and rather than comforting your friend you try to joke him or her out of those "bad" feelings.

In determining whether humor is defensive, the second ingredient to look for is *Content*. Often this is easier to spot than context. Obvious examples include body-shaming jokes; sarcastic, ridiculing or "teasing" observations; and mean-spirited comments. Incidentally, when it comes to verbal punching, I've noticed that aggressors often follow their rotten jabs with a sneering *"I was just kidding! Where's your sense of humor!"* But mean and rude are simply not funny. So ask yourself: is your remark terribly clever or just terrible? (Notice when you're the only one laughing.)

Unfortunately, much of the humor we hear around us does tend to verge on, and frequently never veer away from, sarcasm, teasing, or even shaming behavior, so it's easy to sign up for the general attitude that what's funny ought to be prickly. Be alert, then, for occasions when what you say is clearly hurtful, damaging, attacking, or insulting. At those times, you need to question your intention regarding the "funny" things you are saying—and whether you are actually involved in a self-protective defense.

At first, the only way you will usually be able to determine whether you use humor as a defense *is* to notice the effect of what you say and do. Check out what your hidden (unconscious) intention may be. Do you want to (deeply) wound or at least (lightly) jab others? Are you trying to pull other people closer or keep them at arm's length? In response to your barbed quips, provocative jests, and "hilarious" words, do the

Notice the effect and impact of your "humor"

people around you withdraw and shut down? If they do, begin to feel the distance your defensive "humor" creates.

Outer appearance

Humor is an agile shape-changer, appearing in a wide-range of forms—from shenanigans, banter, quips, jokes, and ridicule, to sarcasm, flippancy, and teasing.

SIGNALS	STORY LINES
Defensive humor can cause you to be . . .	**To feel the internal effects of humor as a defense, try reading this in a sharp, aggressive tone. You may say things like:**
Teasing:	"Hey four-eyes, whatcha got cookin'?"
Shaming:	"You're either deaf or stupid—and I know you're not deaf."
Mocking:	"He's not exactly the sharpest tool in the shed."
Judgmental:	"She's so dumb, she doesn't even know that blondes are supposed to be more fun."
Stinging:	"You could see a lot better if you'd get your head out of your ass."
Provocative:	"As far as I can tell, you never met a liar you didn't want to elect to office!"
Rejecting:	"Yeah, well, if you think I look good now, you shoulda seen me before I looked like a hundred miles of dusty road."
Flippant:	"Hey, it takes a lot of work to do the nothin' I do. Get off my back already!"

Sarcastic:	"Oh, yeah, sure. You'll be rich and famous someday! I'll just sit here and hold my breath!"
Your Signals:	**Your Story Lines:**

We live more by a thrusting wit than by an extended hand

Unconscious intention

Although those of us who defend ourselves with humor may appear to the casual onlooker to be offhand, unperturbed, or even superior, more often we are, in actuality, answering the call of our unconscious. "Protect yourself," it says—either from the intimacy others threaten whenever we let them near, or from the sadness in us that has gone so long unexpressed. And protect ourselves we will, since both visibility (the experience that frequently goes with intimacy) and vulnerability (the experience that frequently goes with expressions of deep sadness) simply feel too dangerous. We choose, therefore, to live more by a thrusting wit than by an extended hand.

Community dynamics

Today humor is probably our most popular collective defense. In fact, stand-up comedians, once relegated to the back burner in the world of entertainment, are now frequently elevated to stardom—considered central to important film-making and made the focus of major television projects.

Why have these funny folk risen to such heights in our esteem? Maybe we're just desperate for some relief from what we perceive as our increasing daily struggles. Tired of the trauma and the drama, we yearn for laughter at any cost. Unfortunately, as individuals, the price we pay for participating in making fun of everything and everyone is often greater than we may imagine.

The point is: we have choices. We can be funny and still be generous. If, for instance, we rudely ridicule marriage (as in the television show *Married with Children*) we undermine marriage; whereas if we gently poke it (as in the television show *Home Improvement*), we enliven marriage. We laugh *and* we learn. If we humorously expose family dysfunction (as in the film *Meet the Parents*), we change our perspective, but if family dysfunction is used to slap us in the face (as in the film *The Royal Tennenbaums*), we give up more than we gain. If we directly but sweetly address our societal fixation on looks (as in the film *All About Cats & Dogs*), we wake up to some of our own constructs, but it we continue to support the idea that the thin and beautiful are more worthwhile and worth more (because that's who we're willing to pay to see in the movies, on television, and gracing magazine covers) we constantly remind ourselves we can never be enough.

Personal sacrifice

As a defense, humor not only passes your personal pain onto others but it also tends to leave you feeling isolated and misunderstood. If, by whatever means, you make it too difficult for us to approach you, eventually we're all most likely to simply go away.

Resource acquired

Practicing humor in any form teaches you to look on the light side. Eventually, when it's used to amuse rather than assault, humor can spare you from taking yourself and the details of your daily life too seriously.

Step 12 in defense busting:
Take the work of growth and discovery seriously, and take yourself lightly!

HIT DEFENSES: CONNECTION THROUGH DOING

The defense of DEPENDENCE

Protecting yourself through excessive reliance on others.

Personal impact

Dependence is, at its worst, a crooked staff that fails to support. It erodes our confidence by rasping in our ear that we can't handle our own life, that we're at the mercy of others, and that we have no personal power. Feeling inept, confused, and helpless, we often find that getting ourselves moving is difficult. We tell ourselves that we have little to offer and also that our connections to emotional, psychological, physical, and spiritual resources are tenuous or even nonexistent. We're inclined to become preoccupied with thoughts and feelings of abandonment, we are nervous about being alone, and we feel devastated when close relationships end.

Often, oddly enough, the more dependent we feel, the more demanding we become—whining and complaining about needing to be certain that we get "what's coming to us" or attempting to manipulate people instead of asking directly for what we want or need. But we do not *see* ourselves as dependent, only as someone who's trying really hard to make things work in a world that's simply too difficult to manage. To discover if you are, in fact, using dependence as a defense, ask yourself this: do you usually feel devastated or incapable of taking care of yourself when *particular* people, places, or things leave your life?

If you
lean
too hard
you risk
falling
over

Outer appearance

We are all dependent on others to some extent—on their approval, acceptance, nurturance, assistance, and information. But when normal, healthy reliance (counting on others' goodwill and appreciation) becomes excessive (and therefore unhealthy), the result is behavior that appears to be clawing, pleading, demanding, self-centered, pitiful, insecure, or chaotic—or even adoring, obsequious, or submissive.

If we use dependence as a defense, others tend to regard us as indecisive, especially because we seek advice at every turn. Initiating projects and other independent activities is often especially difficult.

In addition, we're particularly sensitive to criticism (or *perceived* disapproval). Often we belittle our own accomplishments, but at times we exaggerate them instead, bemoaning the fact that, despite how hard we work, our circumstances remain as difficult and terrible as always.

SIGNALS	STORY LINES
Dependence can cause you to be . . .	**To feel the internal effects of dependence, talk in a pathetic tone. You may say things like:**
Jealous:	"Pat just keeps talking and talking about how great Jackie is. I'm sick to death of it. I need the focus to be on me for a change."
Disorganized:	"Regardless of how much I try, I can't seem to get my life together."
Feeling inferior:	"You're so much better at everything than I am. I just don't know what to do when I'm by myself."
Helpless:	"Jamie's the one who did everything around the house. Now when something breaks, it just stays broken."

Manipulative:	"I know you're really busy and have a full life, but I have to admit I wish I had someone who cared enough to help me."
Confused:	"I don't know where to turn next. Help! What should I do?"
Hurt:	"I guess I'm not much help. I just always feel like I'm always disappointing you. Maybe I should just get out of your way. Would that be better?"
Submissive:	"Honey, whatever you say, I'll do. You're the boss and you know best."
Insecure:	"I don't know the right thing to say. Just tell me."
Fearful:	"I can't be alone. I'm frightened. If you leave me I'll die."
Your Signals:	**Your** Story Lines:

Unconscious intention

Using dependence as a defense leads us to hold one of two unconscious beliefs. We underestimate *ourselves*—which means we believe we're incapable of real accomplishment and that even if we try our best, we'll fall flat on our face. (In this case, we need to realize that this is only an idea we have perpetuated and reinforced, not an irreversible truth.) Or we underestimate *other* people—which means we think that others, in order to feel powerful around us, want us to act as though we are dependent on them. We think that if we *don't* act dependent, they will lose interest and withdraw their caring for us. If we're correct—that those others will abandon us if we don't act needy around them—it probably means we've surrounded ourselves with controlling individuals who only appreciate us when they can act powerful in our presence. In

Your
incapacity
is more
an
idea
than
a fact!

that case, we ought to reconsider whether we really want those kinds of friends. However, if we're incorrect—that is, our friends and family are not only strong but they also truly care about us and *want* us to be our best self rather than being dependent on them—we can safely claim our true power without their abandoning us. They will probably even be relieved at our assertion of independence, since they won't have to feel overwhelmingly responsible for us anymore.

Both of these (unconsciously held) ideas—"I can't do it" and "You *think* I can't do it"—have two corresponding, unconsciously held intentions. The first unconscious intention involves a desperate effort to get ourselves rescued (coupled, unfortunately, with a belief that if we rescue *ourselves*, no one else will come to rescue us!). Another way to say this might be: I play helpless, dumb, small, incompetent, or needy so you'll take care of me.

The second (unconsciously held) intention is to get *everyone* to take care of us. It involves an odd, twisted belief that we can't really depend on any one person, so we're better off presenting ourselves as dependent on *all* people. This way, we figure, we have more of a chance of getting what we need from *someone, somewhere*. We're like the homeless person on the corner who knows that no one individual will provide shelter, so she just sticks her hand out to everyone.

Community dynamics

Many of us seem conflicted with regard to issues of dependence. For instance, how do we help other people, showing ourselves to be good, caring, and noble, without undermining their individual potential and self-reliance? Is welfare, for instance, ennobling or demeaning? Are we, with our social programs and flexible attitudes, supporting or crippling, encouraging or diminishing? All too often, we seem to harm more than we help. When, for example, children who can't even read are passed through successive grades just to get them out of school or perhaps to protect what we regard as their fragile self-esteem, we send our youth into society *less* prepared, *less* autonomous, and *less* self-confident than they might otherwise be. And by overlooking antisocial, destructive, or violent behavior (giving the they-came-from-a bad-home excuse), we encourage eventual dependence on a massive scale (welfare, prison, or crime). Unfortunately, then, community attitudes may often encourage individual dependence.

Dependence undermines personal power

Personal sacrifice

Dependence enforces double jeopardy by undermining personal power and, at the same time, reinforcing your idea that you can't be responsible or self-sufficient. While you're waiting for someone else to do "it" for you, you're likely to neglect the development of your own skills and attributes.

Resource acquired

Dependence forces you into developing a kind of trust—you depend on others, thereby learning that others can be depended on. By definition, then, you learn team-playing.

RACHEL & THE MOTHER KINSHIP
Abandonment
The Threat

I am four years old. It is late afternoon. My mother is in the room with me. She has on a navy blue dress and I have on a yellow dress and red ribbons in my hair. I have obviously done something very wrong, because Mother is angry and frustrated with me and clearly at the end of her rope. She looks at me and says, "I don't know what to do with you. You are so naughty."

She then takes out her small dark-brown suitcase. She starts packing her clothes. She tells me that the only thing she can do is leave me, since I am so naughty. I am scared to death, frozen in horror watching her do this.

This was not the last time Rachel's mother threatened to leave her. Apparently, recognizing how effective her threat was, she employed it all too often thereafter. Probably another kind of child would have stopped taking Mother seriously. Rachel did not—and today she still worries constantly about abandonment. Rachel has a habit of exacerbating this fear by partnering with critical, complaining people who are fearful of commitment. The more uncommitted (and therefore usually rejecting) these people are, the harder she works to please them. She works and works but never feels secure, no matter how hard she tries. Instead, she continually proclaims herself to be a loser. Her unconscious driving ideas are: "People will always leave because I'm basically bad. I don't know what's wrong with me. I must try harder."

Rachel is a typical codependent—doing too much, too often, for too many people. Like water on a dry garden, this can often seem good and even necessary. But just as too much water will drown the garden flowers, the people in the codependent's life can easily be overwhelmed by that so-called caring behavior.

* You throw
  down capes
  where there
  are no
  puddles

* You try to
  do everything
  for
  everybody
  all the time

HIT DEFENSES: CONNECTION THROUGH DOING

The defense of CODEPENDENCE

*Protecting yourself through excessive reliance
on people or things to define your self-worth.*

Personal impact

While using codependence defensively, we usually take one of four primary actions, each of which leads to four main problems and results:

Action #1: We frequently behave in *excessively* helpful ways. *Problem:* Our relationships become unbalanced. *Result*: We're often left feeling unrequited, exasperated, and burdened, thinking we seldom get as good as we give.

Action #2: We're always looking at outcomes. *Problem:* We drain precious juice out of the *process* and forget to appreciate the adventure of daily life. *Result:* Our life seems humdrum.

Action #3: We tend to be caretakers whether or not it's requested, and we are willing to ignore or even defy personal boundaries to accomplish our tasks (both the boundaries of other people and most definitely our own). *Problem:* Caretaking that is unrequested can feel to other people as though we are being condescending and demeaning. We tend to throw down capes where no puddles are present, and people are often only able to say "no" by creating emotional distance between ourselves and them. *Result:* We end up simply feeling unappreciated and slighted—seldom realizing that *our* behavior is what inspired the problem in the first place.

Action #4: We come to believe that people only care about us *because* we do so much for them. Otherwise—we imagine—they would not want us around. *Problem:* We sacrifice a belief in both genuine unconditional love and in our own innate acceptability. *Result:* We feel enormously isolated and unloved.

Outer appearance

What appears to be a loving, generous, helpful, energized offering is actually often over-zealous caretaking that can make us *feel* to others more like a hostage-taker than a helpful friend. In fact, the hallmark of codependence is control, and our need to be in charge of what's happening is often more of a turn-off than a help. Of course, because this controlling effort is coupled with an anxiety to please, we as codependents also often make the best employees, since in our quest for approval, we're willing to work *too* hard and to override our own personal boundaries.

You're often more hostage-taker than helpful friend

SIGNALS	STORY LINES
Codependence can cause you to be . . .	To feel the internal effects of codependence, try reading the following words with extreme passion. You may say things like:
Excessively diligent:	"I believe in *always* going above and beyond the call of duty in every situation!"
Excessively good:	"Is there anything—*anything*—more I can do to help?"
Excessively working:	"What a month! I think I've worked a zillion hours. Well, anyway —it can't be helped. That's the nature of the job! If I don't do it, who will?"
Excessively compliant:	"I know he's confused about our relationship—we broke up but are still having sex! It's hard for me to turn him down. I believe in giving people a second chance."
Excessively caretaking:	"Our son stole our television and sold it to buy drugs. I'm angry, and people say I should turn him in or throw him out, but I just can't put him on the streets. He's my own child, after all!"

Excessively affected by others' opinions:	"Someone said I was coming on too strong—I don't even remember who it was—but maybe I should cool it!"
Excessively controlling:	"I *know* you can stop that behavior if only you want to. If you really love me, you'll try!"
Excessively intrusive:	"I've got some great clothes I think would be terrific on you—much better than the style you're wearing."
Your Signals:	**Your Story Lines:**

Unconscious intention

Codependence leaves us squirming in the muck of what turns out to be our own self-disdain. We are often left feeling dissatisfied with the life we are living, while at the same time we feel disappointingly ineffectual when we try to change others' lives. As codependents, then, we have two unconscious aims, which result in two associated problems:

❖ We want to *do* enough in order to feel as though we *are* enough. The problem is that when we don't feel we are enough, there's no such thing as doing enough. There's only a constant sense of needing to do more.

❖ We're trying to control relationships—both physically and emotionally. We want to be in charge of determining how others feel and think about us. It's probably important to us, for instance, that we're perceived as good and thoughtful individuals. One "helpful" way of effecting this, we (unconsciously) think, is for us to strongly direct the course of other people's lives. The problem is that such efforts, even when they're done kindly and/or insistently, usually don't work very

You're trying to do enough to prove that you are enough

well—which means we're likely to be left feeling frustrated. Also, in the long run, we may not only remain unrecognized for our efforts but also even, perhaps, be resented. The truth is that people only change if they want to, and even then with the application of great personal determination and effort. (Think of one habit or attitude in your own life that you have successfully altered. Doing so probably required some sacrifice and tremendous intention.)

The hallmark of
codependence
is
control

Community dynamics

Originally, the term *codependent* was a specific reference to partners of alcoholics. The alcoholic was dependent on alcohol, and the partner of the alcoholic was dependent on being needed.*

---

* The impact of alcoholism on society has been so enormous as to be incalculable. The connection of alcoholism to personal damage, and thus to psychological defenses in general and to codependence in particular, is covered in a vast body of literature all its own. To summarize briefly: In the beginning, alcoholism was thought of as a radical condition—sometimes even deserving psychiatric institutionalization. Alcoholics—most of whom, it was thought, were older men who had often lost everything to demon alcohol—fell down, drank out of bottles hidden in paper bags in the morning, and were completely debilitated.

Then, after great effort and many defeats, a fellow named Bill Wilson managed to stop drinking and was so amazed and impressed with the effects of sobriety that he wanted to share his "experience, strength, and hope." Shortly thereafter (in Akron, Ohio, in 1935) with the help of a few others, he founded Alcoholics Anonymous.

Many of these newly recovered alcoholics had families who loved them and had been with them through their difficult times, putting up with the broken promises and constant disappointments, picking up the pieces over and over again. In a way, this picking up of the pieces became a kind of a "job" for these sweethearts and family members—a job to which they became accustomed. So when Bill Wilson found sobriety, his wife Lois discovered herself out of that job, relieved of her familiar duties and responsibilities (the so-called support that later came to be called *enabling*). Lois thus found herself in a void. At that point, she reasoned that other partners of recovering alcoholics might be reacting similarly—so she established a support group called Alanon, modeled on the twelve steps of Alcoholics Anonymous.

Remove the "take" from caretaking

But over time, the broader community began to recognize the growing effects of a toxic need for external evidence of personal value, and the term "codependence" became part of our everyday language. (In 1995, the National Association of Codependence speculated that 85% of the U.S. population fell into that category.)

Certainly there are some amazing individuals—society's heroes and heroines—who address the woes of the world first and their own needs second, but codependence is usually not as generous as that. The caretaking behavior of a codependent is more often about "taking" and less often about "caring." As long as we collectively miss this point and continue to encourage codependence as a way of life, individuals gripped by this defense will find fewer models of healthy behavior and diminishing support as they seek to extricate themselves from their own controlling ways.

Personal sacrifice

When you're codependent, you forfeit true self-esteem by thinking your only value is based on what you can do for others and on what other people think of you because of what you do for them.

Resource acquired

Codependence has taught you how to express authentic caring. When this caring comes more from your true desire to support others than from a drive to feel better about yourself, you'll be able to appreciate the ways in which it enhances your life.

HIT DEFENSES: CONNECTION THROUGH DOING

The following three defenses (Therapizing, Controlling, Criticizing) are notable because they tend mostly to be used by people who approach life as authorities—whether they're actually in authority, only want authority, or simply think of themselves as authorities!

The defense of THERAPIZING

Protecting yourself through excessive (often unrequested) advice-giving.

Personal impact

Professional therapists are trained and licensed to therapize. They do it for a living. When you go to a professional therapist you "sign up" for intervention, extremely personal conversation, and even sometimes intrusive advice. But the person using therapizing as a defense often has a personal agenda (fueled by the need for ego-gratification) and pursues that gratification—with or without agreement—tending to storm uninvited into private territory. Indeed, therapizers have the righteous idea that they know how the world should work, and they're anxious to impose that idea on others.

By now our advice-giving has become more of a habit than a part of thoughtful interaction—a habit often reinforced by people around us who encourage us to offer advice and opinions. They do this either because it saves them the trouble of doing their own thinking or because it gives them the attention they crave, while we, at the same time, get to feel smart and important.

Outer appearance

When we're using therapizing as a defense, we are likely to aggressively cross others' personal boundary lines. Sometimes our

You
think
you
know
most
everything
about
the way
the world
should work

suggestions are even correct, but that's not the point, for what often drives us to intervene is not concern but control; not true service and support for others but *self*-service and *self*-support; not the desire to share information but a need to indoctrinate. And that's very much the way therapizing frequently looks and feels to others. It seems to be endless discourse, righteous advice, elaborate counsel, intrusive interpretation, prescription-offering, solution-giving, instruction, insistence, criticism, and controlling commentary. We can seem arrogant, or at least annoyingly self-satisfied. We talk more than we listen, we think more than we feel, and we instruct more than we empathize.

SIGNALS	STORY LINES
Therapizing can cause you to be . . .	**To feel the internal effects of therapizing, read the following words with the tone of an expert. You may say things like:**
Complaining:	"You're just afraid to try harder because you think I'm going to expect too much of you. You need to get over it."
Insistent:	"How many times do I have to say it . . . you're a grown man—and you ought to act like one!"
Advising:	"If you ask me, that relationship is draining you. If I were you I'd get out while the getting is good."
Controlling:	"You should get yourself organized! Your life would improve a thousand percent."
Frustrated:	"My mother never listens when I make suggestions . . . and I just can't get her to understand what I'm talking about. I'm only thinking of what's best for her!"
Analytical:	"You've always been cautious . . . just like your father. Obviously you've taken on his fear. You ought to let go."

Instructive:	"You should stop moving your hands so much when you speak. It makes you look fake."
Intrusive:	"I know it's none of my business but I couldn't help over-hearing, and I think your husband has no right to tell you what to do."
Your Signals:	**Your Story Lines:**

Unconscious intention

Therapizing is a great way to avoid *genuine* intimacy. By focusing on what other people are feeling, thinking, and doing, we're (unconsciously) relieved from having to look at what *we* are feeling, thinking, and doing. Those who favor this defense, frequently come from a background where becoming the "authority" was perceived as the only way to stay afloat.* If you're this kind of person, you probably believe unconsciously that one of your greatest values is your aptitude for managing others and for advice-giving.

As with codependence, we therapizers have a need not only to control how other people *live* their lives but also to control what and how they *think* about their lives. Our idea is that this control can be nicely established if we figure things out (both for ourselves and for them). This, in actuality, is an effort to manage the chaos in *ourselves* that

Therapizing avoids genuine intimacy

You're trying to manage your own internal chaos be wielding external control

---

* The oldest child in an abusive or otherwise awful home often becomes the "good parent" to the younger siblings. According to birth-order experts, older siblings tend anyway to have a "benevolent instructor's inclination" built in, because they learned while growing up that they knew more and had more experience than the younger ones, which was true. Their younger siblings are more apt to be willing to be instructed or to rebel against instruction than is an only child or an older sibling.

leaves us feeling so uncomfortable in our own skin. Thus, our uncon-scious thinking is: "Perhaps my fixing you will fix me!"

Community dynamics

Many people seem to be looking for someone to manage and advise them—someone who can steer their ship and guide their journey. Hosts of radio and television talk shows are elevated to the status of experts who can answer this need. Pop psychologists—the more aggressive and hard-line the better—offer quick answers to complicated scenarios. Even movie stars have stepped down from the silver screen to become political advisors. This tendency to look for simple formulas to live by probably arises from the fact that so many of us feel out of control and are desperate for anything that seems able to manage the intolerable confusion of daily life. The therapizers around us, though sometimes annoying and invasive, seem to have answers to this confusion. Unfor-tunately, what they offer are really only opinions, and very often when we allow those opinions to override our own instincts about what's best for us, we undermine our personal power.

Personal sacrifice

Even in its mildest form, the defense of therapizing tends to sabotage the mutuality that leads to real intimacy in human relationships. This, for instance, is devastatingly obvious with couples when one partner insists on parenting the other (which, of course, requires the consent of the partner in the child role). In such a case, not only does the constant instructing eventually incapacitate the recipient, but it also nearly always announces the eventual disappearance of sexual interest between them (since, in our culture, parent/child incest taboos are much too powerful to allow sex between "parent" and "child").

Resource acquired

This defense teaches you how to discern the true character of situations and to communicate what you've noticed. It's an ability that, when used with consciousness (and upon request), enables you to be a great boss as well as a wonderful friend, partner, or spouse.

HIT DEFENSES: CONNECTION THROUGH DOING

The defense of CONTROL

Protecting yourself by exercising a regulating or directing influence.

Personal impact

Control is the ball peen hammer we use to shape and straighten out the world around us. But paradoxically, the more we swing this tool— the more we try to exercise control (over ourselves or others)—the more beset we are by constant frustration and frequent disappointment. We want our universe and the way it works to be in our control, because we imagine that will make us feel safe. But it doesn't. We keep trying harder but can never entirely succeed, because there's simply not enough control in the world (or *of* the world) to give us this sense of safety. In fact, the more we try, the worse we feel.

Control
corrupts all
partnerships

Outer appearance

Maybe people have said of you, "Oh, you're such a control freak!" when your control-based defensiveness alienated them and became an obnoxious impediment to cooperative interaction. Why would they say such a thing? Because control, brandished as a defense, turns guidance into repression, suggestion into coercion, and regulation into domination. It often has no soft edges at all, and is biting, abrupt, and lacking in compassion. We can recognize it as an inability to delegate and a preoccupation with outcome. When we're being defensively controlling, we often look uptight, shut-down, over-precise, or like we're white-knuckling our way through life.

But control—when it is coated with caring and laced with concern—can also be far more subtle than it sounds in these descriptions. In such instances, control can look much like the previously described Co-dependency, with the difference being that the people we try to control are frequently left feeling (either vaguely or explicitly) as though they've been treated—and how benignly!—as incompetents. This can be confusing to them, since under those (controlling) circumstances, their noticing the source of such discomfort is not necessarily easy.

SIGNALS	STORY LINES
Controlling can cause you to be . . .	**To feel the internal effects of control, try reading the following words in a frustrated tone. You may say things like:**
Self-righteous:	"I'm only doing what I know is right for you!"
Superior:	"I've been working like a dog . . . what in the world have *you* done all day?"
Vigilant:	"Be careful. Most men can't be trusted. Watch your back and don't put all your eggs in one basket."
Bossy:	"It's my way or the highway!"
Critical:	"You need to learn how to follow directions or you'll always be a loser."
Judgmental:	"I'm only going to show you one time how to do this. Try for once to pay attention!"
Coercing:	"Smoking is for idiots. Get with the program!"

Influencing:	"What you need to do is throw her out and change the locks!"
Perfectionistic:	"If you can't do something right, don't do it at all!"
Concerned:	"You're making a terrible choice. I'm just thinking of what's best for you and your future. I'm your mother and I know . . . call it motherly instinct . . . this man's just no damn good."
Your Signals:	**Your Story Lines:**

Unconscious intention

Inside, we're unconsciously driven by a panicky voice that whispers, "Grip the wheel firmly and keep your eyes on the road or *everything* will fall apart." Our fear of a potential breakdown usually begins in early childhood (chaotic households such as alcoholic families are excellent seeding grounds for the sprouting of adult controllers).

On an unconscious level, then, we hope that by strictly governing people, places, and things (and perhaps ourselves through extreme self-control), we will quiet the inside terrors. But the Control defense doesn't work, because *we simply are not in charge* of how people feel or what they do, nor are we in charge of the outcome of circumstances.

This brings to mind the tale of my client, the incredibly controlling Julia. As a child, Julia was regularly beaten so badly at home by her father that she frequently went to school with welts all over her body—even on her hands. Not only was the initial punishment a horror, but Julia also endured the embarrassment of having her welts seen . . . and then ignored—for no one in her school (student or teacher) ever spoke

You're terrified that everything is about to fall apart!

You are not in charge of outcome

to her about either her original bruises, slashes, and cuts, or about the scars on her body that remained afterward.

In fact, Julia's scars were far more than outward and physical. They turned into lifelong inner scars—the kind that dramatically affect every subsequent adult relationship, romantic or otherwise. Of course, like most of us, Julia defended against these scars. At first, she tried to ignore them altogether—the way everyone else seemed to do—but eventually she could deny their existence no longer. At that point, in an attempt to avoid feeling the power and pain of her early abuse, she minimized her remembrances, lightly tossing the stories aside like used tissues. Mostly, however, Julia defended herself by trying strictly to control every aspect of her relationship life, especially where it was related to love. This particular defensive posture is with her even now. With boyfriends, she demands over and over that they explain every thought and action. Most of the men she dates are, naturally, slow to commit and are withholding. Unfortunately, her attempts to control her own resentful feelings toward these men are usually unsuccessful and she's often characterized as inappropriately angry. No matter what, Julia always assumes no one will help anyway and that she'll be alone, fixing everything by herself.

Community dynamics

We all request and even require certain collective controls. These controls are meant to make our lives run more safely and smoothly. Mostly we think of them as "rules." Rules of the road, rules of the game, company rules, family rules, relationship rules. Often it seems easier, if somewhat more complicated, to establish community (safety) rules than it is to create personal (household/family/friendship) rules. That's usually because, as individuals, our vision is so strongly impacted by our history that we often cannot see straight.

Appropriate control offers safe freedom

But in the long run, what we want for our communities is exactly what we want for ourselves—to feel safe but not trapped. We want to know our limits but not be squelched by those limits. We want to feel free but not fearful.

Personal sacrifice

Excessive control undermines spontaneous creativity and, as a result, you become less passionate and more rigid than you might otherwise be.

Excessive control erodes passionate expression

Resource acquired

People who are controlling tend to be extremely confident and responsible, and they are often remarkably direct. These are admirable qualities—when exhibited without the panic that originally initiated the defense or the fear that later sustains it.

HIT DEFENSES: CONNECTION THROUGH DOING

The defense of CRITICISM

Protecting yourself by constantly finding fault.

Personal impact

A person who uses criticism defensively shines a high-intensity spotlight on all the cracks and crevices of life. This is called hyper-vigilance. First, we train our vigilant eye on our own limitations, and then, when we've finished raking *ourselves* over the coals, we turn our sharp, critical vision on other people. This scrutiny of ourselves and others often overwhelms any real sense of appreciation for the life before us. Instead, we are filled with angst—a feeling of apprehension or anxiety often accompanied by depression.

Outer appearance

Criticism appears in subtle forms (eye-rolling, frustrated sighing, and gentle sarcasm) as well as obvious forms (belittling, judging, and censure). As critical people we seem to be insistently scolding, constantly negative, and inevitably disappointed. We keep looking at the holes and not the cheese.

SIGNALS	STORY LINES
Criticizing can cause you to be . . .	**To feel the internal effects of criticism, read the following words in an impatient tone. You may say things like:**
Judgmental:	"You're a mess—straighten up and fly right!"
Perfectionistic:	"I can't seem to find anybody who knows how to do this correctly!"
Belittling:	"I wonder if you could just try to manage a little common sense!"
Irritable:	"Get out of my way and stop bugging me! You make me want to scream!"
Condemning:	"You're impossible. You'll never get a husband with that attitude!"
Censuring:	"Hey, don't complain to me. After all, if you lie down with dogs you get up with fleas."
Blaming:	"We're never going to complete this project on time. Obviously you folks just can't cut the mustard."
Impatient:	"Do the slowest people in the world work at this bank, or what? I've certainly got better and more important things to do."
Disappointed:	"I can't believe you screwed this up again!"

Your Signals:	Your Story Lines:

Unconscious intention

To everyone else, we may seem difficult and painstakingly exacting with regard to the world, but actually we're most dissatisfied with *ourselves*. Other people are merely getting the spillover from our *self-criticism*. We're critical because unconsciously we, ourselves, often feel incompetent, insufficient, and floundering, as if we're perpetually falling short of the mark. Maybe we were constantly criticized as children and came to expect it. Or perhaps we observed our parents frequently criticizing each other (or the neighbors) and thought that's the way people are supposed to talk and think. Or maybe, sensing something was wrong in our home when we were growing up, we decided to pin it on ourselves, and we are now simply reinforcing that idea by immersing ourselves in critical behavior and thought.

Another reason for our insistent criticism is, perhaps, that unconsciously *we're desperate to make the world feel safe for ourselves*. We think that if we can get everything and everybody organized well enough and doing things our way to a sufficient degree, we can avoid the disaster we anticipate.

Community dynamics

A general atmosphere of censure and condemnation can be encouraged in various ways. Two prominent examples today are the unrelenting public flogging of celebrities and the continual micro-examination of the private lives of private citizens (both of which tend to include ongoing media spotlighting of who says what to whom, with the inevitable consequent uproar).

You're desperate to feel safe

Maybe we just know too much now—as we watch the daily progress of wars on television, view the birth of babies on the Internet, witness mock mutilations on cable wrestling, and hear angry couples on sleaze TV publicly assaulting us with the gross details of their collapsing relationships. So much to criticize and point the finger at—and so little time!

Such processes are really reflections of what we in the community desire, for not only do we support these public criticisms and imitate them . . . but we also keep asking for more. Somewhere along the line, we seem to have lost track of what it means to be truly supportive through constructive (albeit uncomfortable) assessment. We have traded gentle, honest evaluation for rude attack. When criticism is constructive, it carefully (and often gently) points out flaws and areas needing improvement—without being vitriolic, demeaning, or righteous. Unfortunately, like so many tools, criticism in the hands of a bad craftsman destroys more than it creates.

Personal sacrifice

Stop looking at the holes so you can appreciate the cheese

Leveling constant criticism at yourself and others saps your feelings of compassion and connection. The vigilance required to locate every flaw and fracture is so consuming that little time or energy is left for intimate, loving experience.

Resource acquired

Attention to what's wrong teaches you . . . what is wrong! Thus, this ability to *discern* helps you see what actually needs to be done. You keep projects running effectively by weeding out what doesn't work and by establishing procedures that lead to clear, purposeful results. In other words, the discernment that comes from having a critical eye is essential for successfully accomplishing tasks and attaining goals.

The hit defenses:
CONNECTION THROUGH THINKING

The following story is about Anne, a beautiful, alluring 36-year-old who still struggles to feel lovable, acceptable, and worthwhile for some reason other than just her appearance. Anne defends (while at the same time perpetuating) her outrageous self-contempt by making the negative assumption that most people are looking down on her (*Projection*). Also, Anne has decided that other people are disgustingly unreliable and invariably untrustworthy (*Judgment*). But because she has such a disastrous self-image, when she measures her own qualities and capacities (*Comparing*) against those she judges, she finds herself coming up decidedly short. To add insult to injury, Anne has chosen to marry a man who reinforces her most negative ideas about herself and about men in general (details below). This choice allows her to spend more time *analyzing* her husband's every word and deed, rather than focusing on her own feelings and needs. She tracks him by checking his private voice mail, reads his e-mails, and goes through his briefcase whenever she gets the chance. All too often, these investigations confirm her worst suspicions.

ANNE & THE FATHER KINSHIP
Sex
Daddy's Hands

When I was around thirteen, my parents divorced. My dad had visitation rights . . . and I always dreaded my time with him.

One sunny day, I remember sitting on the tailgate in the back of my dad's pickup truck. The way his hands were rubbing my chest did not feel right.

I went home and told my mom. She was very upset and called him about the situation. He said I was a liar, that he was only helping me off the truck. Mom didn't say much back to him. After the call, she just looked at me, saying nothing more, and then she left for work.

I was home alone when Dad phoned later to scream at me. He called me every name in the book—a whore, cunt, bitch, and a fucking liar. I shut off all the lights. I was so scared he was going to show up and do . . . something awful.

Today Anne exhibits a great deal of guilt and conflict with regard to her sex appeal. This conflict shows itself in the way she tends to dress provocatively, clearly for effect, while at the same time feeling infuriated when men respond to her.

Now, someone with a different nature might try to bury her sexiness under mounds of fat or to marry a man who was totally disinterested in sex. Anne, however, has chosen someone much like her father—one who tends to deny his own (suspicious) actions while lying about what he does and who he does it with. Also, her husband is the kind of individual who appears to value sex above all else, overriding Anne's protests of discomfort, for instance, and insisting upon public displays of sexuality from her (alluring clothing and physical exhibitions). Of course, we need not feel outraged for Anne—after all, she is *choosing* to acquiesce.

Anne's unconscious driving ideas are: "I am bad. Men are liars. Sex hurts. Sex is sleazy. Sex is all I have to offer anyone. I can't trust anybody, including my own husband. No one cares about the *real* me. I am alone."

The most difficult thing about recognizing the problems inherent in this particular quartet of "hit" defenses (Projection, Judgment, Comparing, and Analyzing) is that when we're in their grip, we experience our thinking as unimpeachable, absolutely reliable, and completely accurate. Claiming an intention to change something that feels so right is truly difficult. In order to accomplish this change, you will most likely need to come to the conclusion that what you're sacrificing far outweighs what you're gaining.

How are *you* adding insult to your injury?

HIT DEFENSES: CONNECTION THROUGH THINKING

The defense of PROJECTION

*Protecting yourself by using other people
as a screen for unconscious thoughts and feelings.*

Personal impact

The way projection works is the way it sounds. Other people are the screen and we are the projector. The picture we project onto that screen involves characteristics—most often the kind labeled negative (like arrogance, untrustworthiness, and meanness), but sometimes even those traits generally considered positive (such as competence, sociability, and intelligence)

Why do this? The reason is that we, along with everyone else, have particular personality "glitches"—things we don't like very much about ourselves. Somewhere along the line we came (unconsciously) to hope that if we ignored these regrettable glitches in ourselves they'd just go away. But they haven't, and won't. "Out of sight and out of mind" does not mean out of operation!

So, inevitably, these buried thoughts and feelings get activated, but because we do not associate them (anymore) with ourselves, we can't imagine they have anything at all to do with us! They must belong, we reason, to *the other people in our lives—all those people **out there***. At this point, therefore, we have become *unaware* that these rejected thoughts and feelings have any connection to us at all. This unawareness perfectly suits our (unconscious) needs. The various aspects, attitudes, and/or behaviors we have mostly lost track of in ourselves are simply gone—projected onto others. "Somebody around here is stupid," we thereby think, "and it's not me, so it must be *them*." Projection thus provided us with a thoroughly natural way to handle thoughts and feelings (in ourselves) we have previously rejected.

After discovering projection, you may feel you are cunning and self-serving, but you are really not, for the distortions we create hide our virtues as well as our vices. This may be especially hard to recognize because, most likely, you've been employing behavior to reinforce that gross misperception for some time now.

In fact, to one degree or another, everyone projects—and reinforces the misperceptions that inevitably follow. By now, the far-reaching effects of this process are likely to have drifted into your life like a silent, corrosive fog. Your vision is clouded, your view is obscured, and your clarity is distorted.

Projection has two reigning principles, which are that *everything feels personal* and that *we seldom realize that we are projecting*.

With regard to the first, we think everything is about us all the time. The truth is quite different, though. In reality, almost *nothing* other people do is actually all about *us*. Very little of what occurs around us and even *to* us is actually *aimed* at us. Rather, most of the time, others are behaving in accord with *their own* inner needs and drives. Those others are usually not even thinking about *us* specifically—including Mom and Dad.

Projection
is
misdirection

When
we're
projecting,
everything
feels
personal

So when you were a child, even the beatings, neglect, outrage, and similar evidences of inappropriateness were not *precisely* about you, but were more about the way those particular misguided individuals reacted to those particular circumstances—according to their own unconscious inner intentions and defenses. This means that *any child* *with your* *natural characteristics born into* *that* *family at the time you were born* *into it would have encountered the same experiences.* Of course, this is simultaneously comforting and discomforting. It means *you* were not exactly the problem, but it also means *you* were not exactly the focus of everything, either—even though you, as a child, wanted to be (and maybe ought to have been) the focus.

With regard to the second reigning principle—that we seldom realize we are projecting at all—we believe we're simply seeing the actual truth. And since we suppose ourselves to be accurate in our assessments and assumptions, we feel justified in basing our subsequent actions and reactions on those assessments and assumptions. Mostly, however, we are *not* thus justified, for instead of a realistic documentary, we're screening an elaborate fiction based on our own private fears, fantasies, and (family) history.

For example, suppose you are passionate by nature. But when you were growing up, your easy-going, placid father and your fussy, detail-oriented mother criticized your passion as disorderly. Seeing that your sometimes stormy ways were not acceptable, you buried them, exiling your passion to your subconscious mind and pretending to be scholarly and philosophical. Now, as an adult, you often find yourself among people you identify as "secretly passionate." You are even critical of them, in the same way your parents were critical of you.

Now—who will you assume is secretly passionate? People who dance and sing and play? Actors? Warriors? Political activists? No. Searching out people who are good candidates for your projection, you

Your reactions are most often based on assumptions and distortions

Take back
the focus
by remembering
you
are the point!

will point your critical finger at scholars and philosophers, proclaiming that they are full of unexpressed passion. And the chances are good that you will not always be wrong. For instance, those academics whom you accuse of hypocrisy may actually (like you!) be closet action heroes. You and the accused, then, are emotional peas-in-a-pod. In other words, just because you're projecting doesn't mean you're completely wrong. But this still doesn't let us off the hook, because how *others* fit the bill is not the point. *We* are the point, and we must realize that whenever we make assumptions about other people, we are actually saying something important about *ourselves*—something to which we probably ought to be paying attention.

Outer appearance

You're probably beginning to understand the ways in which projection encourages and promotes a largely *false* view of reality. Because of the obvious far-reaching nature of this defense, it tends to platform and inspire nearly all the other defenses. The result is two almost simultaneous, allied defenses that can be hard to separate from each other for purposes of understanding and description. The shift from the projection to the defense that *defends* the projection can be so rapid that determining which came first is, again, one of those chicken-or-egg situations.

Projection
promotes
a false
view
of reality

For example, your projection moves you to say to yourself, "She thinks I'm a jerk," which immediately leads you to defensive *Anger*. "Screw her! She's not so great herself." Or alternatively, it could move you in a flash to defensive *Self-Contempt*: "I'm always messing things up. Every time I meet someone great, I act like a moron."

So—especially when you are just beginning to appreciate the tricky consequences of projection—it's best to assume that *most* of what you believe other people think about you is your own projected thoughts and feelings, not the real deal. Start there and you'll have a fighting chance to (eventually) figure out what's yours and what actually belongs to those others.

SIGNALS	STORY LINES
Projection can cause you to be . . .	To feel the internal effects of projection, try restating your thoughts in alternate forms (the italicized sentences offer examples). You may say things like:*
Assumptive:	"They'll never take me seriously." *"I don't take myself seriously."*
Mildly paranoid:	"I'm sure everyone here thinks I'm a jerk!" *"I think I'm a jerk."*
Judgmental:	"Everybody in this business lies." *"I don't trust anybody."*
Misunderstood:	"No one cares whether I live or die!" *"I'm afraid to get enthusiastically involved with life."*
Oversensitive:	"I'm afraid to open my mouth. I know everyone thinks I'm a mess." *"I think I'm a mess."*
Invalidating:	"Men simply don't want strong women like me." *"I'm not comfortable with my own strength."*
Prejudiced:	"If you're rich or beautiful you can get what you want— otherwise forget it!" *"I don't feel I ever get what I want."*

* Since projection can take many surprising twists and turns, the following Story Lines alternatives may not apply to you, but they will alert you to how the tricky process can work.

Your Signals:	Your Story Lines:

Unconscious intention

To investigate this phenomenon clearly, begin with this idea: whatever you imagine others feel and think about you is really what you *unconsciously* think and feel about yourself. Often our most damaging projections began in childhood—initiated by family or peer-member experiences. As usual, our reactions to these experiences and the ways in which we still hold onto them are likely to depend upon our nature.

Consider, for example, the story of my client Joy, now thirty-five years old. When Joy was merely five years old, she was especially petite. At that time, her often inebriated mother found Joy's proportions enormously entertaining and even worthy of ridicule. She routinely brought the small child into her circle of friend and, holding onto Joy's little body as she pulled down her pants, showed everyone how tiny her butt was. She'd say, "You ladies have to see this." As Joy squirmed in embarrassment to hide her "private parts," her mother turned the naked child around and around for her friends to see, while they all laughed.

Today, Joy hides herself emotionally (through Masking and Withholding) and sometimes physically (through Withdrawal). She does this because she still (unconsciously) assumes people want to examine her and intrude in ways she feels are inappropriate. The problem is compounded because, since Joy is exceptionally beautiful, she's sometimes right. Thus, in spite of the wonderful life she has today, Joy still *feels* worthy of ridicule and (unconsciously) assumes others will ridicule her and that she will be powerless to fight back. In these assumptions, she is wrong. Just because other people find her beautiful as well as

Understand the difference between what appears to be true and what is fact

engaging and may want to make her the center of attention does not mean they intend to humiliate her or that she is actually powerless. Eventually, like anyone who is dealing with troublesome projections, Joy will need to understand *the difference between what appears to be true and what is in fact occurring.*

Community dynamics

Once you become aware of the phenomenon of projection and appreciate its range and pervasiveness, it becomes fairly easy to spot, both in yourself and in your community of friends, coworkers, and family. You will eventually even be able to notice the way it works in the larger community we call the world (as when whole cultures self-righteously project their unrecognized inner demons onto other cultures).

A life uncovered can lead to a life recovered

You can begin by recognizing that we all are essentially more involved with *our own* assumptions, fantasies, wishes, and needs than we are with what *others* are really doing or feeling. In other words, most things are just not that personal! And when you are disturbed by conditions around you, you are not likely to be able to change everything and everyone in your world. But you can work instead on changing y*ourself*, and thereby change the way the world seems to you.

Personal sacrifice

When you focus on what you assume others are thinking, feeling, or doing toward or about you, you avoid seeing the responsibility *you* have for the life you've created. Failing to see that responsibility robs you of power.

Resource acquired

Through projection, you have shown to yourself a picture of your own unconscious reluctances, assumptions, fantasies, and fears. A life uncovered can lead to a life recovered.

JUDGE

The defense of JUDGMENT

*Protecting yourself with opinions that tend
to be moral, critical, or righteous.*

Personal impact

As the officious, dark-robed judge, we sit, heavy gavel poised, looking important and as if possessed of superior knowledge. Most of the time, however, this attitude reflects a false importance and bogus superiority that telegraph the overused defense of judgment. This defense tends to assault the self-esteem of those around us by exaggerating their (real or perceived) inadequacies. In doing so, it pushes them away and thereby limits our own ability to connect.

Judgment gives rise to several problems:

❖ It isolates us, for it is divisive by nature. Others may prefer to avoid us altogether rather than taking the chance of being targeted by our judgmental fire.

❖ When we're judgmental, we often make assumptions without sufficient evidence. This encourages us to close our minds and narrow our viewpoints. We tend to be more concerned with substantiating our existing opinions than with appreciating new perspectives.

❖ We often find ourselves in the middle of contention. This position, called everything from triangling and mediating to meddling, can make us seem more like a referee than a caring ally. Some may take advantage of our services (making us feel important), though we are likely to discover that what we get back emotionally is shallow and only minimally satisfying (making us feel lonely).

*Judgment
isolates
us*

*Judgment
narrows
our view*

*Judgment
leaves us
sadly lonely*

Outer appearance

Judgment can lead us to lash out, to be unfeelingly swift and straight to the point (as when, perhaps, we boldly condemn something, someone, or even ourselves as imperfect and therefore inadequate), or it can be more subtle (as when, perhaps, it is offered as caring guidance or as an off-handed suggestion). But judgment, no matter how disguised or perfumed, still makes us appear unapproachable, inflexible and controlling.

SIGNALS	STORY LINES
Judgment can cause you to be . . .	**To feel the internal effects of judgment, read the following words with a tone of superiority. You may say things like:**
Critical:	"I think she's much too old to dress that way!"
Officious:	"Straighten up and fly right. Get a job and stop your day-dreaming."
Didactic:	"Obviously, married people who have affairs don't really love their partners."
Obstinate:	"I don't care what he said or what his so-called circum-stances are—what's right is right!"
Reproving:	"She doesn't deserve a second chance. Throw her out!"
Inflexible:	"I just don't believe working mothers can be very good parents."
Righteous:	"Men simply cannot be as nurturing as women!"
Controlling:	"Yes, I'm the judge and jury. I have to be. I'm doing this for your own good."
Unapproach-able:	"My decision is final. Nothing you say can change my mind."

<u>Your</u> Signals:	<u>Your</u> Story Lines:

Unconscious intention

Just under the surface of our apparent certainty and self-righteous-ness lives a frightened, self-doubting, hesitant person. We're trying desperately to create rules that will make us feel safe. Maybe we think the world's about to fall apart. Perhaps when we were children our world *did* fall apart (someone died, the family moved frequently, there was a divorce). In the face of these events, a set of standards was created in the hope that any future (emotional) devastation would be warded off.

In any case, whatever the background circumstances may have been, we *ourselves*—as is usual with these kinds of aggressive postures—actually feel deserving of the judgment we dispense, and we're making a preemptive strike. We judge lest we be judged.

Community dynamics

We have long loved courtroom drama. Television shows such as *Philly*, *The Practice* and *L.A. Law* (plus older productions like *Matlock* and *Perry Mason*) have taught us about the fictionalized side of judging right and wrong. With the advent of publicly televised and widely-watched legal proceedings (such as Clarence Thomas vs. Anita Hill), we find ourselves privy to the real thing, encouraged daily to judge others' intentions and actions. Then, in the O. J. Simpson trial, we all became authorities and arbiters of right and wrong. In fact, the Trial as entertain-ment grew to be so popular after the Simpson debacle that a new cable television channel—Court TV—jumped into prominence.

Now, in trial after trial—such as those of the Unabomber (Theodore Kaczynski), the Nanny (Louise Woodward), the Oklahoma Bomber

(Timothy McVeigh), and even the President of the United States (Bill Clinton)—we sit in judgment in our comfortable chairs at home. To some extent, this is an exciting development, for as in no other time of history, we are privileged to witness courtroom events as they happen. But in another way, I believe these trials can too easily become an obsessive distraction from our own real lives—a distraction that may undermine our actual *living* of life—while at the same time stimulating the judge who inhabits us all.

Personal sacrifice

When you look through judgmental eyes, the world seems sorely lacking in so many ways—and you yourself are likely to feel your hopefulness and enthusiasm for life diminish.

Resource acquired

You have learned to stand on a firm platform of discernment and self-understanding. Operating from a value system developed through sound processes of information-gathering and contemplation, you have come to appreciate your own clear perspectives. Now you can allow yourself to move through the world with a solid sense of yourself and a clear view of others.

HIT DEFENSES: CONNECTION THROUGH THINKING

The defense of COMPARING

*Protecting yourself by measuring the way you feel
against the way others appear.*

Personal impact

Comparing someone else's *outside self* to our *inside self* is not only exhausting, but it's also self-defeating. Certainly, once in a while we'll

When
we're
comparing
we're not
daring
to get close

emerge the victor in a comparison, but more often than not the people we see or meet or greet *look* better than we *feel*, and we therefore quickly become convinced that we are *less* worthy, more "unlucky" (which generally means powerless to change the way things are), or less capable of prospering, thriving, triumphing, recovering, prevailing, and achieving than others.

Our focus on differences keeps us from feeling intimate. After all, we can't be intimate with someone to whom we feel either superior or inferior. We're too busy feeling alienated.

Outer appearance

People who compare forever watch for similarities and differences, always measuring, evaluating, and noticing who stacks up against whom, and how. Comparing occasionally masquerades as flattery, as when we say: "I don't know how you stay so trim, eating the way you do! I just look at food and I turn into a tub!" But most often it is either plainly self-serving (as when we think we're better than others) or self-demeaning (as when we think we're worse than others).

SIGNALS	STORY LINES
Comparing can cause you to be . . .	**To feel the internal effects of comparing, try reading the following words in a petulant tone. You may say things like:**
Judgmental:	"People always listen to what he says because he has money, and no one wants to hear what I have to say because I'm broke!"
Critical:	"If I had his opportunities, I sure wouldn't act the way he does!"
Vigilant:	"My boyfriend gawks at every woman that walks by, so I feel like I can never measure up."

Victimized:	"Life is easier for everyone else."
Contrasting:	"I always give so much more to my friends than they give to me. It feels lousy!"
Snide:	"If I ran around kissing up like he does, I'd be as popular as he is!"
Testing:	"Do you think I'm as good-looking as she is?"
Flattering:	"Phyllis doesn't understand how lucky she is. If I had her looks, I'd be a star!"
Self-defeating:	"She's so smart. Compared to her I'm a dunce!"
Your Signals:	**Your Story Lines:**

Unconscious intention

We use comparison as a primary defense because we *actually* believe, for better or worse, that we have no equal. Either we think we're head-and-shoulders above most other people or we imagine that we can never, ever measure up to any person. This defense, as usual, can be tracked to childhood.

For example, I remember my client Peter telling me a story familiar to many, about the birth of his baby brother. Peter was seven at the time. He wanted so much to be excited like the rest of the family, but instead found himself angry and scared. "I won't be the only child anymore," he worried. "I won't be the center of attention. There wasn't enough love and attention for me before, so what's going to happen to me now? Will my grandparents love him more than me? He's so perfect. I already make Mom mad because I'm naughty. Now I'm certain she will love him more." Peter never did get over his worry and, as an overachiever, has (unconsciously) spent his life trying to prove his worthiness—comparing everyone else's achievements to his own.

Community dynamics

Society usually supports comparison-making of some kind. Are we richer/poorer, prettier/uglier, younger/older, smarter/dumber, fatter/thinner? Perhaps comparison is a natural inclination supported by our survival-of-the-fittest instincts, which tell us that if we want to "make it," we'd better be the *best*, which, according to society, is likely to mean always to check our wallet, our waistline, and our status! We're all at the mercy of this comparing tendency until and unless we establish our own set of high standards—standards that have both personal application and collective resonance. This means that in order for us to be at our best, both for ourselves and for those around us, we must recognize (and continue to develop) our gifts as well as acknowledge (but not be stopped by) our limitations. In so doing, we create a personal platform of ideas and attitudes that incorporates, to our best advantage, both those gifts and those limitations.

Unfortunately, individuals often fail to establish such standards for themselves. Comparing then becomes a quick and often careless way to figure out how we "should" feel about things. The problem is that our overall self-confidence is undermined when we find ourselves tempted by or attracted to the unobtainable (few of us will ever be as skinny as runway models, as rich as famous athletes, or as adored as movie stars). Spotlighting the most beautiful, for instance, or the richest amongst us, tends to reinforce our shortcomings rather than inspiring us to greater effort. Still, comparing is difficult to avoid and easy to fall back on.

Personal sacrifice

Comparing erects a wall of differences between you and other people, thereby inhibiting your experience of intimacy.

Comparing eliminates sharing

Resource acquired

Like judgment, comparing teaches you how to assess and evaluate. These skills can help you in innumerable ways—from determining the best relationship partner to making the right career choices.

HIT DEFENSES: CONNECTION THROUGH THINKING

The defense of ANALYZING

Protecting yourself through intellectual examination that discounts emotional or intuitive factors.

Personal impact

You are the Tin Man, who focuses on *think*ing and ignores *feeling*. If you only had a heart! Unfortunately for you, ignoring feelings accomplishes very little, for those unexpressed feelings tend to fester and eventually demand attention anyway. This festering can contribute to creating everything from ulcers or constant anxiety to a sense of isolation or explosive outraging.

When we're driven to offer our (often unsolicited) analyses to those around us, we're likely to get one of the following three reactions. One: people feel intruded upon and start to move away from us—which can result in our feeling ignored and/or rejected. Two: people notice the lack of emotional content in our analytical style and feel either misunderstood or not cared about—which can result in our feeling perplexed and frustrated. Or, three: people in our life start to *expect* from us what we routinely give them and begin relying on our analytical skills while

Analyzing keeps us from realizing complete connection

ignoring our (less visible) feeling nature—which can result in our feeling burdened and used.

Outer appearance

Your version is not the only truth

As analytical individuals, we tend to break things down exactly, coolly distinguishing fact from non-fact, and (usually) insisting that our version of the truth *is* the truth. People more accustomed to dealing with a mix that includes emotional and physical factors may feel undermined and less able (or less entitled) than usual to communicate their feelings and perceptions to us. To them, we may frequently *look* helpful, but we probably won't *feel* helpful.

SIGNALS	STORY LINES
Analyzing can cause you to be . . .	**To feel the internal effects of being an analyzer, read the following words in a detached tone. You may say things like:**
Cavalier:	"Sure, your mother's being mean, but she's always mean. Just don't let it bother you."
Examining:	"Romantic hooey! A simple civil ceremony just makes more sense."
Practical:	"I don't believe in getting too excited ahead of time. We'll just wait and see how it all turns out."
Skeptical:	"I know people *say* they've seen flying saucers—but I just don't believe it!"
Demeaning:	"You obviously imagined this choice would please me. But that was idiotic. You should have thought things out more."
Dismissive of feelings:	"Please just put your hysteria on hold for a minute so we can figure this out."

Righteously certain:	"Look, you just need to set aside your pride and ego and understand that, as usual, I'm right about this!"	
Your Signals:	**Your Story Lines:**	

Unconscious intention

We're terrified to access and reveal our feeling self. Analysis helps us avoid that dangerous possibility.

This brings to my mind a client named George, who first entered therapy because Grace, his wife of seventeen years, could no longer tolerate the emotional distance that had developed between them. By the time I met this couple, they were in a sexless marriage and had been sleeping in separate bedrooms for eight years. But their relationship was quite civil, for they were great housemates. And lack of sex was actually not Grace's main complaint. What disturbed Grace was that George seldom revealed (to her or to anyone, in fact) any emotion whatsoever.

George presented himself to me with consistent calm, laying out all the facts, announcing that he had thoughtfully *chosen* this less passionate marriage over another, more passion-filled possibility. As he talked on in his logical way, he began to speak about the chaos in his family of origin. It turned out that his mother had been murdered in cold blood on the front porch of his family home when George was barely twenty. When I asked him in our session how he felt about that death, he said it had not affected him, since he hated her anyway and he had not actually been there when it happened. "I even chose not to return home to the Midwest for the funeral," he said, "so unaffected was I."

This was a typical logical response for George. There is no God because there is no logical proof, he says. Feelings are not logical, serve no long-term purpose, and therefore should be ignored, he maintains. Sure, it would be nice to have (and want) sex in his marriage, but it's no big deal. He has made the logical choice, and that's that, he intones.

Actually, in many ways, George is just fine. He is a thoroughly decent man with a satisfactory job, a sweet (though frustrated) wife, a nice house, and a particular way of life that makes him feel safe. He simply decided long ago that passion was too dangerous to experience. (How this man went about untangling his problem with repressed emotions is another story.)

Like many people, George chooses to run away from his troubling memories and from the feelings that accompany those memories. The problem is not his alone, however, for those who love him often find their own enthusiasm dampened and their excitement repressed when he is around. George may be an extreme example, yet he does generally characterize the type of person who uses analysis as a defense.

Community dynamics

We are encouraged in this scientific, technological age to investigate, examine, and interpret circumstances objectively and to screen out emotional bias. This is meant to promote clear, decisive thinking that is free of prejudice and is followed by reasonable actions leading to well-designed outcomes. It also creates personal psychological imbalances that get reflected in out-of-control communities.

Personal sacrifice

Analysis, when used as a defense, rejects expressions of the heart, leaving you with a dry life that is void of passion.

Resource acquired

Well-developed analytical abilities endow you with the clarity to make cogent, informed decisions.

HIT DEFENSES: CONNECTION THROUGH THINKING

*This, the final thinking defense, can easily go
completely unobserved—except by the defender.*

The defense of MASKING

*Protecting yourself by saying one thing
while feeling or thinking another.*

Personal impact

Finding the face that fits—that's the objective of masking. It doesn't matter to us how far away from our true, honest feelings, thoughts, and desires that "face" takes us, because our need to belong—to be acceptable and accepted—outweighs any other concern. So we sculpt an ideal model of ourselves and mold our own features to fit the model. Originally, being part of the life we wanted seemed like a mission impossible, but once our mask was cemented firmly in place, most of what we thought we wanted became possible.

However, the unfortunate impacts of this defense are twofold.

First, we become so accustomed to our false face that eventually we, ourselves, *forget* we're even exhibiting a facade! This means that after years of defending against visibility (and probably vulnerability, too), we completely lose contact with our authentic self. The problem with this loss of authenticity is that we are thereby robbed of any truly profound or multidimensional experiences. It's as if we're dancing lightly and safely on the ocean's foam but never plunging the depths to see the intense, colorful beauty below. Likewise, living on the surface of ourselves can be safe, but in the long run it is most likely to leave us unfulfilled and longing for more.

The second impact of this defense is alienation, disconnection, and (therefore) isolation. Most of us want to belong and fit in—to be

We wear the face that hides the true (unacceptable) us!

We have lost contact with our authentic self

acceptable (even, perhaps, lovable). This, as I have said, is the provocative intention that encourages masking in the first place. But when the need to belong takes precedence over the need to maintain a sense of personal integrity, this false face turns out more often to separate us from others than to encourage intimate inclusion. As often happens with defenses, we get exactly the opposite of what we think we want.

Outer appearance

In daily life, dissembling is so common that it's considered "normal." Sometimes our behavior falls under the category of being polite. (Someone wonders how you feel—you're tired, grumpy, or sad but—you say "Fine!") At other times, we just think we're being private. (Someone asks, "How did your date go last night?" and you say "Okay," when actually you had an gross, insulting experience.)

Whether through artifice, pretense, bravado, distraction, compulsion, humility, or the myriad other possible concealment methods, we cloak ourselves in what feels to us like an *appropriate* public face. We look fine; we just don't feel fine. We're hoping we'll be able to hide out and protect ourselves from criticism, disdain, and the disappointment of others. We have confused invisibility with invincibility.

We've confused invisibility with invincibility

SIGNALS	STORY LINES
Masking can cause you to be . . .	**To feel the internal effects of masking, try reading the "saying" words and the "thinking" words in two completely different tones. You may say (and think) things like:**
Compliant:	*Saying*: "I'd love to help." *Thinking*: "I'm so exhausted, I just want to pull the covers up over my head."
Inauthentic:	*Saying*: "What a great outfit." *Thinking*: "She's such a bitch!"

Consciously lying:	*Saying*: "I paid $50,000, but it was worth it!" *Thinking*: "It really only cost $35,000, but they'll never know."
Misleading:	*Saying*: "Sure, no problem—I'll handle it." *Thinking*: "I'm such a fraud—I have no idea what I'm doing!"
Codependent:	*Saying*: "I'll do anything to make you happy." *Thinking*: "I hope this makes him appreciate me."
Secretly overwhelmed:	*Saying*: "Love all the gifts! You guys are the best!" *Thinking*: "If anyone knew how I really felt, they'd throw me to the wolves."
Dissembling:	*Saying*: "No, it's not you. I just realize I'm not ready for a relationship right now." *Thinking*: "I can't wait to get away from this loser!"
Your Signals:	**Your Story Lines:**

Unconscious intention

We are afraid that at our core, something is truly wrong with us. We therefore carefully hide our "real" self to keep other people from getting too close, which we're certain would result in a confirmation of our worst suspicions. But we also want to be a part of things—to be included and to be connected. Masking gives us a way of participating without suffering (deadly) close scrutiny. We simultaneously want to belong *and* to avoid being found out. We dissemble, then, in order to promote safe association.

You dissemble in order to feel safe

Community dynamics

Hiding one's "true self" (from friends, family, or coworkers) as well as withholding honest ideas and feelings is, to some degree or another, common to everybody. Stated and unstated standards, protocols, and requirements exist, and we tend to adjust our behavior to accommodate ourselves to these rules—to go with the flow. This camouflage, in part, is what often seems to hold the fabric of civilized society together—but what price do we as individuals pay?

Certainly, if most people were thwarting society rather than trying to find ways to get along, things would likely be even more chaotic than they already are. However, when the demands of masking undermine an individual's creative potential, as well as his or her more deeply-felt opinions, perhaps (as a society) we are striking a bad bargain by encouraging it.

Personal sacrifice

You probably began this process of covering up early on—as soon as you found out what was acceptable and what was not. Initially, it allowed you to feel included. If your school crowd particularly disliked someone, you learned to act (often without *really* thinking about it) as if you also had an aversion to that person. This need to belong continues throughout your life, and masking eventually seems like an *essential* aid. But while allowing you to feel safer in your relationships, masking can also obscure your uniqueness. Disclaiming that uniqueness can leave you feeling confused and uncomfortable in your own skin. Suddenly you feel lost, even when you seem to be on the right track—unseen in full view, unheard in full voice. Part of the intention of this book is to inspire you to remember your true self—the face behind the curtain.

Resource acquired

Masking teaches appropriate social graces (how to get along in the world), containment (the ability to keep things to yourself), and

Heal
by
revealing
the face
behind
the curtain

adaptability (how to fit in under diverse circumstances). As always, however, when the shield outweighs the warrior, the warrior falls.

When the shield outweighs the warrior, the warrior falls

THE RUN DEFENSES

The run defenses:
DISCONNECTION THROUGH FEELING

The following "disconnection through feeling" defenses—Shame, Self-Contempt, Fear, Victimization, Withdrawal, Depression, Terminal Uniqueness, and Spirituality—are among the most common ways of avoiding interaction with other people. (Spirituality, though probably the least-used defense in this group, is becoming more prominent these days. It is particularly tough to catch, since it often hides behind otherworldly piety or metaphysical double-talk.)

The story of Tommy's Taunting offered below nicely elucidates the way in which several of these disconnection-through-feeling defenses (when combined with a particular type of personality) might show up early on.

TOMMY & THE CHILD KINSHIP
Relationship
The Taunting

I was twelve or thirteen. It was a nice spring afternoon and I was riding my bike home from a flea market where I had picked up some Playboy *magazines. Halfway home, I noticed that I was being followed by an ancient, souped-up, gray car that made a loud, low noise as it rumbled along. Four Caucasian boys about sixteen to eighteen years old were in the car. They all had long blond hair and wore white T-shirts.*

I was instantly intimidated and rode up on the sidewalk. I started pedaling fast. They stayed nearby, driving alongside. Soon they began calling me names like "Chink," "Slant," "Nip," and "Jap." They were yelling at me and laughing. I pedaled as fast as I could, because I knew if they caught me, I was dead meat. They followed me as I rode around the corner to my house and ran with my bike into the side yard near the trash cans.

They locked their brakes right in front of my house and skidded to a halt. Then all four jumped out and were standing around their car, taunting me to come out and "fight like a man." They said they were going to kick my ass.

At that moment, all I could do was cower in fear behind my side gate. The boys saw me hiding. Then I heard them laughing as they got back in their car and peeled out. Why had I been such a coward? Why couldn't I stand up to them? When the fear wore off, I wanted so badly to kill them. I swore to myself that if I'd a gun, I would have killed them all. I never told my folks.

This story paints a picture of a healthy but naturally reticent boy who grew up to be a fear-based, self-contemptuous, withdrawn, self-conscious man. Today, at age twenty-nine, Tommy still keeps emotional secrets and seldom speaks up for himself—except when he has angry outbursts. He carries enormous shame, both about his ethnicity and about himself as a man, which leads him to constantly expect rejection. Because he is not assertive by nature, this shame he feels immobilizes him and he finds pursuing his dreams difficult. Tommy's favorite pastimes include shooting on a range and hunting. His unconscious driving ideas are; "I should be ashamed of my heritage. I'm outnumbered. I need to stay armed and vigilant. I can't speak up because people are dangerous. No one likes me anyway."

Notice particularly how all of the "disconnection through feeling" defenses use a separation strategy for self-protection. In many cases, the Story Lines for these defenses live inside the unhappy mind of the defender and emerge into public view only if the stresses of a particular situation call them forth.

Try to imagine how easily you could be pulled from the first to the last of this defense series. Perhaps the process would sound like this: I am filled with <u>Shame</u>, which leads me to feel <u>Self-contemptuous</u>. In the face of this Self-contempt, I find that I am uncomfortable inside myself . . . and in the world. This discomfort leaves me riddled with fear. I deduce that I am afraid because I am being <u>Victimized</u> by an unfeeling world. My answer to that victimization is to <u>Withdraw</u>. The more I withdraw, the more <u>Depressed</u> I get. I know I am all alone in the extent to which I feel these feelings—certainly no one else experiences the depths of difficulty I do—which, I realize, makes me <u>Unique</u>, so unique that it's killing me (that is, it's terminal). The only answer is faith in the unseen. Thus, I will cling to <u>Spirituality</u> like a shipwrecked sailor to a raft.

RUN DEFENSES: DISCONNECTION THROUGH FEELING

The defense of SHAME

*Protecting yourself through your all-pervasive
sense of basic defectiveness.*

SHAME

We come now to *Shame*, possibly the most unrelenting, deeply effective defense of all. More than any other defense, shame keeps us stuck in our stories, not only in light of its own gnarly impact, but because of the way it is so often either the inspiration for (or the true source of) a vast number other defensive problems. It's so powerful, in fact, that it can even promote and perpetuate itself! Shame begets shame. Therefore, it's essential for *all* readers to assume some (major) relationship to this topic.

Personal impact

The word "shame" is routinely used today and has even become a common reference point for many people (perhaps due largely to author John Bradshaw, who popularized the word and concept with his best-selling book *Healing the Shame that Binds*). But what is shame? What does it mean? It certainly ought not to be confused with simple embarrassment (as when we're momentarily inappropriate or clumsy), nor should it be lumped in with the (fleeting) uncomfortable feelings that can arise from making public mistakes. Shame is far more devastating (and lingering) than these. Far more. It is, in fact, a profound, deeply-rooted poisonous vine that (when it's around our own throat) strangles our sense of personal worthwhileness, or that (when it's twisted around the throats of others) effectively and nearly instantly reduces their self-esteem to the point that it may appear to have vanished altogether.

By definition, *Shame* is a sense of fundamental, essential defectiveness—a feeling that we are, at our core, broken and unfixable. It's much like that slimy old horror-movie monster, the creature from the Black Lagoon—a deadly beast that splashes through the murky surface (often at the most inopportune times) to do its worst! Certainly, if this belief in fundamental and essential defectiveness has a stranglehold on you, you already have a sense of its potential for (interior) devastation!

Outer appearance

Shame as a defense is easy to spot (both in ourselves and in others). We know it when we *feel* it in ourselves (we're extremely embarrassed, outrageously self-conscious, and/or depressingly demeaned), and when

You
think
you're
broken
and
can't
be
fixed

We say
to ourselves:
"I'm
not okay
so you
don't get
to be okay,
either!"

we *see* it in others (they look abashed, "caught," or maybe just simply scared). Think of the ways this awful experience is most commonly (and casually) characterized: "He's so shamefaced." "You ought to be ashamed of yourself." "What a shame that is." "Shame on you."

As Shame-filled individuals, we tend first to twist and turn in the dark shame-waters before us. Then, with so much shame to spare, we start to drag others down with us. And drag them down we do—usually through outrageous arrogance, obvious contempt, and/or flagrant condescension. It's ugly but effective. We blame, reproach, and discredit. By the way, I do not mean to imply that we do any of this with malice of forethought. Instead, as usual, we're being run by something bigger than we are—by the mammoth machinery that has grown up inside to defend us.

Of course, the most devastating way we employ this defense is by turning it toward ourselves. To manage this, we most often use self-sabotage and self-degradation, both of which can be brought about through either negative *thinking* (as in "I'm worthless, useless, can't do it" and "What's the point? I should just give up") or negative *behavior* (as in *Procrastination, Compulsivity, Demeaning self-talk,* and *Withdrawal*).

Right away, you can start exploring the way *Shame* works in your life. You can examine both your *self* shaming and your *other-*shaming methods. Striking at the heart of this monster can begin to free us from stuckness NOW!

SELF-SHAMING

SIGNALS	STORY LINES
Self-shaming can cause you to be . . .	**To feel the internal effects of self-shaming, read the following words in an embarrassed, withdrawn, pitiful tone. You may say things like:**
Self-pitying:	"People think I've got it all together. If they only knew what a disgusting mess I am!"
Self-rejecting:	"Don't bother yourself. I'm not worth the trouble."
Embarrassed:	"I hope no one asks me any questions. I'd be completely and utterly humiliated, since I have no idea in the world what I'd say."
Covering your face:	"Oh, God . . . don't look at me . . . just don't look."
Lowering your eyes:	"I can't stand the way those people are looking at me. I just want to hide."
Negative:	"There's definitely something wrong with me. I'm just a big loser."
Hopeless:	"I'll never get anywhere. I've screwed everything up my whole life. I've just been wasting time."
Your Signals:	**Your Story Lines:**

OTHER-SHAMING

SIGNALS	STORY LINES
Other-shaming can cause you to be . . .	To feel the internal effects of shaming others, read the following words in a contemptuous tone. You may say things like:
Reproachful:	"If I have to work with that guy one more day, I'll be sick!"
Discrediting:	"Hey, your contribution is minimal to say the least!"
Degrading:	"Face it—you'll never amount to anything!"
Contemptuous:	"I don't even know why I married you. You're such a loser."
Derisive:	"Why don't you get your fat butt off the couch and do something useful!"
Blaming:	"It's your fault we have nothing."
Accusatory:	"You're not even trying to understand. What a waste of my time!"
Invalidating:	"When I want your opinion, I'll ask for it!"
Ridiculing:	"Can you believe what a pig that woman is!"
Your Signals:	**Your Story Lines:**

Unconscious intention

The shame defense is most often supported by the same concept that serves as the very definition of shame itself: *something is _really_ fundamentally wrong with us, and we are irreparably flawed.* And we're (unconsciously) out to prove it!

Thus, we see ourselves as irreparably damaged and imagine that hiding this damage is paramount. Failure to do so, we think, will most certainly lead us to be discarded, unloved, abandoned, or reviled (or to suffer some other similar, terrible fate). This is typified by Joe, who as a small boy was constantly punished by his father for imperfectly done chores and other minor infractions. An example: once Joe was made to go into the bathroom he shared with his two brothers and sit cross-legged on the linoleum floor very near the toilet, facing the wall. His father fussed about how close Joe's knees were supposed to be to the wall, about his posture, and about how quietly motionless he was required to remain. For a long time, Joe sat on the cold floor crying. After about half an hour, his older brother Keith came into the bathroom to pee. Keith was surprised to see Joe sitting there, gave him a light kick, and asked him what he was doing. Joe cried as he told Keith that Dad had put him there, saying if he moved he'd get into even more trouble. Keith shook his head silently and left. A long time passed. Joe hoped his mother would come, but she never did.

Eventually, of course, Joe was released from his bathroom prison. Unfortunately, this did not release him from his prison of shame and self-contempt—a place of confinement in which, to this day, he still resides. Clearly, Joe knows something's wrong. Dad thought it was something *about* Joe. His brother thought so, too. Having no information to the contrary, Joe came to believe they were right.

As has been previously noted, the *other*-shaming tendencies we exhibit come mostly out of shame overflow—when our shame bucket is too full and it splashes onto others. We may also simply be dealing with an experience of the idea that misery loves company.

Shame strangles the very life out of you!

Community dynamics

Our entire society flaunts its relationship to shame. We name, blame, and shame! The public degradation, disgrace, and dishonoring (shaming) of prominent personalities—including politicians, celebrities, and criminals—is a commonplace news event. We are actually, collectively, passing on to those around us the shame we ourselves feel inside—imagining this passing-the-buck procedure will make us feel better. Of course, it does not work. As usual, the shame we pass on becomes the shame we witness, which becomes the shame we emulate. Ashes to ashes. Shame to shame.

Personal sacrifice

The most obvious cost of shame is that it prevents you from believing that you (and the world around you) are worthwhile.

Resource acquired

Shame, like all other defenses, has gifts to offer when it's used with consciousness. For instance, it may protect you from an inflated ego, thereby helping you maintain healthy modesty.

RUN DEFENSES: DISCONNECTION THROUGH FEELING

The defense of SELF-CONTEMPT

Protecting yourself by using excessive expressions of self-disdain.

Personal impact

As individuals steeped in self-contempt, we are submerged in a dank, stagnant pool. The black waters wash over and over us until we feel ourselves drowning. For some reason, we want everyone else to know what we *already* know, which is: we stink.

There are two particularly awful aspects to this insistently negative position. First: the more we complain about ourselves, the more *we* come to *believe* our own complaints. Second: the more we put ourselves down, the more likely we are to *convince other people* that something is truly wrong with us! Just for a moment, consider the possibility that the only thing really, fundamentally wrong with you is your *idea* that something is wrong with you!

The only thing
<u>really</u>
wrong with you
is
your idea
about yourself!

Outer appearance

Self-contempt shows up in many obvious forms, such as self-directed negativity (as when, with yourself as the target, you engage in derision, mockery, or other despicable inner commentary). Or it may even appear as self-sabotaging behaviors (such as compulsivity, sloth, or depressive withdrawal). In addition to these clear examples, certain other behaviors or attitudes, more difficult to identify, also suggest self-contempt, such as the bravado that usually accompanies a bullying disposition.

But whether we are bullying braggarts or mocking self-haters, we are most likely to either surrender to the depression that often accompanies our outrageous self-contempt or, instead, to override our insistent self-doubt by working tirelessly to "appear" comfortable and capable.

Your motto
is
"never
enough"

SIGNALS	STORY LINES
Self-contempt can cause you to be . . .	**To feel the internal effects of self-contempt, read the following words in a deprecating tone. You may say things like:**
Comparing:	"I just don't seem to be able to do anything right. I'm sure someone else could be more helpful to you."
Scorning positive outcomes:	"Why should this turn out any better than usual!"

Negatively self-talking:	"What an idiot I am."
Minimizing:	"Don't make a fuss! Anyone could have done that!"
Rejecting care:	"Please don't waste your time."
Rejecting compliments:	"You like this outfit? Thanks, but I was just thinking I look like a horse today."
Helpless:	"Life's passing me by and I'm just a big ol' loser!"
Self-despising:	"I don't know why you bother . . . I'm just a pain in the neck and not worth the trouble!"
Your Signals:	**Your Story Lines:**

Unconscious intention

Because self-contempt often rests squarely on the shoulders of *Shame,* we are apt to notice that, to some degree, the unconscious intention driving them both (and even the way they are expressed) are similar. Hopefully, this similarity will reinforce our understanding of how they both work.

Self-contempt is fueled by one of two different and opposing (unconscious) "beliefs." The first is that *we are truly contemptible*—so contemptible that we must advertise the fact. The second is that *we are truly extraordinary*—so extraordinary that other people will feel diminished by our greatness and therefore be repelled by us. This second (and far more difficult to accept) possibility offers a striking example of an important concept: whatever is manifesting in an obvious *outer way of being* is inevitably balanced by an equal and opposite *inner way of feeling*. Thus, the braggart uses flamboyant bravado to compensate for feelings of extreme low self-esteem. Underlining this idea is essential, for it will serve as a cornerstone for all of your change-directed efforts. Please pause and consider:

Step 13 in defense busting:

Realize that all conscious feeling and thinking themes are inevitably balanced by equal and opposite *unconscious* feeling and thinking themes. Look for the opposites in yourself

Community dynamics

Society as a whole appears to know very little about how to deal with problems of self-contempt, especially when those problems show up in the most obvious forms—like drug-use, alcoholism, and other compulsivity, or with people involved in violently abusive relationships (here both the abuser and the abused are self-contemptuous!). The community observing these problems may be complaining, scoffing, and even fearing these manifestations, but seldom does that same community arrive at any real or viable solutions. Perhaps there *are* no grand solutions, because maybe such problems must be tackled one person at a time. However, instead of focusing on how better to punish related crimes (the drug user's robberies, the alcoholic's car wrecks, the sex addict's public bathroom rendezvous, or the abuser's violent explosions), we might choose to start with an acknowledgment of the actual most common *source* of these difficulties (home and surrounding environment). In this regard, investigation of early-life emotional states and circumstances could be the key to change. In any event, fundamental education (starting in elementary school) about what makes us tick (and break down!) certainly promises to help us more than it hinders us.

Personal sacrifice

When you're brazenly self-contemptuous, achieving intimacy with others is often nearly impossible. You shove yourself away from other people with your can'ts and won'ts. You reject loving attention by insisting on your own unworthiness. Eventually, infected by your negativity, observers think maybe you're right. Perhaps you *are* less wonderful and capable than they think you are!

You're shoving life away with can'ts and won'ts

Resource acquired

While at times self-contempt can undermine both self-actualization and intimacy with others, it can also, in other instances, act as a safeguard against ego-inflation. Likewise, its more benign cousin—self-doubt—when judiciously employed, can serve as an important modifier, teaching you modesty.

RUN DEFENSES: DISCONNECTION THROUGH FEELING

The defense of FEAR

*Protecting yourself through persistent feelings
of eminent (emotional or physical) danger.*

Personal impact

Fear-based individuals assume the plane will crash, the job will collapse, and the relationship will disappoint. Doom is their demanding master and gloom their frequent companion. Their glass is half-empty and their loaf remains half-baked.

Sometimes when fear intrudes, we feel a quiet, ongoing, anxious concern, causing us to tiptoe toward situations while over and over looking carefully to the left and to the right. Then, at other (more excruciating) times, there's just an awful, stark terror that absolutely paralyzes our legs and, in fact, our entire being. We cannot think of moving, of taking a new turn, or of developing a fresh plan. We can focus only on the fear and on what that fear threatens.

This particular defense displays itself in a wide span of expressions—everything from mild, nagging anxiety that pokes us in the gut (we just *know* disaster lurks and sulks around every corner) to brow-furrowing vigilance that eats at our brain like an unstoppable Ms Pacman. Perhaps public speaking terrifies you, or being caught making mistakes horrifies you, or appearing inappropriate mortifies you! You fret: *What do other people think of me? Does anybody really like me? I can't let them know, see, or realize that I. . . .*

Defensive fear can even drag us to the very edge of ourselves and, in the process, gobble up all the space inside. In these cases, we might find ourselves in the grip of extreme phobic responses (such as agoraphobia, which is fear of leaving home; or claustrophobia, which is fear of confined spaces). In fact, this debilitating defense can even go so far as to support and sustain an irrational, morbid horror of death (perhaps showing up as hypochondria).

All in all, this awful defense (which like so many others was probably initiated by disruptive childhood circumstances)—whether appearing in its benign or its aggressive forms, tends continuously to beat us down until eventually we most resemble the broken-jawed, punch-drunk boxer who stayed too long in the ring.

Fear
beats us up
and
keeps us down

Outer appearance

Certainly you may be well aware of the depth and scope of your own fears; you may even have some sense of their effect on your life. But oddly enough, spotting the fearful person sitting next to you is often not as easy as it might sound. For instance, consider Rachel—a rich, powerful, beautiful, articulate, fun, widely-loved woman. At first glance, Rachel seems to have and be all the things most of us yearn for.

Unfortunately, what Rachel *feels* is quite different from how Rachel *looks*.

This woman is afraid of crowds, of parties, of speaking in public, of making a mess, of disorder in general, and of having her true feelings seen and heard. In fact, she's afraid of visibility of any kind. She worries all the time, therefore—about seeming perfect and sounding perfect. To the casual onlooker she may *appear* clear, strong, and active, but in truth her life is constantly undermined by her own relentless inner terrors.

To recognize fear in friends, acquaintances, and family, try noticing the ways in which they too-frequently alter or cancel plans, especially when those plans involve new activities. Also listen for the sounds (and the "feel") of *excessive* worry (both in yourself and in others), particularly as it relates to how anything (well, everything!) is going to turn out. You may even try tuning in to the music underneath the words. For example, does "I'm afraid to fly" have a simple, natural ring to it, or do you think, for particular individuals, it might translate as, "Every time I get on a plane, I'm sure it's going to crash and I'll die"?

SIGNALS	STORY LINES
Fear can cause you to be . . .	To feel the internal effects of fear, try reading the following words in a panicky tone. You may say things like:
Anxious:	"I'm terrified to fly. So I'll engage in rituals like tapping on the plane three times, drinking, taking drugs that put me to sleep, or calling psychics to be sure it's a good day to fly."

Phobic:	"I'm afraid to use public restrooms. I always think some-one will be watching me or I'll pick up some dreadful disease or something else strange. I hate it so much I'm willing to forgo travel so I won't have to use those kinds of facilities."
Irritable:	"Get off my back. I'll ask you to marry me when I'm good and ready!"
Hesitating to risk:	"I hate my job, but it's the only thing I know."
Passive:	"I stay away from conflict at all cost."
Avoiding:	"You go ahead. I'd rather just do my own thing."
Inactive:	"I don't like to travel very much. I prefer staying close to home."
Controlling:	"Disorganization makes me nervous. I need to know the plan."
Denying:	"I'm not going to the doctor. I'd rather not know."
Resistant:	"I'm comfortable where I am. I don't like change."
Hypochondria-cal:	"I can't meet you for lunch. I'm on my way to the doctor again. This time I *know* something is really wrong!"
Your Signals:	**Your Story Lines:**

Unconscious intention

Everyone feels reasonable and appropriate fear from time to time (as when a loved one is sick or when a familiar lifestyle is threatened by job change, money loss, or moving). But when we are fear-*driven*, life often revolves around a series of our anxious concerns. Like someone riding an arcade merry-go-round, we mentally turn and turn and turn—always landing where we started—getting nowhere.

What drives fear is complicated. If, for instance, in just one specific area we were to find ourselves afraid (even in the extreme), we could manage it and be done with it. That is, if we were afraid of flying we could simply chose *not* to fly. Unfortunately, fear often refuses to be contained, tending rather to spill over from one spot to another, like gravy on a plate.

Several red-flag warnings will help you determine when fear is an aid in recognizing that appropriate safety measures need to be taken—or when it is, in fact, defensive. The first red flag involves *excessive* amounts of time and energy being given to making certain *you are the one in control* (inside and out). You have probably felt that way for as long as you can recall. Remember way back, when in the midst of great difficulty, you started turning your focus to what *appeared* manageable (how smart you sounded when you spoke, how good you looked, how neatly organized your things were, how much you ate). At that point, this focus (unconsciously) gave you the sense (to some degree) of sitting in the stillness of the hurricane's eye. All around you, while things crashed and clanged, you focused your worry on the after-effects. Mostly, even while the storm was still raging, you concentrated on figuring out how to replace the broken glassware and when to start the clearing process. Now, as an adult, you apply this procedure to your current circumstances. Perhaps the stakes seem even higher now, since back then your behavior was more a response to the way other people chose to conduct your life; now it's about how and what *you* choose. As luck (or the unconscious!) would have it, your fear level has risen to accommodate the higher-stakes nature of the game.

Thus, our first driving (unconscious) intention is *to make everything turn out the "right" way*, which equals *our* way. To do this, we think we must keep our eye not on the ball we've thrown but on where that ball is going. Where will it land, who might it hit along the way, and how will people who've seen the throw feel about us? We think if we concentrate enough on the ending, we will remain in charge. However, we are not in charge. Not of endings anyhow—only of process (steps along the way). We are not the ones in the pilot's seat and we have no real authority over what people think when they see and hear us. But because somewhere deep inside, we actually already know this, all of our efforts to control outcome only bring you increased anxiety instead of relief.

The second red flag is another common unconscious intention supporting the defense of fear: *we are driven to undermine our own personal success.* The question follows: what unconscious ideas and/or needs are driving this undermining procedure? Three come quickly to mind: We are (unconsciously) afraid of doing better in the world than our parents did, because that would mean we are betraying them. We have a need to satisfy the negative messages our families gave us. And we wish to avoid the difficulties and responsibilities we anticipate that real personal success will bring.

But what's to explain why already wildly successful people are (or remain) fear-based? It's curiouser and curiouser. Once again we must look to the father/mother kinship, for it turns out that most often in these cases the unconscious driving voice is parental, so no matter how things appear on the outside, the so-called powerful individual is just as stuck in the old *I-don't-deserve-it* story as a person who is more obviously struggling. The intention of the defense, then—no matter who's using it—is to flagrantly undermine joy in order to maintain the (childhood/parent) status quo. *You may get it*, the dark throaty demon whispers, *but you'll never enjoy it!*

Fear
is
just
a
feeling
and
not
a
fact

The worst part of all this is that for many people, fear gets all puffed up and begins strutting its stuff around like a self-impressed peacock. Before we know it, the demon has grown into a god. Like it or not, we find ourselves building temples to it and bowing at its altar. But what we need to know is that, in fact, *fear is just a feeling*—neither of greater nor of lesser importance than other feelings. It is not more substantial than hope nor more gripping than lust nor more terrible than grief nor more powerful than compassion. And the great news is there's an antidote for fear—and that antidote is called is faith.

The antidote for fear is faith

Community dynamics

Every day we get to witness how our communities (nationally or globally) handle *real and palpable* fear (such as war, AIDS, or economic collapse). Unfortunately, though, when it comes to many of the issues that can be truly fear-provoking, we often spend more time and effort arguing than trying to fix the problem. Who's to blame? How did it happen? Who's to blame? Is the problem at hand a worthy focus? Who's to blame? We argue in this way mostly because we, as individuals, feel basically powerless to affect the situation in any truly viable way. We talk where we cannot act.

Meanwhile, on local levels, we are confronted daily with widespread hysteria. Media reports of crime, death, and disaster support and perpetuate this hysteria. Again, we tend to fight the fear with useless argument, having no idea where to turn or what really to do.

On a happier note, this faith antidote seems to have been discovered by more than a few of us. Perhaps the national upsurge of religious and spiritual interest reflects this discovery. Flowers growing up in the manure. We may be learning that, when faced with terrible dread (either personal or communal), we do have a choice. We can attempt to flee—or stand (with faith in hand) to face the dragon.

Personal sacrifice

Fear discourages risk-taking, robbing you of the stunning rewards of provocative, or instructive, or powerful, or exhilarating new adventures.

Resource acquired

Fear, the ally that can serve but must not rule, encourages you to look before you leap—a helpful procedure if you're to avoid a sudden fall into the chasm.

RUN DEFENSES: DISCONNECTION THROUGH FEELING

The defense of VICTIM

Protecting yourself by focusing on feeling cheated, fooled, abused, or ignored by people and/or circumstances.

Personal impact

Like a punished puppy trembling in the corner, victims feel weak, insecure, and unsafe. They imagine themselves to be preyed upon, duped, and suckered by a dangerous world in an unsupportive universe. They're quick to express a sense of powerlessness, even in the most ordinary of circumstances—and when they're faced with unusual or unforeseen difficulty, they can easily collapse.

The more we complain, the weaker we feel and the worse things look. We undermine our own innate capacity by choosing reaction over action, often trying to enlist others into our negative thinking. This (we hope) will move them to say those golden words: "Oh, you poor thing, you got another lousy break, didn't you? Life's not fair, is it!"

Outer appearance

Of course, overwhelming circumstances can make a victim out of anyone—temporarily. Perhaps this is why it's so easy to point the finger to outside influences—the causes and reasons we identify as answering the question "why?" In fact, the Victim defense is the "Run" version of the "Hit" defense of Blame. "It's not my fault," we can hear the victim cry. "I'm at the mercy of circumstances" (which means: everyone and everything else is to blame).

When we claim victim status as a defensive posture, one of two things is usually happening. Either *our victimization is self-generated* or *our victimization (so-called) is more perception than fact*. In the case of self-generated victimization, we look like those individuals who can't pay their rent because (while stuck in Depression) they've chosen to watch TV all day rather than search for work; or the abused spouse who (while stuck in Fear) hangs around for more abuse; or the morbidly obese overeater who (while stuck in Compulsivity) has constant physical problems associated with the obesity. (As you can see by these examples, the defenses are often intertwined—serving and perpetuating each other. It's always helpful to notice which cluster of defenses you yourself use most.)

With regard to victimization that is more perception than fact, examples can be seen in the slow-working employee who believes she can't get ahead because she's female (when the truth is that her work is simply awful), or in the man who thinks women leave him because he's not rich (when the truth is that he's just an unpleasant person), or the entrepreneur who thinks his income keeps falling because "business is bad all over" (when the truth is that he can't get his work and his thinking organized efficiently enough to do well).

You remain a victim by learning to play the blame game

SIGNALS	STORY LINES
Victimization can cause you to be . . .	**To feel the internal effects of victimization, read the following words in a pathetic tone. You may say things like:**
Complaining:	"You don't understand how hard things are for me. I never catch a break."
Confused:	"I feel like giving up. I don't know which way to turn."
Sacrificing:	"I do everything for you and what do you do for me?!"
Blaming:	"If you just listened to me, I wouldn't need to yell!"
Fatalistic:	"It's not my fault nothing ever turns out right. The worst things always happen to me."
Pouting:	"He acted interested and then never called. It's always that way with me!"
Feeling powerless:	"I keep hitting my head against a brick wall."
Resentful:	"I should have seen it coming. How could I have believed a woman would ever be given a real chance in this business!"
Pessimistic:	"What's the use? The world's against me!"
Wanting rescue:	"Someday the right person will come along . . . and I'll be able to be happy."
Comparing:	"Other people have all the luck. They've got families to help them. I don't."
Your Signals:	**Your Story Lines:**

Unconscious intention

As victims we unconsciously hold several (usually erroneous) beliefs:

❖ *We do not experience ourselves as having genuine authority over the way our lives are developing.* This often leaves us feeling too small for the job (of living), fragile, incompetent, and greatly put-upon. Secretly, we're desperate to be rescued from the impossibility of it all. We may simply have decided that since *we* are unable to triumph over life's obstacles, perhaps someone else can do the triumphing for us.

❖ *We believe we're actually the focus of <u>everything</u> that goes wrong in our lives.* This follows from an immature, self-centered belief that the world revolves entirely around us. In actuality, there is a young age at which such narcissistic thinking is appropriate. Apparently, however, the victims' emotional growth stopped at that age and they therefore never come to realize that life is not reflecting or targeting them personally. The earthquake isn't *their* fault, the car-jacking wasn't aimed specifically at *them*, and even the boss's bad mood is (usually) not inspired by *them*.

❖ *Unconsciously, we're throwing a psychological temper tantrum.* We stomp our feet and think, "Why me? Why should *I* have to do it? I've already had a tough life. Someone else should fix this for me. I can't. I won't!"

Community dynamics

As far as society goes, huge numbers of people—from the homeless to those who have suffered domestic violence or molestation to women (simply due to their gender) to African Americans (simply due to their ethnicity) to the poor (simply due to their financial status)—fall into this victim category. The wide-ranging nature of this description most likely arises to a great extent out of our overall desire to think of ourselves (and to be thought of) as "good people." Unfortunately, this is a misunderstanding of actual goodness and of the way goodness works. The truth is that assigning "special" status to those who have experienced misfortune does more to relieve our own sense of powerlessness (or maybe our guilt over having a better life) than it does to actually help those at whom we direct our pity. It's a behavior that could more easily be described as self-aggrandizing than as compassionate.

Many people who are interested in so-called "victims' issues" may be reacting strongly to the (unconscious) sting of their own early (usually ignored), unresolved personal traumas related to feeling victimized. Often in these cases, focusing on another's victim drama is easier than revisiting one's own. Thus, we should be alert for occasions when our true motive is to rescue our own sagging self-esteem. We can do more harm than good if our "help" falls into the category of enabling rather than that of assisting, since the recipients of our largesse may tend to stay stuck in hopeless, unproductive lives instead of growing and developing self-fulfilling and society-fulfilling resources. So in the long run, we feel better, they get worse.

Therefore, treating people as perennial unfortunates, misfits, or incompetents undermines their potential and, eventually, short-changes society as a whole. The temporary feeling of superiority we get is no more authentic than the "help" we are giving those others. Everybody loses this game.

Personal sacrifice

By believing yourself to be a victim and behaving as if you have no choices (which is always far from true), you renounce the personal power you might otherwise use for the betterment of the situation about which you are complaining.

Resource acquired

You have learned to depend on other people. Applied in a healthy way, this capacity makes you a great team-player.

RUN DEFENSES: DISCONNECTION THROUGH FEELING

The defense of WITHDRAWAL

Protecting yourself through emotional and even physical retreat.

Personal impact

Withdrawal is the camouflage that protects us as we trek through the battles of our lives. We pull ourselves back under the cover of brush so the enemy cannot spot us. It's effective! Just recently a client reported his boss's comment: "I really like having you here. I know you're doing your job, but at the same time I can almost forget about you altogether, because you're so quiet. It's great." But being forgettable does not feel as good to us as it sometimes looks to others!

It's hard to be seen if you're never heard

Typically, those who choose this particular defensive path are congratulated for being unobtrusive. Usually the invisibility starts early. Parents may reveal this pattern when they say, "Oh, he was always such an easy child . . . so quiet and good—no trouble at all." Meanwhile, that individual, now grown and living an uncomfortable life, is working hard (either in a therapeutic setting or in other, perhaps less effective ways) to resolve anxiety-provoking issues such as buried aggression and thwarted self-expression.

Check out your own history. At first, you probably stayed quiet and separate, because that seemed like the best way to be. Your reticent, and/or supersensitive nature encouraged it, and the strained circumstances around you (such as, family mandates and peer-member pressures) demanded it. But what began as a simple protective device has, at this point, lowered a heavy, velour-like curtain over everything in your present life—a curtain that darkens your experience of both your relationships with others and your feelings about yourself.

It's an insidious process, this system of withdrawal—appearing to be much gentler on our (inner) system than it really is. Our silence is far from golden, for it's actually tarnished and is destroying us. The less we talk, the harder talking gets to be, even when we want to talk. Once we're silent for long enough, we begin to feel (and be) overlooked. At that point, asking for and getting what we want—and even ultimately knowing *what* we want—becomes increasingly difficult. We feel so frustrated and faltering that we finally come mostly to reject interaction with others altogether. Now we are truly as lonely as we have always perceived ourselves to be.

Outer appearance

Withdrawal can make us look removed, reluctant, unavailable, moody, or simply shy. To some observers, we may even appear to be snobbish or arrogant, but of course we're really just afraid, perfectionistic, or depressed (to name only a few possibilities).

Some will romanticize our reticence, assuming that "people like us" have a great deal to say, but only to "special" listeners. Others will merely be annoyed and—especially if they are inclined to activate their own blame or victim defenses—treat our withdrawal as personal rejection. Either way, we lose.

SIGNALS	STORY LINES
Withdrawal can cause you to be . . .	**To feel the internal effects of withdrawal, try reading the following words in a quiet monotone. You may say things like:**
Procrastinating:	"I'll do it later. I've got plenty of time."

Your silence is not golden— it's ruining your life!

Rejecting:	"I don't want to discuss it. Let it go." ✗
Disengaged:	"I just don't know what to say . . . whatever you want is fine."
Isolating:	"Leave me alone. I need my space."
Silent:	". . . . ."
Reluctant:	"No, you go to the party without me. I won't even know anybody there."
Sulking:	"No, I'm not still mad, but I just don't feel very much like having sex tonight."
Removed:	"I don't like to get involved. It's not my business."
Vague:	"How do I feel? I really don't know."
Retreating:	"It's not that I don't care—I just hate fighting, that's all. I'm a lover not a fighter."
Your Signals:	**Your Story Lines:**

Unconscious intention

As with everything, withdrawal often begins early and continues until it becomes a well-developed habit. This "habit" however, is propelled, like all defensive measures, by the unconscious intentions that drive it. In this case there are a number of possibilities. Through our withdrawal:

❖ We're aiming to lodge an angry protest declaring "I just won't share my thoughts and feelings with you at all. You don't deserve it!"

❖ We're asserting a demanding plea that reports "If you really care about how I feel and what I think, you'll work hard to find out."

❖ We're expressing a pouting self-contempt that says "I have nothing important to share."

❖ We're fostering an accusation that proclaims "You don't really want to know me anyway." Or

❖ We're making an insistent declaration that announces "I am powerless. I have no other choice."

Needless to say, such covert forms of communication are likely to leave us essentially high and dry. Eventually, people around us will tend to get fed up, burned-out, resentful, or respond hopelessly when the option of helping or rescuing us comes up. All too often, at that point, we are driven even further into our dark defense.

Community dynamics

As a community, we often support withdrawal by seeing it as a virtue. This (silently) supportive posture with regard to the nonparticipating portion of our population is reinforced by the way we tend to grease the squeaky wheel—a process during which we often throw a spotlight on the troublesome while at the same time overlooking the unseen potential contributors who live all around us. Would it help if we celebrated the quiet heroes? If we insisted on their being seen as vivid, valuable people of substance? Perhaps by encouraging the revelation of uniqueness that is defined by exuberant authenticity rather than by brash, eccentric rebelliousness, we could discover hidden treasures and untapped resources among us.

Personal sacrifice

While you may cause no trouble to others, you often stifle your own creative, contributory, inventive self-expression.

Resource acquired

Among other things, practicing withdrawal teaches you restraint—giving you the ability to appear (and often to be) unruffled by upheaval. This makes you a person who can help others calm down in times of disturbance or crisis.

RUN DEFENSES: DISCONNECTION THROUGH FEELING

The defense of DEPRESSION

*Protecting yourself through feelings of emotional,
mental, and/or physical paralysis.*

DEPRESSION

Personal impact

Depression, the cloud of gloom that shivers above us, casts an ominous shadow over our days and a damp threat over our nights. Currently, this "problem" is most often approached from the biochemical angle, with an emphasis on the associated inherited/genetic factors or other physical considerations. For purposes of this discussion, however, biochemistry and its importance will take second position, while we direct our focus on the psychological aspects that might lead this condition to be considered a defense—both the underlying issues that support the defense as well as the choices (howsoever unconscious) that perpetuate those issues.

"Choices?" you may exclaim. "What choices? I really feel awful. Who would *want* to feel this way?" But the hypothesis we are presently exploring is that depression is not unlike other (unconsciously) chosen feelings, thoughts, and behaviors. Depression, then, is meant to defend the same personal, emotional turf that you first began defending as a child. Now, you're in a kind of post-traumatic shock state, but we call it depression.

Like many other defenses, depression shows up in a wide range of different forms—from mild gloom to abject misery. When we're dejected, we are drained of energy and can't imagine changing either our circumstances or our outlook. To some extent, we don't even *want* to. On top of that, the worse we feel, the more discouraged we get. Eventually, then, as depression chews away at our foundation like a ravenous, oversized termite, our self-esteem collapses and we fall in upon ourselves—helpless and hopeless.

The worse
we feel
the more
discouraged
we get

Outer appearance

Overall, when we talk about being "depressed," we're generally referring to one of two states. The first (and most common) is simple sadness, fatigue, or irritability (more a creation of passing circumstances than true depression). In such instances, we might say things such as, "I'm down in the mouth . . . out of it . . . blue. Oh, I'm so depressed." In fact, at those times we are more often describing a transient emotional circumstance than presenting true clinical information.

The second reference to depression includes states that can be either temporary (inspired by specific circumstances such as the death of a loved one) or long-term (inspired by biochemistry). In either instance, anti-depressant medication may be required.

The sort of depression being addressed here, however, precisely fits neither category (although we may find shades of the others mixed in). It is more than a product of particular circumstances and may be initiated as much by intense feelings as by biochemistry. Nevertheless, our appearance or demeanor may strongly resemble depression in its other forms, since we are likely to look and to feel distracted and confused. Our tendency in the face of these discomforting feelings is to hide out (isolate). We're frequently riddled with anxiety and often blanketed by inexplicable sadness.

When we're in this state, we have little energy and we tend to drag ourselves from place to place. In fact, at times we find it difficult to get moving at all. To some, we might appear sorrowful and melancholic. If we're lucky, we simply find ourselves unable to concentrate. But when we are being run by the most aggressive and pernicious version of this defense, we may find ourselves robbed of appetite, deprived of sleep, and strangled in our ability to work.

SIGNALS	STORY LINES
Depression can cause you to be . . .	**To feel the internal effects of depression, read the following words in a gloomy monotone. You may say things like:**
Lethargic:	"I just don't want to get out of bed."
Sad:	"I cry all the time and I don't even know why."
Hopeless:	"I don't want to try anymore. What's the point?"
Helpless:	"I should get organized but I don't know where to start."
Discouraged:	"No matter what I do, I still feel as if my life is never going to be the way I want it to be."
Isolating:	"Better not come over. I wouldn't be very good company."
Lacking energy:	"This place is a pig sty, but I can't seem to get myself motivated to clean it."
Sleeping badly:	"I'm up and down all night long."
Eating badly:	"Well, I guess the good news is. . .I've completely lost my appetite."
Humorless:	"I don't find that—or much of anything—funny right now. Thanks for trying."

Your Signals:	Your Story Lines:

Unconscious intention

Depress your feelings, depress your feelings, depress your feelings—and eventually those underlying (unmet) feelings depress you. "What *unmet* feelings?" you moan. "Isn't depression itself enough of a burden?" Actually—no, for depression's (unconscious) intention is truly to help us avoid making contact with deeper feelings (of terrible fear and horrific anguish). Somewhere, at some time, we decided those (other) powerful emotions were much too difficult to endure or confront.

But our avoidance has caught up with us. Actually, for some (largely unfathomable) reason, this may show up in our in early adulthood (that is, our twenties or thirties), when previously unidentified concerns typically begin trying to bubble up, causing ripples on the (apparently) smooth surface of our lives. Maybe this occurs because, until then, we tend to assume our lives will, at some later time, (magically) begin to look and be better. So we just go along with things, waiting for *the* moment when our lives will begin. Now we (unconsciously) decide that moment has come and gone—without us. "Life is not showing up the way I imagined," we say to ourselves. At that point, we begin feeling hurt, mystified, and even shocked. We close the blinds, pull down the shades, and hope it will all just go away.

Of course, no discussion of depression would be complete without including the well-known "*yikes*" response to midlife. Many people at that point come to a psychological screeching halt. "*This is not what I thought it would be,*" they shout. "*Where am I going? Where have I been? What's happened to all those dreams and plans? Have I wasted all this time? Do I have enough time left?"* These kinds of dismal questions obviously have the power to ignite in us hysteria, fear, deep sorrow, and ultimately depression.

Regardless of how and where all this began, the depression that follows often closely resembles a low-grade fever that suddenly spikes into dangerous territory. We're wise, therefore, to recognize the threat of (psychological) infection—an infection based on our disappointment about the way things are turning out (or about how little power we think we have to make them turn out a different way) that takes all of our energy. We're exhausted. Still, staying on the surface of ourselves to avoid the profound grief, the devastating fear, or the intense rage that lives deep inside seems like a better (unconscious) choice. So we continue to give ourselves over to the defense.

Community dynamics

Twenty years ago, a diagnosis of depression was restricted to a very few, extreme cases that often required hospitalization. But lately, this has become a diagnosis for the many. Not only are people less ashamed to acknowledge some degree of depression, but this designation has (especially among wealthy, successful people) also become fashionable. Herbal remedies (such as St. John's wort) as well as doctor-prescribed anti-depressants are routinely advertised on television—indicating how widespread the audience for them must be.

As a result of this new attitude toward depression and the proliferation of widely prescribed drugs such as Prozac, Zolaf, and others, society, overall, finds itself to be a co-conspirator supporting the neglect of extremely important (deeply-lodged) feelings. The problematic outcomes are plenty. Not only does the individual obviously suffer (by giving up personal power and productivity), but since depression also puts a stranglehold on passionate, creative responses, the community suffers as well.

Personal sacrifice

Depression limits your ability to greet, meet, and treat life in an engaged, enthusiastic way.

Resource acquired

Depression teaches many things, not the least of which is compassion for the sometimes dark moods of others.

RUN DEFENSES: DISCONNECTION THROUGH FEELING

The defense of TERMINAL UNIQUENESS

Protecting yourself through your feelings of being completely different from other people and through your ideas that you are therefore misperceived by them.

Personal impact

When we defend ourselves with feelings of terminal uniqueness, the important element is not how strange or unusual we may (or may not) appear to others, but rather how completely different, misunderstood, and/or extraordinary *we* feel ourselves to be. This feeling of difference actually brings us a significant sense of satisfaction and personal well-being (although at this point we may not yet realize this is true). We tell ourselves that the facts of our life story describe either the most horrific of events or, alternatively, represent the most benign experiences anyone has ever lived through. *Emotionally*, we experience our history as unprecedented (even if *intellectually* we understand it is not). We are already certain that we don't (and can't) fit in, and our defense of

You feel
separate and
therefore
not equal

Terminal Uniqueness nicely encapsulates our feelings of isolation, alienation, and unacceptability.

Outer appearance

The defense of terminal uniqueness is usually exhibited through one of two personality styles.

The first is that of the *show-off*. When we're one of these, we will do anything to prove our uniqueness. We're willing to look outlandish, foolish, and even bizarre. Sometimes, however, we merely seem superficial or artificial.

The second is that of the *hider*. When we're one of these, we keep our "outsider" feelings a secret. We might look like we're blending in and are part of the crowd, but inside we feel completely alienated.

But whether we show off or hide out, our feelings are the same—that we don't fit in!

You think you'll never fit in

SIGNALS	STORY LINES
Feeling terminally unique can cause you to be . . .	**To feel the internal effects of terminal uniqueness, read the following words with a peevish, irritated tone. You may say things like:**
Misunderstood:	"People don't quite get where I'm coming from."
Disconnected:	"It's easy for him—he's normal. But I've always marched to the beat of a different drummer."
Judgmental:	"Yeah, I wish I had his problems. He should try walking in my shoes for a day!"
Comparing:	"Hey, I'm just not like other people."
Critical:	"What a moron! He's like all the rest!"

Self-deprecating:	"I'll never be as smart as other people."
Victimized:	"Nobody struggles the way I do!"
Alienated:	"I'm sure my family found me on their doorstep or something. I'm nothing like any of them."
Your Signals:	**Your Story Lines:**

Unconscious intention

We most likely choose Terminal Uniqueness as a method of defending ourselves because:

❖ *Deep inside we feel so ordinary (or stupid or ineffectual)*—so lacking in special qualities—that we're afraid we'll get lost in the crowd. We're certain, based on the information provided by our feelings, that nothing we can do will ever be enough to get us included. We hope that as our so-called uniqueness is interpreted as remarkable, we ourselves will be seen as remarkable. And/or,

❖ *We're terrified of the intimacy* that's involved with feeling truly connected to others. Perhaps we believe the intimacy will suffocate us, so we reject those who offer it; or maybe we're afraid that people will discover how unworthy we believe ourselves to be and be repelled. We leave ourselves out, then, before we can be left out.

Community dynamics

We all want to feel unusual, special, and matchless—and at the same time to fit in. This is no easy matter. Gang members do it by fitting in with each other (wearing special garb, speaking in particular ways, using

You fear
getting lost
in the crowd

For you
rejection
is a
preemptive strike

meaningful handshakes), while at the same time and by means of the same mechanisms, standing out from the broader community.

Perhaps so-called "minority uprisings" are merely mass expressions of terminal uniqueness. As the protesters say, "You must treat me differently and regard me as special because I am _____ [and they fill in the blank with one of more of the following: their age, religion, ethnicity, skin color, national origin, gender, sexual preference, or socioeconomic status]."

What later turns into a defense can easily begin as a simple part of developmental staging—an aspect of a process the great Swiss psychiatrist Carl Jung called "individuation." Individuation is the development of our own special "voice"—which differentiates us from our family and our peers. However, this developmental process is thoroughly unlike the defense of Terminal Uniqueness, which distorts our sense of being (*wonderfully* distinct) individuals into feeling of being (*horribly* distinct) outsiders. An inability to recognize this difference may indicate that our individuation process is incomplete.

You must learn that there is a big difference between horribly different and wonderfully distinct

Personal sacrifice

Terminal uniqueness as a defense robs you of a deep sense of belonging.

Resource acquired

Feeling terminally unique can teach you to seek out, investigate, and value the rare, uncommon qualities that truly distinguish (but do not *separate*) you from others. Eventually you can learn to be proud of what's *authentically* different about you.

RUN DEFENSES: DISCONNECTION THROUGH FEELING

The defense of SPIRITUALITY

Protecting yourself through the use
of excessive religious or spiritual referencing.

Personal impact

Certainly in our own mind, our spirituality is not defensive. In fact, we think, we are operating from good (perhaps even lofty) intentions, so it's all the more mystifying when, at times, others tell us they feel ignored, overwhelmed, disrespected, invalidated, unheard, and/or even repulsed by the way we "come at" them. This, of course, is in the mostly rare circumstances when people actually have the courage or self-regard to speak up about our way of presenting ourselves and our "spiritual" position. More often, people hesitate to confront us in these circumstances—perhaps not wanting to seem (spiritually) disrespectful or not wishing to get into one of those aggravating religious arguments that goes nowhere and upsets everyone. Meaning this: we "spiritual types" are not always so easy to confront!

Our style comes in part from the fact that we are passionately committed to our ideas—but this does not ameliorate the effect of our presentation. We think our point is the *only* point, so we dismiss other people's spiritual opinions. That's bad enough, but even worse is the way we offhandedly offer our superficial (and often simplistic) religious solutions as an easy fix for other people's intense struggles and crises. At those times, we come off as righteously condescending.

Indeed, our spirituality provides for us a sturdy platform on which to stand and even may offer a soothing caress for others to lean into. But when we present that spiritual perspective in a holier-than-thou way, it

We think
our point
is the
only point

has the effect of separating us from others and, in some ways, from the very concepts we espouse.

Outer appearance

We talk as if faith, or belief, is an all-purpose salve that should relieve people of *every* problem or unwanted feeling—a magic conviction, experience, or collection of principles that is guaranteed to save everyone from difficult situations. We're quick to offer spiritual solutions or cosmic remarks—often while minimizing what others are feeling in the face of their heart-wrenching circumstances. We seem to believe that spiritual understanding is superior to other types of understanding, and we sometimes get indignant (or more likely condescending) when our listeners don't appreciate the profound statements we're making. The problem is that our approach tends more to repel than to convince, particularly to the degree that it ignores or diminishes matters we regard as "less than spiritual." There's an old saying: "Be sure you don't get so spiritual that you're no earthly good."

Be sure you don't get so spiritual that you're no earthly good

SIGNALS	STORY LINES
Spirituality as a defense can cause you to be . . .	To feel the internal effects of defending through spirituality, try reading the following words with an inflexible tone. You may say things like:
Self-righteous:	"If you'd only listen to what I'm telling you, your life wouldn't be such an unholy mess!"
Minimizing feelings:	"Death is merely a part of life, you know. You'd best understand that God has a plan. It's time to move on."
Condescending:	"I have the personal ear of the Creator, so if you're smart you'll listen to me."

Intellectualizing:	"You know better than to feel so irritated with your wife. Stop yelling. Think about the spiritual consequences of your actions."
Flippant:	"Hey, maybe it's just your karma!"
Convincing:	"I know we're *supposed* to fall in love and be together, because I've had a clear God-sent vision that tells me so."
Proselytizing:	"Unbelievers go to hell."
Sanctimonious:	"I don't know why you're mad at *me*. After all, what I did was obviously the will of God."
Your Signals:	**Your Story Lines:**

Unconscious intention

Spirituality that reflects a sense of being deeply and profoundly connected to the heart of the universe can be the source of the highest kinds of development. If anything, such spirituality promotes authentic humility, for spiritual people tend truly to appreciate their place in an awesome and creative cosmos. Spirituality as a defense, however, is something else. It tends to be narrowly intellectual and, like so many other defenses, is often used as a cover. But *what* does it cover? Underneath, deep within us, our seeming spiritual confidence is likely to be covering up screaming doubts about the value and truth of spirit forces and effects. This screaming doubt—so powerful and demanding that we're frantic to drown it out—claws desperately at us in our silent moments, demanding proof that there is indeed something beyond us, that our faith makes sense, that our existence is not meaningless, and that we are not alone. We attempt to convince others in order to convince ourselves.

Community dynamics

Oddly and wonderfully enough, spirituality has recently enjoyed a comeback and is once again fashionable. This is reflected in popular movies like *Michael* and *Contact*; in best-selling nonfiction like *The Soul's Code, Care of the Soul, Conversations with God,* and *The Celestine Prophecy*; and even in prime-time television programs such as *Touched by an Angel.* In addition, many people who once would never have been attracted to spiritual or religious ideals flock to hear speakers like Depak Chopra teach Eastern perspectives about the mind/body/spirit connection or Marianne Williamson explain *A Course in Miracles.*

A growing number of people seem to recognize a desire to connect to their inner, spiritual beliefs—beliefs that are intuitively available but have probably not yet emerged developmentally. Such individuals frequently discover that these beliefs combat an increasing sense of worldly helplessness by offering them something beyond transitory, often uninspiring materialism.

Personal sacrifice

When you use spirituality as a defense, you give up the possibility that your spiritual views will have any real impact on your listeners, who often get turned off by your proselytizing.

Resource acquired

Your deep awareness that a profound and real aspect of the universe exists beyond space and time, and that such an aspect is immediately available to the attentive, spiritually-awake person, can engender in you (and even *from* you, when rightly presented) a sense of extraordinary comfort and confidence.

> ### *The run defenses:*
> ### *DISCONNECTION THROUGH DOING*

The first three "disconnection through doing" defenses (Chaos, Compulsivity, and Counter-dependence) are based on the (unconscious) logic that, for you, being constantly in motion is a terrific defense against just about anything. Chaos shows how frantic behavior can masquerade as (sometimes useful) activity. Compulsivity shows how unrelenting behavior can masquerade as exciting activity. Counter-dependence shows how purely achievement-oriented behavior can masquerade as successful activity.

The final four "disconnection through doing" defenses (Procrastination, Withholding, Physical Illness, and Dissociation) are based on the (unconscious) logic that avoidance is the best defense ("Put off, hold back, rest up, and flee the scene," your psyche says).

SUSAN & THE CHILD KINSHIP
Body-Image Shame
The Birthday Party

I was nine. It was the month of my birthday. Jackie, who lived down the block from me, came over to tell me that she and her friends were giving me a birthday party. I was surprised and excited, for even as a child I was extremely overweight and had become accustomed to being left out of things.

When I got there, I was greeted with a party environment. I was thrilled, because the other kids were not usually that nice to me. With great anticipatory excitement, I said hello—but before I knew it, the kids were yelling and laughing at me. "Who would throw a party for you?

You're just a big fat pig. Big fat pig. Big fat pig. Ha ha ha ha ha ha ha ha!" They threw tomatoes at me. They laughed and laughed. I started screaming hysterically.

I ran home, and when I got there I told my mother what had happened. I was still hysterical. She just looked at me and shook her head. I asked her, "Aren't you going to do something? Please do something!" She said "Just let it go. They aren't worth it."

Today, at the age of forty-four, Susan is a woman who enters into any kind of relationship with great suspicion. The relationships she chooses—which tend to be chaotic and unreliable—substantiate her fears. Over and over again, she comes to the conclusion that she must do everything by herself.

Susan is extremely self-conscious about her body and has used her lifelong struggle with morbid obesity to explain her feelings of separation, her expectation of ridicule, and her deeply held belief that few people truly care. Her unconscious driving ideas are: "People are not to be trusted. I will always be fat and worthy of ridicule. Relationship is not worth it. No one will ever defend me."

Many other elements in her upbringing contributed to Susan's experience of the world, including an abandoning father, a suffocating alcoholic mother, and her own exquisite natural sensitivity, which caused her to perceive the world with vastly heightened intensity. Actually, this extraordinary sensitivity may have been the key element in most of her struggles, for her weight has long been her primary way of attempting to protect herself from the consequences of her sensitivity.

RUN DEFENSES: DISCONNECTION THROUGH DOING

The defense of CHAOS
Protecting yourself through vast, disordered confusion.

Personal impact

Life feels out of control—the storm is raging, the captain has fallen overboard, the sails are ripped, and there's no land in sight. Everything that can go wrong seems to go wrong, and we feel constantly overwhelmed, inadequate to the tasks before us. Worse still, we often infect others with our sense of desperate confusion.

Outer appearance

Chaos throws us into a whirlwind of self-destruction

We can hardly miss noticing people who use chaos as a defense—their relationships, career, environment, and even physical health appear in some way to be impacted. The chaotic individual seems constantly to be choosing paths that (perhaps obvious only to onlookers) are destructive—including unhealthy partners, loathsome jobs with damaged and damaging personnel, ill-conceived living situations, compulsive behaviors that perpetuate devastation, disorganized ways of living, and unbalanced friendships.

SIGNALS	STORY LINES
Chaos can cause you to be . . .	**To feel the internal effects of chaos, read the following words in a rapid, panicky tone. You may say things like:**
Disorganized:	"Everything is such a mess. I can't get anything in order."
Overwhelmed:	"Yikes! I just don't know where to start!"
Lacking clear purpose:	"Who knows what's going to happen? I'm just trying to get by."

In catastrophe:	"I can't believe this happened to me again! Every time I turn around, something is going wrong."
Expecting catastrophe:	"Everything always falls apart anyway. Why bother trying?"
In uproar:	"I'm usually running around like a chicken without a head!"
Out of control:	"I just want to scream!"
Compulsive:	"He's in my life . . . out of my life . . . in my life! I can't make up my mind. We break up . . . everything seems to be over . . . then I can't stop thinking about him and I end up calling!"
Desperate:	"Help! I can't keep my head above water."
Your Signals:	**Your Story Lines:**

Unconscious intention

The defense of chaos is most often inspired by one or both of two primary unconscious needs: ❖ *Our need to stay small*—that is, we're terrified of really growing up and facing an adult life. We turn to chaos, which requires so much of our attention that we're left with little energy for growth; and/or ❖ *Our need to avoid vulnerability*—because chaos keeps the noise level in our lives up so high that it overwhelms any healthy vulnerability we might be tempted to express. We are thus protected from the possible (or expected) pain of such matters as relationships, a truly challenging career, unpleasant memories that need attention, or, in general, confrontations with reality. As long as we're spinning out of control, we don't have to face the feelings associated with any of these matters.

Community dynamics

To many of us, the foundations of our everyday world seem more and more to be turned upside down. Chaos erupts as our rules for living become fuzzy or are obscured—rules for the way men and women are "supposed" to act together (when do we have sex? who pays the check? who stays home with the kids?); rules for how to get ahead (is hard work enough? is political correctness essential?); and rules for social intimacy (when is getting personal getting *too* personal?). Even our many opportunities can throw us into consternation (anyone can become either a millionaire, a business owner, or homeless . . . can get married or not . . . can have children or not . . . can have a career or not). This plethora of choices, as wonderful as it is in some ways, has added fuel to the fires of social chaos. On top of that, people are living longer (actuarials show the average life span to be seventy-three years for men and seventy-seven years for women), and in response many young people are taking their time, often far too much time, figuring out where their lives are going. And then—we get married and divorced more often, have several different careers in our lifetime, and tend to investigate or even become involved in various different religions. Where we used to be stable, we are now veering, swerving . . . and sometimes teetering. When this social chaos (that's connected to the fast-paced times in which we live) ties into our personal defense through chaos, the result is, naturally, more chaos.

Personal sacrifice

Chaos sabotages success by making it extremely difficult to establish and accomplish goals.

Resource acquired

Chaos teaches you how to stay afloat in the tumultuous sea called life.

RUN DEFENSES: DISCONNECTION THROUGH DOING

The defense of COMPULSIVITY

Protecting yourself through impulsive, repetitious,
self-defeating behavior.

Personal impact

Recently a client, after a year of sobriety, wrote the following:

I don't know if you have ever in your life flirted with
compulsion, toyed with addiction, or invited shame in "just for
a while." They seem like harmless enough entertainment when
they first arrive and have a look around. But then they want to
wrestle with you and with your life. When they do, they win
consistently and want to keep going long after you're exhausted.
One holds you down while the others taunt you, and soon your
blood is boiling with shame, regret, and a desire to grapple
those bastards one last time <u>and win</u>. But you cannot win, of
course, and the only option is to start clawing up the floorboards
and tunnel out through the basement. If you've never had that
experience, perhaps it is hard to imagine. To be drawn toward
a goal you don't want, act in a way you'd swear "isn't you,"
and be caught in a tide you can't reverse. Powerless, yet mindful
of the fact that <u>you</u> started it.

Inside, we feel an irrepressible, clamoring need that doesn't give a
hoot about our future! It only hopes that *more* (of whatever) will make
us feel better right now. Yet the fix never fixes, and we just keep getting
emptier and more dissatisfied. Whatever the focus of our compulsion—
be it drugs, alcohol, sex, money, fame, work, beauty, fitness—that
compulsion is always more important than the circumstances and obliga-

You operate
from the hope
that
MORE
will
make you
feel better

tions in our lives. We are lips-pursed, hands-on-the-hips children stomping loudly in the middle of the room, demanding that we get what we want when we want it—and when we want it is *now!* Eventually other people feel rejected or left out and begin leaving us, or at least start complaining. Since we often find this more annoying than helpful, we tend to spend our time with those who share our compulsive bent.

We want what we want when we want it— and when we want it is now!

Outer appearance

Mild cases of compulsivity can show up as extravagance and flamboyance ("Shopping just makes me feel good") or even optimism ("I really believe if I play often enough, I'll win the lottery!"), but in the extreme, it simply looks like rampant addiction, often accompanied by flagrant delusion ("I don't drink *that* much!"). Since our focus is on satisfying our compulsion, anything that gets in the way is ignored or rejected. We can look inflexible, preoccupied, and *driven*.

SIGNALS	STORY LINES
Being compulsive can cause you to be . . .	**To feel the internal effects of compulsivity, read the following words with an insistent tone. You may say things like:**
Excessive:	"Just one more and then I'll stop. I know what I can and can't handle!"
Procrastinating:	"I'm going to quit smoking [eating, drinking, overworking, gambling, etc.] tomorrow."
Denying:	"You don't know what you're talking about. I'm in control of my drinking. I only want to take the edge off."
Helpless:	"I just can't stop."
Chaotic:	"No matter how hard I try, everything in my life keeps falling apart."

Needy:	"Look, I know the way he treats me is wrong. But you don't understand. I *need* him!"
Angry:	"Get off my back. It's my life!"
Driven:	"I know you don't think she's good for me but I don't care what happens . . . I have to be with him!"
Irrationally repetitive	"This time will be different!"
Your Signals:	**Your Story Lines:**

Unconscious intention

Compulsive behavior is stimulated by the (unspoken) promise that the object of our compulsion (food, drink, money, sex, relationship, work) will fill the void growing inside us. This void thus turns out to be the actual problem, which makes the compulsivity only a *symptom* of that problem. Unconsciously you think, "I'm not enough, and the only way I can feel like I am enough is to *get* enough." But for the compulsive person, there's no such thing as enough, and until the *source* of that self-negating belief is dealt with directly, the compulsive behavior is likely to continue. That's why so often when an individual contains or manages one kind of compulsion, the compulsive urge shows up in another form (you stop drinking alcohol and start overeating; you stop overeating and start overspending; you stop overspending and start overworking).

You think if only you can get enough, you'll feel like enough

Community dynamics

Compulsives are everywhere—smoking, drugging, drinking, gambling, working, acquiring money, spending money, eating, sexing, or clinging to relationships the way barnacles cling to the sides of ships!

Likewise, our cultural heroes seem driven by urgent, controlling forces that demand power, prestige, and money. Meanwhile, advertising and commercialism loom before us with promises of total fulfillment. They reel us in with fantasy then return us to our daily lives—where we're more dissatisfied than before. Compulsive behavior is our (inadequate) answer to that dissatisfaction.

Our romance with compulsivity (and its companion: addiction) goes way back. Rent an old movie from the thirties or forties, for instance, and notice that nearly every character smokes and drinks. Then, from the sixties onward, note that films emphasize the furious pursuit of unhealthy relationships. Today, compulsivity of all kinds is still being celebrated (cigarette addiction among teens and preteens is on the rise, while alcohol addiction and drug addiction proliferate; even heroin is making a comeback). Of course, our addiction to food and the resultant obesity are visible all across the land.

While the aforementioned are obvious compulsive expressions, others are just as widespread if not quite as recognizable to most people. For instance, look at the way gambling is glamorized—sometimes presented as family-friendly (Las Vegas), tantalizingly innocent (the lottery), or entertainment for the big boys (Wall Street).

In fact, compulsivity is so pervasive and widespread throughout society that many of us are like fish swimming in the ocean who don't even know they're in deep water.

Personal sacrifice

There's a hole in your bucket!

Compulsivity guarantees daily discontent and ongoing frustration because—there's a hole in your bucket. And no matter how much or how often you pour "stuff" into it, everything runs out the bottom and your bucket never fills up.

Resource acquired

Compulsivity instills in you a desire to reach for the stars—a longing for more—and an unwillingness to settle for less. It prepares you to appreciate abundance.

RUN DEFENSES: DISCONNECTION THROUGH DOING

The defense of COUNTER-DEPENDENCE

Protecting yourself through stubborn self-reliance.

Personal impact

Work, work, work—do, do, do—achieve, achieve, achieve! We are the ones who get more done than anyone else. Problems only seem to arise when others try to help. Our response to their efforts is usually to be rejecting and to insist on doing it all ourselves. We are likely to convince ourselves that we're doing everything because <u>we</u> *are the only ones who can do anything right.* But doing everything by ourselves leaves us feeling completely alone. On top of that, mainly because of our attitude and high-level drive, other people in our lives often see themselves as (at best) unable to please us or (at worst) incompetent.

You think you're the only one who can do anything right

Outer appearance

This defense is hard for us to address, let alone give up, since we usually credit our (total) autonomy for many of our successful achievements. To many, we appear strong, proud, and capable, partly because of the way we firmly tolerate but little interruption when we're on our way to accomplishing our goals. Over time, though, our inner resentment and sense of personal burden grow like mushrooms in the damp night. As a result, a time is likely to come when, to associates and friends alike, we will appear irritable, hassled, harried, and perfectionistic. Of course,

You're a constantly moving target who's hard to hit

our "I can/must do it all" defense will not allow us to accept help. Finally, we find ourselves completely exhausted.

SIGNALS	STORY LINES
Counter-dependence can cause you to be . . .	**To feel the internal effects of counter-dependence, try reading the following words with a prideful tone. You may say things like:**
Unable to delegate:	"By the time I explain how to do the job, I could have done it better myself."
Hesitant to ask for help:	"It's hard for me to ask for anything."
Disgusted about the idea of dependence:	"She doesn't even work! That would drive me nuts. I just can't stand to be around her."
Untrusting:	"I find that people let me down most of the time."
Rejecting nurturing:	"I like to be alone when I'm sick."
Perfectionistic:	"I get crazy when things don't go just the way I planned."
Superior:	"If you want something done, ask a busy person like me to do it."
Lacking intimacy:	"It's hard to find a man who can deal with a really strong woman. I intimidate most men."
A workaholic in denial:	"Look, I work like a dog because the work has to get done, not because I want to be the one doing it!"
Your Signals:	**Your Story Lines:**

Unconscious intention

As a counter-dependents, we're thoroughly committed overachievers who, deep down below the surface busyness, believe our diligence and excessive efforts amount to . . . nothing much. In fact, our constant racing pace is fueled by a low-rumbling anxiety. We must surpass all the rest and outlast all the others, this anxiety tells us. Or else what? Or else, perhaps, like so much smelly trash, we'll be discarded by those with whom we must deal. Or maybe we'll be discovered as the fraud we know ourselves to be. In the end, we feel more desperate than determined— more driven than purposeful.

Underneath it all you feel more desperate than determined

Most likely, our early memories are full of double messages, like "I love you unconditionally except when you act like a stupid idiot!" Perhaps, if we were raised in an atmosphere of unpredictability and unsafe circumstances where the rug was always being pulled out from under us, we felt rejected by the very people who were supposed to love us most. All of this devastated us, and now (unconsciously) we probably believe that one more horrible experience will damage us beyond hope of recovery, or maybe even kill us. So we're running from that (inevitable) awful, permanently damaging experience. We dance as fast as we can—hoping the frantic rhythm of our dance will distract our attention from the (disturbing) memories, while at the same time heading off future pain at the pass.

Community dynamics

Self-reliance is regarded by most Americans as a primary virtue. We are taught that we must get to the goal on our own steam, stand on our own two feet, pull ourselves up by our bootstraps, and count only on our own resources. In other words: be proud, upright, and independent.

We live in a society where the more we produce, the more respect we garner. Self-sufficiency is seen as contributing to this high productivity.

Usually, the more we prove we can do it all, the more accolades we get. Thus, the counter-dependent, in a way, by ferociously pursuing autonomy, embodies the very essence of American know-how.

Personal sacrifice

Your counter-dependence robs you of the opportunity to experience fulfilling partnership.

Resource acquired

The counter-dependent learns resolve, self-reliance, and initiative. You know how to get the job done, and to get it done right.

RUN DEFENSES: DISCONNECTION THROUGH DOING

In the following section, I discuss the defense of Procrastination at considerable length. I do so in the hope of emphasizing three points: this is an exceedingly common defense; it's seldom taken very seriously; and because it's a high-impact defense with major ramifications in your life, it should be taken seriously.

The defense of PROCRASTINATION

Protecting yourself by putting things off until the last minute.

Personal impact

Procrastinators are slow but not so steady. We not only don't win—but we often don't even finish the race! We're lethargic and frequently have difficulty getting ourselves moving. This is because:

❖ We decide that what's in front of us to do (whether it's requested by others or self-assigned) can definitely wait until a later time. "After all," you may think, "what's the rush?" or "I have more important (or more interesting) things to do right now!" A *rebelliousness* is probably attached to our hesitation as it relates to requests of others; a *sabotaging* element is likely to be attached when our own intentions are involved.

❖ Our relationship to time is confusing and vague. When tasks must be accomplished, we either think we will have plenty of time to get the job done or we convince ourselves that the timing itself is simply not right and that *our* timing is better.

❖ We get an adrenaline-like rush as we sprint to the finish line to complete any project we've delayed, especially when a deadline that originally included plenty of time for completion is now only hours or even minutes away. We also tend to rely on this stimulation and its exhilaration for inspiration.

Outer appearance

All of us procrastinate now and then—by not getting invitations or holiday cards out at the right time, hesitating to return certain telephone calls, or putting off unpleasant personal confrontations. But those who *perpetually, habitually* procrastinate—who seldom finish projects or who dawdle along the way and/or are constantly late—tend to cause ongoing, sometimes serious problems, frustration, and even anger, both for themselves and for their friends, mates, and colleagues. Procrastinators make all kinds of excuses, but eventually no excuse is good enough.

SIGNALS	STORY LINES
Procrastination can cause you to be . . .	To feel the internal effects of procrastination, read the following words in a languorous tone. You may say things like:
Overwhelmed:	"I never seem to have enough time to do everything that needs to be done."

Late:	"I really tried to get here. I thought I could do just one more thing."
Withholding:	"Sure, I'll tell you what's happening—when I'm good and ready!"
Appearing lazy:	"I just lay around on the couch all day. I couldn't seem to get myself moving."
Avoiding:	"I'll get to it later."
Delaying:	"I'm just about to start the project. Don't worry—I always work better under pressure!"
Reneging:	"I need to cancel our date again, but I promise I'll make it up to you!"
Irritable:	"Get off my back! I'll do it when I do it!"
Your Signals:	**Your Story Lines:**

Unconscious intention

Procrastination
is a *choice*
not a condition

Procrastination is not, as many say, mere "laziness." In fact, what's called "laziness" (and is regarded as an uncontrollable, despicable condition with which one is unalterably stuck) is really a reflection of *how we adjust our priorities*. If our "priority" is to laze about on the couch, we do so because we have determined that lying around is far more important than fixing the screen door. It's not a pathological condition or a tragic circumstance of our lives. It's the result of decisions we've made.

Procrastination is
not laziness—
it's adjusted
priorities

Rather than reflecting a decision based on convenience, procrastination reflects our response to habitual *fear.* In fact, we are mostly not aware of having made any decision at all. This fear, sometimes great and sometimes small, is always and inevitably unconscious. In this case, there are two primary fears:

❖ Fear of *success*—which involves our *ability* to accomplish what we have set out to accomplish, along with the "what's next?" factor. (Example: "If I succeed with this project, everyone's going to expect more and more of me, and I don't know if I can measure up" or "If I return that call, I might get caught in a personal connection, whereupon I'll be swallowed up and disappear.")

❖ Fear of *failure*—which involves our *inability* to accomplish what we've set out to accomplish as well as our confronting the incompetence factor. (Examples: "If I try, I'll fail and everyone will hate me. So maybe I won't try at all, or I'll wait until the very last minute. Then if the project doesn't turn out well, it will seem that's just because I didn't have enough time" or "If I return that call I might have to reveal a personal truth [like that she made me mad the last time we spoke], and then she's going to hate me and I'll have blown the relationship entirely. So I'll put off the confrontation [forever] because I'm so bad at handling things like that.")

Community dynamics

The problem is that as a community, we tend to send out mixed signals with regard to procrastination. For instance, we generally expect (of ourselves and each other) high levels of productivity, but all too frequently the training ground we offer our children for developing their sense of being productive, having an active imagination, and being involved with living, is an electronic babysitter—the TV. Later, when those same children become teens and slug along—procrastinating with chores or homework (especially by spending inordinate amounts of time playing video games or watching television), we are horribly dismayed.

Even worse, perhaps, is our own adult attitude about nurturing or supporting our most passionate dreams and desires—particularly when a life-partner is involved. We put off our fun ("When we retire . . .") and hold off on our life ("Someday we will find time to . . ."). Is this a sneaky way of co-signing a procrastination defense with that partner? Certainly it can be said that American society (as reflected by our work habits and expectations) pays more attention to what's good for the general public than what's right (and perhaps healthy) for the individual. Of course, the whole is made up of its parts, so it behooves us to be clear, both about the messages we are sending and the behaviors we are encouraging.

Personal sacrifice

Procrastination undermines productivity, therefore limiting your personal success and corroding your feelings of competence.

Resource acquired

Procrastination teaches you to slow down and pace yourself—a helpful ability in a world that too often asks you to maintain a state of unending urgency.

RUN DEFENSES: DISCONNECTION THROUGH DOING

The defense of WITHHOLDING

Protecting yourself by holding back emotionally and/or physically.

Personal impact

Being confronted by this defense in others is often an excruciating experience, as anyone who has ever chased a withholding individual for resolution, dialogue, or comfort will quickly confirm! Yet while it can be exasperating to witness, being the person *doing* the withholding is even more horrible. The worst part is that this behavior tends to reinforce itself, so the more we withhold, the more we need to withhold . . . or the more we withhold, the more incapable we are of speaking up.

The more we withhold the more incapable of speaking we become

Outer appearance

As withholders, we are often uncommunicative—having successfully learned to suppress both our impulses and our enthusiasm. We tend to refuse conflict, preferring to escape rather than to confront. This makes us look like anything from cowardly to arrogant or shy. Actually, we are merely quieted by our own habit of silence . . . and by the fears that sustain that habit.

SIGNALS	STORY LINES
Withholding can cause you to be . . .	**To feel the internal effects of withholding, try reading the following words without inflection. You may say things like:**
Silent:	"I just need my space. I have nothing to say."
Lacking sexual desire:	"I simply have no interest at this time."
Benumbed:	"I don't know what I want. I can't seem to get excited about anything."
Inhibited creatively:	"I feel stuck. I have a few ideas, but then they just fall apart or I don't have the energy to make them happen."
Uncommunica-tive:	"I don't want to discuss it further. I've said all I'm going to say on the matter."
Isolating:	"You go—I'm just not in a party mood."
Indifferent:	"I don't really care what you do."
Apathetic:	"If you want a divorce fine—it's your call!"

Your Signals:	Your Story Lines:

Unconscious intention

Deep down, we are usually fuming and sputtering about the early-life circumscriptions that hindered our expression and halted our development. We feel desperate about what we now experience as emotional paralysis and are incensed about what we feel are lost years, missed opportunities, unsatisfying relationships, and, above all, a misunderstanding world. We usually respond to this anger in one of two ways: either we convince ourselves that we are constrained—that there's a muzzle on our mouth and a noose around our throat—as a result of which we are often incapable of contributing (our thoughts, feelings, or intentions) to others; or we conclude that we've simply arrived at a better method of interaction—one that includes the freedom to figure things out for ourselves in our own good timing. So we hold on and hold tight until (or so we think) we're really ready to "share." Of course, that time seldom comes.

Community dynamics

Withholding frequently looks like *politeness,* and as such is often supported and even requested by society, and (as is also true about the defense of Withdrawal), we as a society inevitably put our attention on those who make the most noise—though we don't necessarily like them for it. By contrast, less intrusive people get less attention, so in a way it might be said that they are overlooked. This means that people who make the most commotion about their dis-ease (whatever it may be) get the most funding, while the quiet ones often lose out; or rioters get more attention than peaceful marchers; or professional community provocateurs are covered constantly by the press while quiet behind-the-scenes community leaders are seldom recognized. Criminals get our attention, while law-abiding members of society usually go unnoticed. Loud and forceful so-called leaders of social and political groups look like they're representing their "people," while often the really effective leadership is being exercised by those who work quietly behind the scenes on important collective issues, getting little press. The point is that all too often we are, as a society, out of balance and out of whack!

Personal sacrifice

The first and most obvious thing you give up when you withhold is visibility. Overlooking you is easy, since others have no idea what you're thinking or feeling. You fade into the background, and only a faithful few are likely to bother discovering who you really are inside the silence.

Resource acquired

At its best, withholding teaches restraint—a wonderful, useful quality that most people, especially compulsives, would do well to learn.

RUN DEFENSES: DISCONNECTION THROUGH DOING

The defense of PHYSICAL ILLNESS

*Protecting yourself through constant, nagging,
repetitive experiences of body problems.*

Much speculation has occurred among medical professionals as well as the lay public with regard to the mind/body connection. Many well-respected physicians, psychologists, and metaphysicians have joined in profound explorations of this mind/body link. Among them are authors such as Larry Dossey, M.D., whose many works on this topic include

Healing Words and Beyond Illness; O. Carl Simonton, M.D., a pioneer in the treatment of cancer through visualization and guided imagery; and Joan Borysenko, Ph.D.,cofounder of The Harvard Mind-Body Clinic.

Current thought among experts such as these is that <u>matter</u> is influenced by <u>mind</u> far more than might be recognized at first glance, and that achieving harmony between the mind and the body is a key to enhanced mental, emotional, and physical health. Various methods are proposed or recommended for bringing about this harmony, including biofeedback, hypnotism, visualization, behavior modification, prayer, and meditation. Even traditional medical personnel have begun to embrace the possibilities of working with the mind/body connection (sometimes enthusiastically, sometimes tentatively).

Especially with regard to the defense of Physical Illness, I invite you to consider and investigate, as open-mindedly as you can, these possibilities for yourself. Do this especially if you seem to get ill either more often than those around you or in circumstances that routinely disrupt your life or the lives of others. If you do not believe such a mind/body link exists, or if you wonder how something so tenuous as the mind can be used to affect something so substantial as the body, I ask that you approach this inquiry with a certain suspension of disbelief and a sense of adventure.

Personal impact

Physical illness as a defense involves constant and/or recurring physical problems. It is not the same as a neurotic *fear* of present or future sickness (hypochondria), but is the direct experience of *actual* illness right now. Illness works well as a defense because it's so *real*, it's so (apparently) *not* our fault, and it gives us a perfect reason to be inactive ("My bad back makes it impossible for me to go to work today"), to have our own way ("I feel another cold coming on. Could you stop by instead of our going out?"), or to gain sympathy ("I can't believe I'm sick again. I feel like I'll just never be well!"). We usually feel powerless to fight whatever ails us. Perhaps we respond by being secretive or by becoming vigilant—anxiously watching for signs, hoping we can stop the intruder before it strikes again and before we're forced to go to the doctor or to self-medicate. Or maybe we live in fear and doubt (in which case we are actually exhibiting a Victim defense in its early stages). We think such things as: "Why me? Why am I always the one who gets sick? It's not fair."

Outer appearance

Certain individuals fall ill more often than others, getting every cold, every flu epidemic, every newly reported allergy, and every *everything* that's going around. Others constantly worry about getting everything that's going around. Both are likely to be exhibiting the illness defense. Those of us to whom this description applies tend to get sick before important events and at especially inopportune times. Friends and colleagues begin to expect the disappointing phone call canceling the date or meeting—along with our usual explanation: something's coming on, the chronic backache has returned, the ever-threatening allergy has struck again. If you think you might be using physical illness as a defense, first check out how often you get sick and for how long. Then notice if your bouts with (seemingly) different illnesses tend to involve similar complaints and have similar repercussions in your life. Please be aware, however, that you ought not to minimize any symptoms you have or fail to seek appropriate professional assistance. In fact, ignoring symptoms might even be another manifestation of the defense itself ("I don't need to see a doctor. I already have some pills from last time").

SIGNALS	STORY LINES
A physical-illness defense can cause you to be . . .	**To feel the internal effects of a physical-illness defense, read the following words in a complaining tone. You may say things like:**
Mystified:	"I don't know what's wrong with me. I've been sick a long time!"
Minimizing:	[In answer to others' observations of your continuing illness:] "Oh, it's nothing. My resistance is low and I'm fighting off something."
Secretive:	[Thinking:] "I'm not going to tell anyone about it this time. They'll just make a big deal out of it."
Canceling plans:	"I have to cancel our date. I'm really, really sorry, but I'm sick again."
Victimized:	"You can't possibly understand how hard it is to be struck down by chronic fatigue. I just can't lead a normal life."
Hypervigilant:	"That sounds like fun, but I'm not willing to take any chances. I've got an important week coming up. I'd better lay low for now."
Your Signals:	**Your Story Lines:**

Unconscious intention

Moving through life with balance is no simple matter. From my perspective, the psyche—*wanting* us to achieve the balance we need—is our best ally. The problem is that sometimes our psyche must take drastic action to get our attention so it can bring about that balance. For instance, if we're forever rushing through life, perhaps the only way we can be slowed down is to be knocked down! A stark example of this might be found in the Epstein-Barr patient. Medical studies have established a simple, typical profile for those diagnosed with this illness: they are type-A (aggressive, *extremely* active) females.

Illness can reflect many unconscious concerns and attitudes.

❖ Illness sets the stage for rescue. When we're rescued, we feel cared about by and connected to others, which gives us permission to evidence a sort of dependence of which we are otherwise afraid.

❖ We believe we're "too much" for other people to be near comfortably. We fear that if we express ourselves completely, we will overwhelm everyone around us. Then they will go away and we'll be alone. If we're sick, we think you're less threatening, which allows people to remain near us.

❖ When we were growing up, we got real attention only when we were sick. We still (unconsciously) hold onto illness as a potential attention-getter. Illness, then, is something we (unconsciously) use in an effort to gain power over other people (their time, energy, and attitude toward us).

❖ Illness can give us permission to avoid responsibility ("I'm too sick [or even too potentially sick] to do anything or go anywhere").

❖ Illness can be a (covert) way of expressing anger or fear.

Community dynamics

Holistic medicine, which deals with mind *and* body and their relationship rather than with the body alone, is clearly gaining favor with the general public today. Its acceptability and popularity can be recognized by how frequently people go to either holistic medical doctors (those who include an awareness of factors other than just the body) or alternative practitioners (such as herbalists, acupuncturists, and acupressurists). We in the Western world seem finally to have discovered what other cultures (notably those in the East) have recognized for centuries—that the body is often an outer reporter reflecting the events of the psyche, and that attention to the workings of the psyche is necessary if the body is to enjoy stable and long-lasting health. Luckily, as Westerners incorporating Eastern approaches, we have the advantage of examining *both* traditional medicine and alternative interventions.

Personal sacrifice

An illness defense sabotages every area of your life, especially your career and relationships. Regardless of how successful you are in these areas, you could probably be more so if you weren't sick as often as you are.

Resource acquired

Illness can teach you how to access your capacity for courage and resolve, as you plow ahead through your life despite being physically limited.

RUN DEFENSES: DISCONNECTION THROUGH DOING

The defense of DISSOCIATION

Protecting yourself through an emotional separation from everything and everyone—including separation from your own physical self.

Personal impact

We operate as if in a dream, often moving habitually through the thick fog of our lives like one of those sci-fi creatures that's only barely awake enough to do the mad scientist's questionable deeds. Our benumbed body ambles along, following the instructions of our robotic brain, while our feelings lie sleeping in a separate chamber of the laboratory. Meantime, we watch all.

Dissociation for defensive purposes is easy to take on, difficult to notice, and challenging to disrupt. It's nearly always an exclusively interior process, with emotional disengagement as its unconscious aim. When it's most successful, this disengagement causes us to lose contact not only with others (which we may experience as a kind of emotional deadness), but even with ourselves (which we probably experience as a disconnection from our own body). This deadness/disconnection makes us appear, at times, to be more a witnessing camera than an involved participant.

Just in terms of their descriptions, it might be easy to mistake the troublesome defensive (or pathological) state called "Dissociation" with the often-sought meditative state called "witness" consciousness (a refined transpersonal experience). They ought not be confused, however, for the defense is (unconsciously) employed to *protect* the psyche, while the meditative state is (consciously) achieved to *enlarge* and *expand* the psyche.

We might most easily notice ourselves using this defense in the sexual arena (where we would seem to leave our bodies and *watch* ourselves "perform"), though such defensive self-protection can also occur under other circumstances (like when we're "outside" ourselves watching a business meeting we're attending or when we're observing ourselves on a date). In such instances others might regard us as "spacy," inattentive, distracted, disinterested, aloof, or bored.

Outer appearance

From the outside, Dissociation can be difficult to discern. On rare occasions, however, it can be easily identified—as when someone responds to us with glazed-over eyes or a blank stare.

SIGNALS	STORY LINES
Dissociation can cause you to be . . .	**Dissociation is a silent but deadly internal process. Feel the Story Lines creep through your brain. You may *think* things like:**
Detached:	(during sex, thinking) "The cellulite on my thighs is ridiculous!"
Inattentive:	(while your partner is spilling her emotional guts, thinking) "It's hard to concentrate on what she's saying. I wish she'd stop crying and get to the point."
Distracted:	(while driving, thinking) "Oh, my! I have no idea how I even got home—I must have been driving on automatic."
Bored:	(while at a dinner party, thinking) "This is the most boring topic in the world. I'll just shut up and wait 'til they're all done talking. What a waste of time these people are."
Appearing disinterested:	(while on a date, thinking) "1 feel completely outside myself—watching. Like there's a couple having dinner and I'm overhearing them."
Appearing invulnerable:	(while at the funeral of a supposedly dear friend, thinking) "I'm just going to scream if I don't get out of here. Meanwhile, I'll keep my feelings to myself."
Apathetic:	(while attending an important business meeting, thinking) "I don't care one way or the other how this problem gets solved."
Your Signals:	**Your Story Lines:**

Unconscious intention

The defense of dissociation is tricky, because while we might actually convince ourselves that we merely feel apathetic, bored, distracted, and invulnerable, our problem is more serious. What's likely is that (rather than being disinterested or uninvolved) our "boredom" is a defense against a primitive terror (a terror that, as usual, most likely began in childhood). We fear total destruction, either through involvement with other people or by the intensity of our own feelings. Enemies, therefore, are everywhere—within and without. And the biggest enemy of all is emotion.

Initially, our dissociation probably occurred only now and again, when we (unconsciously) related specific difficult life-situations to original (terrifying) circumstances. Then, when we realized that not revealing our inner state made us feel infinitely safer, we began to employ the technique more and more often. Now, a majority of the time, we watch from around the corner of our lives, waiting, always waiting— for the sputtering internal fires that (unconsciously) threaten to consume us, to finally die down altogether.

What this defense announces, then, is not our lack of involvement, but rather, in fact, our *over-involvement*. We protect ourselves by first separating from others and then by separating from ourselves. The (unconscious) thinking in this case is, "If I stay disconnected, I can't be damaged!"

Community dynamics

In general, society tends to support our staying distant from most uncomfortable personal feelings, or at least it supports our restraint of expression. We are encouraged to "take it on the chin" and "buck up." This hesitation to identify with any kind of extreme emotional vulnera-

To you emotion is an enemy

bility and a preference for a stoic "get through things without exposure" attitude certainly support those who use the Dissociation defense.

Perhaps the (unconscious) societal fear is that more feelings equal less dedication to production (and the more you produce, the further you and the economy can get). Implicitly, community mandates like "the less said the better" and "don't air your dirty laundry in public" translate easily to that which is defensively dissociative, such as "Don't let anyone know you *have* any laundry to do! In fact, it's best even to keep that knowledge from yourself." As a result, many of us find ourselves wandering robotically through our lives.

Personal sacrifice

Dissociation robs you of the true connection, genuine enthusiasm, and ecstatic responses that are reflections of an impassioned life.

Resource acquired

Dissociation teaches you the detachment that can make you a wise, helpful, impartial observer.

> ### *The run defenses:*
> ### *DISCONNECTION THROUGH THINKING*

MARY & THE FATHER KINSHIP
Abandonment
Choosing Sides

It was the day my father left the house for good. He requested that I put all of his things in the car before he drove off. He came into my bedroom and asked me to make the decision that instant if I was going with him or not. He kept telling me to go with him. He kept asking me to decide.

I just stood by the dresser in shock. I wanted to go with him but knew I could not leave Mom alone. I told him I would stay with Mom. He was crying. I was in shock—not believing what was happening. My father was leaving me.

I did not see him for years after that.

Today, twenty-seven-year-old Mary, still guilty about choosing Mother over Father, is convinced that she must sacrifice herself to some amorphous "higher good." That sacrificing results in her frequently seeming burdened by others' needs and feeling over-responsible for the outcomes of situations—both her own and other people's. At the same time, she believes herself to be powerless and small. This conflict often paralyzes her, while simultaneously encouraging a rejection of intimate primary partnership. She's skeptical, believing relationships usually turn out to be more trouble than they're worth.

The way Mary's traumatic childhood situation was handled was typical in her family, where little healthy conversation occurred and inappropriate requests were constantly made. Because her own nature was to be conciliatory, she usually felt the need to (perfectly) respond to these requests, however inappropriate they were. Her unconscious driving ideas now are: "I'm the one in charge here. Every time I make a decision someone gets hurt. I have to fix everything myself."

The following "disconnection through thinking" defenses are all about processes that go on in your head. Intellectualizing *and* Skepticism *make you feel smart by keeping you occupied with how things work.* Paranoia, Guilt, *and* Confusion *make you feel incompetent while keeping you occupied with how things don't work.* Obsession, Fantasy, *and* Perfectionism *drive you to self-consciousness, while keeping you occupied with how things could work. And* Denial *just allows you feel righteous about your point of view.*

RUN DEFENSES: DISCONNECTION THROUGH THINKING

The defense of PARANOIA

*Protecting yourself by assuming that people
and/or circumstances are against you.*

Personal impact

"Paranoia" is used here in its popular (and most common) sense to denote a *defense*. The same word, used clinically, identifies a major personality disorder, the profound mental illness described as psychosis characterized by a persecution complex so extreme that it may lead to violently disruptive antisocial behavior. Used as defense, however, paranoia means something quite different. For our (defense definition) purposes, the term refers to excessive vigilance where we assume people are more likely to be foes than friends. As individuals in the grip of this defense, we tend to make mountains out of molehills, feel overwhelmed by our own disappointment with others, display an argumentative, irritable reactivity, and bear grudges for a long time.

Paranoia is one of those experiences that reinforces itself. The more concerned we feel, the more guarded our thinking gets, and the more cautiously we act; then the more cautiously we act, the more guarded our thinking becomes. We spend much time trying to figure out who's to blame—for our disappointments, losses, failures, and even the simple discomforts in our lives. We look for confirmation of our most negative beliefs. Eventually all of the guarding leads us to feel anxious and to *expect* trouble. This brings us to:

What we expect is what we get

Step 14 in defense busting:
Notice how expectation leads to manifestation. In other words, what you expect, you get. So if you're watching every step you take because you expect to fall—you can expect to fall!

Outer appearance

Paranoia as a defense can appear as a vile self-consciousness that harasses us into hypervigilant worry about how other people view us and think about us. We are driven to constantly look over our shoulder, guard against impending danger, and shield ourselves from prying eyes. Often, there is a combativeness about us, for we're always preparing for a good fight.

We pride ourselves on being objective, rational, and unemotional, but others often see us as rigid and uncompromising. We're critical of

You're always
preparing
for a fight

others, yet when similar criticism (even an extremely benign version) is leveled at us, we find it difficult to take. In response to such criticism, we're quick to become angry and then to counterattack. Also, we often appear to be secretive and guarded. Actually, we're just reluctant to confide in others, because we think the information will eventually be used against us.

SIGNALS	STORY LINES
Paranoia can cause you to be . . .	**To feel the internal effects of paranoia, try reading the following words with a contemptuous tone. You may say things like:**
Judgmental:	"I don't think people can be trusted to do the right thing."
Vigilant:	"I believe it's smart to keep your eye on the ball and your finger on the trigger."
Wary:	"I like to get the lay of the land before I make my move."
Lonely:	"No one really gets who I am."
Expecting disaster:	"This is a dangerous world. Don't kid yourself. It's important to be on your guard!"
Self-conscious:	"I feel like my boss is scrutinizing my every move!"
Secretive:	"I hate it when everybody knows my business!"
Argumentative:	"I'm a loner—so what?"
Rigid:	"Hey—I just know how I like things to be. What's wrong with that?"
Blaming:	"Where's my watch? This time I'm sure someone took it."
Your Signals:	**Your Story Lines:**

Unconscious intention

The defense of paranoia usually has two unconscious aims:

❖ The first aim is to prevent our experiencing harm from a world that we see as *mostly* threatening, dangerous, and out-of-control—a world we think of as more bad than good. We have an extraordinary fear of intimacy and the demands it might make on us. Our vigilance, then, is our safety net. As always, a chaotic childhood usually initiates this defense.

❖ The second aim is to protect us from negative thoughts and behaviors we believe are aimed at us *specifically*. This idea that other people are focusing on us—that we're at the center of other people's universe—indicates that we're looking out at the world through very immature eyes. At one (very young) time in life, of course, feeling like the world revolved around us was natural. But in a healthy, supportive environment, we would have outgrown and moved beyond that developmental stage. However, if we find ourselves still stuck in such self-consciousness, it probably means that, in order to compensate for early feelings of *extreme insignificance*, we assigned ourselves feelings of *extraordinary importance*. By now, this is an old idea.

Community dynamics

We lock our doors, put alarms in our cars, watch our back, and look over our collective shoulder. Indeed, when we are attentive to daily news reports, our maintaining an intelligent, balanced response to (rightful) feelings of being threatened can be difficult, and we may even feel derelict if we *don't* become hypervigilant or "paranoid" these days. Plus, it does not help that enforcers of "political correctness" cause much of what we say (and do) to be scrutinized then reinterpreted, misinterpreted, or distorted, which requires from us yet another kind of constant vigilance.

Vigilance is your safety net

Things weren't always this way. Even though many of us were taught early on that other people are out to get us, that this is a survival-of-the-fittest, dog-eat-dog world, and that we'd best be on alert in every way—we didn't experience the collective fear and anxiety that stalk us today. Even in big cities, people used to leave their doors unlocked and walk through the park at night. Of course, since 9/11/01, national (even global) "paranoia" is at an all-time high. Still we must, in the interest of living in awareness without paralysis, recognize the difference between wise watchfulness and an infatuation with dismal possibilities.

Personal sacrifice

Probably the worst part of paranoia is that it overwhelms any faith you might have in the goodness of life and makes you feel as if you must control everything around you in order to stay safe.

Resource acquired

Paranoia teaches you to be wary and to stay alert.

RUN DEFENSES: DISCONNECTION THROUGH THINKING

The defense of GUILT

Protecting yourself by thinking you have done a bad thing.

Personal impact

Guilt
is a
watchful
policeman

When we compare our thoughts or actions to a standard of *presumed* appropriate functioning and then fail to meet that presumed standard, guilt arises. Like a watchful policeman, this defense limits what we might do and punishes what we have done.

Outer appearance

Guilt can often be detected in the endless complaining we do about our own behavior. When we drone on and on about our shortcomings and about the errors of our ways, listeners eventually stop wanting to console us and, instead, tune out.

To the people around us, our guilty behavior or attitude might be regarded as intriguing (since they want to figure out what we've "done" that's so terrible) or it might be off-putting (since they feel uncomfortable with our self-consciousness), or it might stimulate their own feelings of guilt.

Perhaps we're the kind of "guilty" person who is constantly regaling the world with tales of our good works—which turns out, suspiciously enough, to look like we're trying too hard to please others. Also we tend to be over-helpful, attempting to fix everything and everyone whose lives we intersect. Those around us may confuse this behavior with true goodness but, in fact, we are often just defensively guilty and looking for absolute absolution.

SIGNALS	STORY LINES
Guilt can cause you to be . . .	**To feel the internal effects of guilt, try reading the following words in a pathetic tone. You may say things like:**
Over-apologetic:	[With regard to sneezing—or a billion other minor, involuntary things:] "Sorry . . . sorry . . . so sorry!"
Regretful:	"Can you ever forgive me? I know you say I apologize too much, but I really feel terrible about this."
Remorseful:	"I just can't stop thinking about the accident. No matter what anybody tells me, I keep thinking I could have done something to avoid it!"

Comparing:	"I feel bad about having so much when so many people in the world have so little."
Penitent:	"I'll do anything to make this up to you!"
Overly responsible:	"I feel like it's all my fault this relationship fell apart."
Your Signals:	**Your Story Lines:**

Unconscious intention

At first glance, we look like people who really think we have done bad things (or who have had "unacceptable" thoughts). But (unconsciously) this viewpoint is often actually a way of trying anxiously to avoid or ward off certain feelings—feelings (that began in childhood) of enormous, angry disappointment toward others and/or in regard to a nearly unendurable sense of personal inadequacy ("They let me down because I'm really, really, really not worth their love [or respect or attention or time]").

Indeed, great dis-ease comes with our guilty thinking, and to comfort ourselves we'll try anything. At times, perhaps, we flaunt our guilt, hoping we can get others to repudiate our reasoning. In other instances, we stew in it, hoping those same others will notice and rescue us from our guilty morass.

Shame is the engine that drives your guilt

Two main (unconscious) drivers are usually connected to this defense. The first such driver is a form of *Shame*. While *Shame* itself reflects who we see ourselves to be *at our core,* defensive *Guilt* focuses on our thoughts and on our behavior. Therefore, because guilt brings attention to what we *do* (thereby taking the attention off of who we *are*), it gives us a (false) sense of authority over our lives. In other words, managing behavior most certainly seems easier than managing essence.

Of course, we seldom actually change the dreaded behavior that's obsessing our guilty minds (even if we supposedly can change it). We simply spend an inordinate amount of time *thinking* about changing it. Regardless, guilt fails to address the real problem (of Shame) anyway. Mostly it just turns out to be like one of those children's games where you hammer the peg down on one side of the board only to have it pop up immediately on the other side of the board. Similarly, even if we can and do change the particular behavior engendering the guilt, the shame still keeps popping up.

The second (unconscious) driver of defensive guilt is an inflated ego. This ego tells us that (in spite, perhaps, of evidence to the contrary) we have nothing—*nothing at all*—to feel guilty about. This often misled ego insists that it's *other people* who are really at fault and to blame. Our psyches, then, like the mother or father who says "Better not get too big for your britches," intends to keep that self-serving, bloated ego in check, for fear that otherwise our behavior may get out of hand. This second driver is an example of the equal/opposite perspective presented earlier (see Defense Busting: Step 13, p. 148), in which we, the "guilty" person, think and act in a way that is pretty much the *opposite* of how we actually (unconsciously) see the situation.

Either way (driver #1 or driver #2), much of the so-called "bad behavior" we monitor and temper through our guilty thinking is involved more with our imagination than with reality. In other words, for the most part we're better than we think! But by now we imagine that if we can only be more perfect, we'll *feel* less afraid and actually *be* less loathsome. People, then, we reason, will respond accordingly.

You're better than you think!

Community dynamics

Guilt serves society by acting as a constraining and containing monitor of behavior. It comes to us through religious communications (teachings about right and wrong), family messages (instructions passed down from earlier generations), and societal mores (guidelines about "proper" ways of living in the world). We clearly need conscience monitors in order to have a world that functions well, but a little guilt goes a long way!

Personal sacrifice

Defensive guilt makes it *impossible* for you to appreciate the good work you do and the progress you make. It thereby undermines your experience of joy and celebration.

Resource acquired

By forcing you to acknowledge your own imperfections, guilt keeps your ego in check and your feet on the ground.

RUN DEFENSES: DISCONNECTION THROUGH THINKING

The defense of CONFUSION

Protecting yourself through emotional and/or intellectual ambivalence and disorder.

Personal impact

Confusion as a defense is the mental blizzard that makes even simple solutions to simple problems incomprehensible. We're in a mental swirl, truly believing that our disordered lack of clarity is unavoidable and unchangeable. At times, our overwhelm completely paralyzes us—and appropriate action truly does become impossible. When that happens, we usually shut down and give up.

Outer appearance

When we defend ourselves through confusion, we're often seen as sitting on the fence, weighing all the odds, mulling things over, and examining the (seemingly) endless, complicating factors. We frequently lack direction and are unable to plan ahead.

As confused people, we tend to speak in shoulds and coulds ("I should decide, but *everything* looks good" or "I could make a move, but what if it's the wrong decision?"). To others, we may even appear fundamentally addled or at least jumbled. Unfortunately, our confusion can start to feel like a communicable disease to those around us, and they intuitively move away to avoid infection.

SIGNALS	STORY LINES
Confusion can cause you to be . . .	**To feel the internal effects of confusion, try reading the following words in a frustrated or halting way. You may say things like:**
Unable to decide:	"I've test-driven ten different kinds of cars. Every sales-person tells me a new story. What should I do?"
Lacking focus:	"I don't have any idea what direction I should go in my future. How do people figure this stuff out?"
Resigned:	"I guess I'll just have to *do* something—but who knows what?"
Numb:	"I'm so mixed up. I don't even know how I feel about anything anymore!"
Overwhelmed:	"My head's going to explode if I have to think about this problem any longer! I can't do anything more. I'm stopping."
Muddled:	"What's going on here? Will someone please clue me in?"

Your Signals:	Your Story Lines:

Unconscious intention

Confusion is a protection against the fear we have of testing our personal competence. We see such a test as a lose/lose proposition. If we're terrific and capable, we might be faced with responsibility we don't feel ready for. If we're terrible and incapable, we might be cast out as failures. Confusion, then, lets us stay small, invisible, and irresponsible. As long as we can't figure things out, we don't have to take any sink-or-swim actions.

Community dynamics

The everyday world is often confounding, discombobulating, bewildering, perplexing, and chaotic. In the face of this fact, mystification and confusion about your own general direction and personal purpose seem reasonable. After all, if the world around you is in such a mess, how can *you* be expected not to be? But, in fact, we each must be responsible for sorting out our personal dilemmas and for establishing lives that, we hope, will contribute to setting things straight in our communities.

Personal sacrifice

To confusion, you sacrifice the clarity of thought, feeling, and perception that can fuel and empower your life.

Resource acquired

Although confusion causes delays, mixups, and even personal agony, it also disciplines you to examine alternative possibilities, explore all of the angles, and consider things carefully before you act.

On the fence is a painful place to sit!

RUN DEFENSES: DISCONNECTION THROUGH THINKING

The following three "disconnection through thinking" categories—
Denial, Skepticism*, and (especially)* Intellectualization—*cause you to*
appear to others as self-confident and self-assured. Of course, deep
down you know the truth.

The defense of INTELLECTUALIZATION

Protecting yourself through excessive analyzing,
pondering, mapping, exploring, and investigating.

Personal impact

Defensive intellectualizers scrutinize, probe, and inspect—all too
often ripping the heart out of things and leaving behind a colorless,
passion-drained corpse. The people to whom we (sometimes proudly)
display our intellectual skills frequently seem insulted by and even
rejecting of our detailed insights. This, naturally, is a mystery to us, since
we are reasonably certain that what we have to offer is invaluable. "Why
are other people so emotionally reactive to the truth?" we frequently
wonder. The sad thing is that the aggravating way we hold ourselves
separate from (and above) others eventually drops us smack dab on our
ifs, ands, and buts. At those junctures, our immediate community is
deprived of our authentic ability to comprehend situations and we're left
holding the empty emotional bag.

Outer appearance

We defend ourselves by using our minds to control people, things,
and circumstances, often over-complicating matters in the process.
Rational thought, we believe, is a stable constant and therefore is the
superior alternative to feelings, which we perceive to be distracting,
unpredictable interruptions to a sturdy, steady walk through life.

You believe
thinking
is better
than feeling

Others generally view us as goal-oriented—much more interested in the analysis of facts than in being connected with actual people. We frequently underestimate our effect on your listeners, who mostly feel more attacked than informed. Too often, we appear to others as detached and lacking in compassion.

SIGNALS	STORY LINES
Intellectualiz-ing can cause you to be . . .	To feel the internal effects of intellectualization, read the following words with a tone that is devoid of any feeling whatsoever. You may say things like:
Arrogant:	"You don't seem to have the slightest comprehension of the importance of the point I'm making."
Analytical:	"Okay. Your relationship's over and done with. Stop feeling sorry for yourself and let's figure out what you need to do next."
Unfeeling:	"If you would just look at this thing logically, you'd realize that you're making a mountain out of a molehill."
Instructing:	"If you know smoking is bad for you, just stop."
Rigid:	"I don't have time for games."
Controlling:	"Exactly what direction are you heading in with all this self-investigation? Stop blowing things out of proportion. Just figure out the problem and fix it."
Harsh:	"I was just making a suggestion. What's the big deal? You're being too sensitive."
Critical:	"Hey, jobs come and go. How are you ever going to get your life on track if all you do is sit around feeling sorry for yourself?"

Your Signals:	Your Story Lines:

Unconscious intention

Actually, though passion is usually regarded as being purely emotional, it is not necessarily so—for, in fact, *any* process can be passionate. *Imbalance* is the true problem—one neatly disclosed here in the defense of intellectualization. Early on, we (unconsciously) chose to direct our (extraordinary) passion into mental endeavors because we were hoping for freedom from the trouble created by our natural emotional intensity. Perhaps, when we were children, members of our family ridiculed our expressiveness, or maybe we felt that intensity brought us unwanted (negative) attention (at school, amongst peers). Our response was to shove this dangerous zeal into tiny storage boxes and lock them safely away in the dark recesses of our unconscious minds. Now in our lives, the zeal gets neatly arranged into carefully constructed concepts. The good news is that we're still driven by that (unconscious) passion—only it's passion that currently takes form as passionate thought.

Community dynamics

A strong emphasis on rationality is frequently promoted as a worthy goal—especially (is this a surprise?) by and among the highly educated. Yet even when such an approach seems appropriate (appearing not to reflect imbalance between thought and feeling), we need to ask some questions. At what cost is rationality favored? Are other kinds of intelligence being ignored? What of *emotional* intelligence? *Musical* intelligence? *Athletic* intelligence? *Social* intelligence? *Intuitive* intelligence? *Creative* intelligence? *Psychological* intelligence? *Spiritual* intelligence?

Until we find a way of both appreciating and integrating the panoply of forms intelligence can take, we will find ourselves and our communities being less than we, and they, can be.

Personal sacrifice

The main problem with this defense is that you get so involved with your own (often over-detailed) thinking that you're unable to connect—either with others or yourself.

Resource acquired

Your well-developed ability to analyze things rationally allows you to unravel the twisted, tangled knots of daily living.

RUN DEFENSES: DISCONNECTION THROUGH THINKING

The defense of DENIAL

Protecting yourself by refusing to accept (an obvious) truth.

Inner impact

We stand, brow furrowed—mystified by the way certain circumstances seem repeatedly to occur in our lives. *Why do these things keep happening?* you ask. *Why?* In addition, we are startled and perplexed by observations others have frequently made to us regarding our behavior or personality—because we do not recognize their observations as valid in terms of how *we* think of ourselves. If this describes you, you are in active defensive denial.

Outer appearance

We're rejecting, disagreeable, contradictory, and combative when dealing with information about ourselves. Those around us often make efforts to penetrate our thick, well-built walls of defense, but as we

If more
than two people
say it,
you ought to
consider it!

steadfastly disavow any knowledge of what's going on, they often feel as if they're on a mission impossible. Eventually, even the best of friends, relatives, and coworkers are likely to get frustrated and go away.

SIGNALS	STORY LINES
Denial can cause you to be . . .	**To feel the internal effects of denial, read the following words in a surprised tone. You may say things like:**
Rationalizing:	"I really don't eat that much. I'm just big-boned!"
Disavowing:	"Hey, you have no idea how hard it is until you've walked a mile in my shoes. Stop judging what you don't understand!"
Contradicting:	"What are you talking about? I'm just trying to have a little fun!"
Rejecting input:	"I know what's best for me. Just leave me alone!"
Resistant:	"Why do you people always harp on my drinking? I just drink to take the edge off. I can stop whenever I want to."
Mystified:	"No, I have no idea why these things keep happening to me. I guess it's just the way the cookie crumbles."
<u>Your</u> Signals:	<u>Your</u> Story Lines:

Unconscious intention

As with so many defenses, Denial is first and foremost (unconsciously) intended to keep away horrid personal pain. In addition, it's designed to protect us from *change*—a change we expect will be

You're
operating from
false
faulty
beliefs

unendurable and even more devastating than our current (difficult) experiences. This change, we (unconsciously) assume, will land us right in the center of long-avoided, deeply-feared feelings of emptiness and worthlessness.

Most of the time, in the unconscious recesses of our psyches, we are perfectly aware of what we're doing and what the effects of our behavior are likely to be. But in order to conceal *from our conscious self* how deeply unacceptable, troubling, and/or destructive that behavior (or thinking or feeling) is, we create a "false belief"—a belief that enables us to continue as we are. This turning away (even unconsciously) from truth varies in nature from what's called *repression*. Repression is a process based more on the idea of (unconsciously) protecting ourselves from being overwhelmed by unendurable emotional memories or information than on avoiding facing the truly helpful uncomfortable behavioral facts.

Community dynamics

Denial, which we encounter both as individuals and in our communities, is probably the most difficult defense to acknowledge—and for obvious reasons. Accepting what you cannot see, what you have intentionally hidden from yourself, is difficult! I am not talking here about deviousness or spin-control or power plays or outright lies. I am talking about people who genuinely advocate their proactive or reactive positions even as they lose awareness that those positions *are* just positions—and not necessarily uncontested and obvious truth. In politics, for example, denial is blatant, as everyone passes the buck, points the finger, and reviles and accuses opponents. Schools, school officials, and parents resist being accountable for the outcome of education. Governmental agencies constantly complain about not having enough money to serve people's needs adequately, while citizens scream and yell at the same time about excessive government intervention as well as an aggressive tax burden. Gun control advocates blame guns for societal violence and gun proponents say guns don't kill, people do. Everybody's right and no one's wrong.

Personal sacrifice

When you're in denial, you give up the possibility of change—for what you don't acknowledge, you can't address and you certainly can't fix. Denial keeps you stuck in patterns of behavior, thought, and feeling that are damaging, thereby limiting both your perspective on the present and your ability to plan for a successful, healthy future.

Resource acquired

While working with the mechanics of denial, you may miss a lot of what's going on, but you do develop the ability to arrive at specific points of view, make decisions, and then stay focused and clear about what you have determined to do.

RUN DEFENSES: DISCONNECTION THROUGH THINKING

The defense of SKEPTICISM

Protecting yourself through excessive, pervasive negativity and doubt.

Personal impact

As skeptics, we quickly and deftly question information that does not match our own carefully constructed viewpoints. We scoff heartily at those who fall prey to dangerous mythologies—ideas like trusting in life, depending on other people, and believing in "higher [non-human] powers." We laughingly point a finger at those who have faith in the political process. We often even ridicule the notion of "true" love. All-

You're positive that it's best to be negative!

in-all, we are certain that wise vigilance in every area is more important than anything else.

Outer appearance

Those who know us generally think of us as negative, doubting, and nay-saying—and as people who reject most new information. Our skepticism can be obvious (via sarcasm, ridicule, or snide remarks) or subtle (via silent looks, knitted brows, or pursed lips). Either way, the people around us frequently feel their elation minimized and their natural enthusiasm about life undercut—and with good reason, for our attitudes often drive the luscious feelings of magic, wonder, and mystery into the shadows. Many times, then, others pull away from us—not knowing exactly why they've done so, but feeling that retreat is necessary for their own well-being.

SIGNALS	STORY LINES
Skepticism can cause you to be . . .	**To feel the internal effects of skepticism, read the following words with a snarl. You may say things like:**
Ridiculing:	"UFOs! Next you'll be telling me you're getting messages from your radiator!"
Contemptuous:	"We're born, we live, we die. The idea of a God somewhere is just a cop-out—a way to make yourself feel better!"
Self-righteous:	"I'm not willing to discuss my views. I know what I know, and I'm actually not interested in what you have to say about them."
Irritable:	"Oh, please! No more of your romantic hooey!"

Didactic:	"My point is obvious and indisputable. I see no reason for argument."
Rational:	"Why do you keep asking me how I *feel* about this? How I *feel* is irrelevant. I'm tired of your psychobabble."
Cynical:	"Don't believe a word that 'abundance' guy says. Try to realize that every silver lining has a cloud!"
Rejecting:	"This way always worked for me before. I see no reason to change."
Your Signals:	**Your Story Lines:**

Unconscious intention

As defensive skeptics, we have grave doubts about *everything*—doubts that usually began in the midst of traumatic childhood events. We most likely developed our vigilant perspective back then in an (unconscious) attempt to override our own interior intensity. *After all*, our psyche reasoned, *passionate belief is much too dangerous. If I let myself think the world is a magical, trustworthy place, I'll be annihilated!* So one might say: scratch a skeptic and find a fervent true believer just under the surface. Our skepticism also acts as a sharp instrument to cut away the dread and anxiety of unwanted surprise.

Community dynamics

In a sense, being skeptical is the American way. Infidels, free-thinkers, those who scoff at or are suspicious of organization and concentrations of power—all to some extent are skeptics and doubters. In fact, America was established by such as these—who rejected an environment of intolerable political and social orthodoxy and, as a result, created a more satisfying life in a new land. But *constant* defensive skepticism can become oppressive, dampening the fires of creative expression and innovation. In regard to the community and social institutions, it can encourage people to become cynical and to presume that *none* of the community's officials have the best interests of ordinary citizens at heart.

Personal sacrifice

Skepticism can undermine the exciting (personal and professional) explorations, dreams, and wondrous revelations that often occur as a result of faith and trust.

Resource acquired

Like everything else, skepticism *itself*, moderate or otherwise, often has its virtues, for it keeps you alert and guards you against dangerous naivete. As the followers of Jim Jones might say, better a dollop of skepticism than a cup of punch.

RUN DEFENSES: DISCONNECTION THROUGH THINKING

The defense of OBSESSION

Protecting yourself through repetitive focus on an idea, feeling, person, or thing—a focus that most often overrides all other thinking.

Personal impact

Obsession is an all-consuming process that leaves us feeling like a chaotic mess. When we're consumed by obsessive thinking, we behave as though we are insistently, absolutely, irrevocably, frantically committed to a particular way of thinking. ("Without him my life is unendurable" or "If I were to lose my [money, house, relationship, job position] I would be nothing.") In fact, obsession is one of the most difficult defenses to work with because it's *purely* a mental pursuit (although it often involves physical behaviors). That is, if you're an alcoholic you can get rid of all your liquor, or if you eat compulsively you can make certain only healthy food is in the house, or if you're addicted to gambling you can stay away from casinos. But even if we avoid the object(s) of our obsession, our obsessed *mind* goes everywhere we do! It's easy to understand, then, how obsessions can become overwhelming, dominating, and eventually even degrading. They are like the ravenous dog who smells meat on your hand.

When our efforts to "get what we want when we want it" seem futile, as they usually and ultimately will, we are left feeling abandoned, forsaken, and forlorn.

Outer appearance

Obsession is the "disconnection through *thinking*" version of the "disconnection through *doing*" defense of Compulsion.

When we're in the grip of Obsession, we're consumed by a need to fulfill our desire, act on our feeling, or have the object or person we "need." In our mind, we review conversations, remember incidents, and repetitively practice future dialogue. At first, our obsessions can be kept secret, even for long periods of time (relationship with a mistress, self-destructive eating habits, involvement with pornography, private or shameful fears we think about regularly). Usually, however, as obsessed individuals, we become so absorbed, engrossed, and intense regarding the object of our obsession that talking to us about anything else becomes difficult for others, and they will have the choice of either joining with us in our obsessive conversation or getting away from us altogether.

Obsession is distraction

SIGNALS	STORY LINES
Obsession can cause you to be . . .	**To feel the internal effects of obsession, read the following words in a frantic tone. You may say things like:**
Preoccupied:	"I can't think about anything but him!"
Rejecting:	"You just don't understand how important she is to me. Stop butting in."
Paranoid:	"I know he's with someone else—and I have to find out . . . I'm going to drive by his house again!"
Hypervigilant:	"I could tell from the body language that something weird is going on! I need to find out what it is."
Desperate:	"I'll do *anything* to win her back!"
Sentimental:	"In my head. I just keep running the tapes . . . remembering all the great times we had together! It's killing me, but I can't stop."
Compulsive:	"I called her fifty times . . . I know she's there . . . but she won't answer my calls. I'm just going to keep calling until she picks up the phone."
Isolating:	"Leave me alone—I need time to think."
Your Signals:	**Your Story Lines:**

Unconscious intention

Originally, our focused attention (which later became defensive Obsession) was (unconsciously) intended to be a temporary salve—a distraction from terrible feelings of inadequacy and worthlessness. We thought that if only we could acquire "it"—the object or experience we craved—we'd feel better about ourselves. Needless to say, we never got "it" and if perchance we did, we never felt better about ourselves anyway. Nonetheless, our hyper-focused ways turned into habits. Unfortunately, while those habits came nowhere near resolving our deep-seated self-esteem issues, they did hugely complicate those issues.

Community dynamics

Society supports a variety of obsessions. We scramble frantically up the corporate ladder; worry lest we fail to outclass the neighbors; struggle to develop flawless, youthful bodies; pursue "perfect" relationships with "ideal" people; and seek awesome sex with amazing partners. We buy, buy, buy . . . aspire, aspire, aspire . . . chase, chase, chase . . . and lust, lust, lust (just as ubiquitous advertising urges us to do). A widely accepted notion is that more is better and less means we are . . . failing. This is likely to change only as increasing numbers of us individually recognize the futility of the endless chase. Then, with our inborn capacity for focused intensity—the ability to be relentless in our search for fulfillment—we can learn to seek *genuine* (personal, professional, and community) betterment for ourselves and even be role models for others . . . instead of doing what we often do now, which is to brutally flog ourselves with our own dark, unrelenting need.

Personal sacrifice

Obsession can be so all-consuming that you have little time left over for actual living.

Resource acquired

Obsession has trained you to focus. Now you can use this ability appropriately to concentrate your efforts in circumstances that enhance rather than ensnare you.

RUN DEFENSES: DISCONNECTION THROUGH THINKING

The defense of SELF-ABSORPTION

Protecting yourself through excessive self-centeredness.

Personal impact

"You're so vain," goes the popular 1972 Carly Simon song, "you probably think this song is about you!" If Self-Absorption is a defense we use, our passion for attention is unlimited. We're completely self-focused, and we want everyone else to be focused on us, too. Our excessive need may present itself negatively or positively.

You're trying hard to prove how special you are

As a self-absorbed person who demands to be the *positive* center of attention, we seem *exceedingly* self-confident, sometimes even to the point of behaving in a grandiose manner—conducting ourselves with an elaborate, heightened sense of our own importance. Often we're especially anxious about our appearance, particularly about remaining youthful. We need to feel special and are preoccupied with either thinking about or even actually attaining the unlimited success, power, brilliance, beauty, or ideal love that would prove how unique we truly are. We are ravenously ambitious, but seldom satisfied with our accomplishments.

You think it's all about you

As a self-absorbed person who craves *negative* attention, we're fast to proclaim our unworthiness and self-contempt to anyone within earshot. We consider *our* pain, discomfort, grief, or depression to be worse (and more important) than anyone else's. Often, we are unable to put our own concerns on hold for even a few moments to focus on the lives, deeds, and feeling of others, who therefore tend to experience us as draining and selfish.

Outer appearance

In addition to our considerable (positive or negative) needs, we tend to exhibit a style that is either noticeably passive or noticeably aggressive. If it's passive, we are likely to appear disconnected. If it's aggressive, we probably seem pompous, arrogant, bored, self-righteous, and contemptuous. Both postures include a lack of empathy for others (when we visit a sick friend in the hospital, we either spend the whole time thinking about how generous we're being or complaining about *our* problems). Yet we're excruciatingly hypersensitive to other people's opinions about *us*.

We tend to be exhibitionistic and to need constant admiration. In relationship, we focus primarily on *our* needs, only paying attention to our lovers when that proves to be a way for us to look and feel better. We often express emotions in exaggerated ways (excess ardor, nonstop sexual seductiveness, temper tantrums), being charming one minute and rageful the next. The rage is most likely to occur when our sense of entitlement (and unreasonable expectation of special treatment) is thwarted.

On the other hand, we may frequently wear a mask of cool indifference, while at the same time being stealthily exploitative with friends—taking advantage of their goodwill or befriending them in the first place mostly because of what we think we can get from them. We are usually unconscious of this exploitative side, for we think of ourselves merely as a "good and caring" friends. The only way for us to know if we're being inspired by a self-centered agenda is to notice how reactive we get—*inside or out*—to other people's responses to us. For instance, do we (even secretly) get furious when friends don't thank us sufficiently, or do we get (exceedingly) resentful when we feel a lack of total repayment (for good deeds or generosities)?

SIGNALS	STORY LINES
I am self-absorbed when I am . . .	**To feel the internal effects of self-absorption, watch yourself with your mind's eye as you read the following words with a dramatic flair.**
Seductive:	"When I look at you, I see myself. You make me feel so beautiful, I want to kiss you . . . all over."
Hypersensitive:	"I know you do a lot for me, but somehow, underneath it all, I just don't believe you *really* care."
Ambitious:	"Hey, all's fair in love and war. It's survival of the fittest!"
Rageful:	"You're a stupid, small, insulting man who clearly does not understand me. If you did, you'd never make that choice!"
Complaining:	"I spent a fortune on plastic surgery, physical trainers, diet doctors, and clothes—and all I get is one jerky man in my life after another!"
Exhibitionistic:	"If you've got it, flaunt it, I always say. And I do!"
Acting entitled:	"Hey, you're lucky I'm even bothering with your family, as difficult as they are!"
Indifferent:	"I know I should read the paper once in a while, but I just can't get interested."
Self-pitying:	"I'm afraid. I try so hard—harder than anyone I know. I work diligently, but I just can't get ahead. What's wrong with me? What's *wrong* with me?"
<u>Your</u> Signals:	**<u>Your</u> Story Lines:**

Unconscious intention

Whether it's revealed in a positive or a negative way, our self-absorption most obviously discloses how profoundly *unimportant* we unconsciously feel ourselves to be. This is another good example of the equal/opposite principle in action (see Defense Busting: Step 13, p. 148). When we must constantly prove we're exceptional (whether exceptionally great or exceptionally terrible), it indicates our actual (unconscious) belief that we are *not* exceptional at all.

We're riddled with insecurities—trying to deal with not just one perceived weakness, but with many—and we feel as though our literal *survival* is at stake. We think that if we can only get enough praise, power, prestige, and attention, we'll be okay. We're like flowers that need constant bright sun to thrive. Other people are that "sun," and when they shine their light on us, we're alive. But when they turn their attention to anything or anyone else and their light goes away, we suddenly feel deprived of nourishment and begin to wilt. Our intention, then, is not so much to get more attention than anyone else (although that's what we *seem* to want) as it is merely to survive and thrive.

Being the center of attention makes you feel alive

Community dynamics

Defensive self-absorption is a benign version of the psychological condition called *narcissism*. But just as Paranoia (the defense) is quite different from the personality disorder called paranoia, so is Self-Absorption (the defense) quite different from the personality disorder called narcissism. Despite this fact, the word "narcissism" (which might actually apply to only very few people) has now entered the culture with a corrupted meaning as a common term for anyone who is even slightly self-involved ("Oh, he's such a narcissist") and has thereby lost its original and more serious meaning. Thus, in informal conversation, many people now use "self-absorbed" and "narcissistic" interchangeably.

We typically declare that self-centeredness is annoying and that self-involved people are disagreeable. But, in fact, we're often collectively ambiguous in regard to this quality, since even as we hesitate to approve of what looks like selfishness, we encourage and reward various distasteful, self-centered, self-aggrandizing behaviors, especially in the fields of entertainment and sports, where many people—particularly impressionable youth—find models of how to behave in this complex world of ours. We also promote, protect, and encourage the self-absorbed behavior of other stars, all kinds of stars—business stars, medical stars, financial stars, political stars, and science stars—along with their often outrageous, attention-getting antics. Perhaps we do this because we feel that a little personal glory is reflected onto us by their prominence, or we somehow recognize that they may be acting out hidden parts of ourselves we're afraid to express.

Personal sacrifice

Your self-absorption requires that you sacrifice true compassion for others—as nearly every ounce of your energy is taken up by your effort to prove how special you think you are.

Resource acquired

Self-absorption teaches you to look at yourself carefully, which can offer you important self-awareness.

RUN DEFENSES: DISCONNECTION THROUGH THINKING

The defense of FANTASY

Protecting yourself through a preoccupation with illusory notions.

Personal impact

Fantasy is a magician who distracts us with his trickery so we won't need to face the realities of our own lives. The defense of fantasy—whether it involves fantasies about flawless sex, worldwide fame, outrageous fortune, a perfect relationship, an ideal home, a perfect body, or anything else—uses us up, drains our energy, and undermines our genuine abilities. Sexual fantasy, for instance, can take up so much of our attention that we're left unable to function in our daily routines, since we spend every moment daydreaming about who and what we want or would like to have happen. Because our fantasy life *always* outclasses, outdistances, and overshadows reality, nothing ever seems to turn out quite right. Fantasy thus leaves us feeling constantly dissatisfied. Employment, relationship partners, friends, and/or other specific circumstances inevitably disappoint us. We compare and then complain. We usually feel as if we are getting the short end of the stick, holding the half-empty glass, and sitting on the not-so-green side of the fence. Indeed, from our perspective life is letting us down.

Fantasy picks you up and then drops you off into dissatisfaction

Of course, fantasy in its everyday uses can be extremely helpful—your boss is a creep and you briefly entertain the idea of knocking his block off, or you see a great-looking person walking down the street and for a moment visualize what dating him/her would be like, or you drive through wonderful neighborhoods dreaming of a big new house. By way of such normal and exciting fantasies, we can experience relief, excitement, or even renewed hope. However, when we *consistently prefer fantasy experiences to real-life experiences, the impact on our*

You feel like life is letting you down

potential for ongoing satisfaction can be severely disturbed. At that point, then, fantasy has developed into a defense.

Outer appearance

This very private defense is not always easy to recognize in others. Almost the only way to do so is to listen for conversation that circles (too often) around future possibilities—especially when those references hardly seem like "real" possibilities at all. ("Someday I'll get a big schooner, leave everything behind, and sail around the world"; "All I'll need is a huge club and ten minutes with that guy"; "Every day I expect my *perfect* prince to appear.") Sometimes, fantasy-driven individuals who have a little insight into their excesses choose to acknowledge what's going on by giving it an affirmative, even boastful spin ("I'm a dreamer" or "I'm an incurable romantic.") Of course, these might also be anything from simple, immature exaggerations to correct self-assessments, so listen for accompanying statements that hint of impossibly fanciful imaginative flights, and also look for attitudes of overall dreaminess and lack of attentiveness.

SIGNALS	STORY LINES
Fantasy can cause you to be . . .	**To feel the internal effects of fantasy, read the following words in a dreamy tone. You may say things like:**
Disillusioned:	"Damn! I really thought this was it! I thought I'd finally found my perfect mate."
Daydreaming:	"I've figured out exactly what I'd do if someone gave me a million dollars! Look, I wrote it all down."
Focused on outcome:	[About first date]: "I really mean it this time! I know I've said that before, but this seems like it may be *the one.*"

Perplexed:	"No matter how hard I try, all of my relationship partners have ended up having something wrong with them! I just can't figure it out!"
Oblivious:	"No. I don't read the newspapers or listen to the TV news. I prefer the more pleasant topics I can conjure up in my own head!"
Disappointed:	"I thought getting this new car would make things look brighter. Well, that lasted about a day."
Resentful:	"Nothing ever turns out the way I expect it to!"
Perfectionistic:	"I just want everything to be right! What's wrong with that?"
Futurizing:	"Someday my prince will come . . . and rescue me from this lousy life."
Your Signals:	**Your Story Lines:**

Unconscious intention

To us, reality feels both difficult, uncontrollable, and unrewarding. It has probably felt that way since early in our lives. We (unconsciously) defended against a sense of being out-of-control then and we do it still—often experiencing tremendous confusion as a consequence—as we have created (or escaped to) alternate realities where we could maintain an *illusion* of control. We are still drawn to this kind of escapsim, not fully seeing it as the *illusion* it is—one that merely provides temporary and inauthentic relief—not a long-term solution.

Community dynamics

Artistry has many faces. Daydreams, flights of fancy, fiction, myths, stories, and visions—all of which are conceptions of the mind, images drawn by the imagination, and all of which appear in a multitude of expansive forms, including prose, poetry, music, dance, sculpture, painting, drawing, film, and even games (of mind and body). These creative flights, which uplift, inspire, entertain, provoke, encourage, revile, enlarge, and amuse us, are usually not evidence of inappropriate fantasy involvement. But, as with distortions of any imaginative process, some *versions* of this creativity can be used compulsively and indiscriminately, causing problems both for ourselves and for the community at large. Excessive fantasy engagement prevents us from taking the kind of real-life actions that would allow our fantasies either to *become* our realities, or to be recognized as impossible dreams that need to be dismissed.

Personal sacrifice

This defense is debilitating, in that it infects you with discontent, disappointment, and resentment toward the circumstances and people in your real life. Besides that, it all too often sucks up time that would be better devoted to creating *actual* (beneficial) experiences.

Resource acquired

If you lack the ability to fly on the wings of imagination, this universe becomes a dry, colorless, taste-free zone devoid of all things beautiful. Appropriate fantasy, then, is the stuff of a great life.

RUN DEFENSES: DISCONNECTION THROUGH THINKING

The defense of PERFECTIONISM

Protecting yourself by insisting upon <u>excessively</u> high standards.

Personal impact

Like an unerring heat-seeking missile, we perfectionists home in on and seek to destroy all apparent flaws and errors in ourselves and others, howsoever minuscule those flaws and errors may be. We must make certain that everything we do is absolutely, positively, unquestionably right and successful. Unfortunately, this need is a setup for self-contempt—for there are few times and few places where we will be absolutely, positively, unquestionably right and successful! Thus, the hallmark (and inevitable result) of perfectionism is dissatisfaction. This means that if we're accomplished in using this defense, we're probably also proficient at paralyzing self-criticism. Constantly reaching for the impossible usually leaves us frustrated, disappointed, and negative. And when we impose our perfectionistic inclinations on others, they also tend to feel criticized and inadequate, and will likely welcome the opportunity to spend their time with someone who is less demanding.

Perfectionism is a set-up for self-abuse

Outward appearance

Perfectionists come in all forms—from anorexics and CEOs to anorexic CEOs. To spot them, don't look for someone in a particular profession, socioeconomic level, or state of mental health. Look for certain *attitudes*, such as control, complaint, and ingratitude.

As perfectionists, we may: (a) appear to be merely dedicated hard workers—people who want to do the best job possible; (b) appear to be do-nothing individuals (we prefer to do nothing at all rather than to make a mistake); (c) try so hard to be absolutely, perfectly beyond criticism

Nothing's ever perfect therefore you're always left holding the disappointment bag

that we take forever to finish a job; (d) seem overwhelmed with our own lives (because we're trying all the time to do so much so perfectly); (e) appear to be bragging or thinking we really *are* superior (because we speak of our own perfectionism with a slight smile); and/or (f) be completely unappreciative of others (since nothing anyone else does is good enough, either).

SIGNALS	STORY LINES
Perfectionism can cause you to be . . .	**To feel the internal effects of perfectionism, try reading the following words in a tight-lipped tone. You may say things like:**
Driven:	"If something's worth doing, it's worth doing right."
Frustrated:	"Oh, forget it! This will never be good enough."
Holding black/white perspectives:	"Everything was going along fine, totally fine—then the soufflé fell and ruined the entire evening."
Dissatisfied:	"Everyone tells me I'm already too thin. I wish they'd just leave me alone. When I look at myself, all I can see is how far I need to go."
Competitive:	"I have to do better than anyone else. I just *have to!*"
Critical:	"I like everything about her but her nose. It's too big. I don't think I can spend the rest of my life with that nose!"
Overwhelmed:	"I know eventually this job will fall apart. Maybe I should just give up right now."
Complaining:	"I can't seem to find an assistant who's able to do things right, so I have to fire one after the other. . . ."
Unappreciative:	"Here, let me finish that. You know how life is: if you want something done right, do it yourself!"

Your Signals:	Your Story Lines:

Unconscious intention

We're driven by our idea that anything shy of a flawless performance will result in abandonment, rejection, or ridicule (any of which, to our psyche, usually lands us in the center of our aloneness, or—we [unconsciously] imagine—might even equal death). In addition, when *others* fail to be perfect in our eyes, we feel personally disrespected, undermined, and let down. This leads us to the erroneous assumption that we'll never be able to depend on anyone—which once more leaves us feeling oh so terribly alone.

Often much anger lies underneath our perfectionistic maneuvering. We whisper to ourselves through gritted teeth, "I'm going to get it totally right this time. *Then* they'll see how great I am!" This anger, which is sometimes deeply buried, is reported by the perfectionist through many behaviors—some subtle and "ordinary" (like snappishness and criticism as a response to even minor disappointment) and others more extreme (like physical twitches and tics or self-induced vomiting [bulimia]).

As an example of how the toxic effects of perfectionism can manifest in, and sometimes cripple, several generations at once, I present Paula—an anorexic/bulimic woman who believed that because her mother and father "truly loved her," she had no right to feel anger or regret about the behavior they exhibited when she was a child.

After much work in therapy, Paula realized that she had spent many years denying her own angry responses—to her mother's extraordinary perfectionism (plastic covers on all the furniture, excessive neatness, not allowing children in the living room because they were too messy, extreme emphasis on being "a smart lady") and to her father's constant apologetic, submissive reaction to her mom's unending criticism of him. But Paula had also adopted many of the qualities she most loathed in her parents, including a perfectionism of her own. It revealed itself in her extreme attention to cleaning, a do-more-do-better attitude toward herself in her job (which ended up translating to "I can never do enough"), her intent to develop a perfect body (which led to both starving and vomiting), and a contempt for and distrust of many of the men who came into her life. (I was especially interested in how the vomiting seemed to answer two problems at once for her. It helped her work toward a "perfect" body and it gave her a way to express her anger, since vomiting is a violent, rejecting process.)

You try to control what you feel by controlling what you do

As Paula later realized during her therapy, when the bulimia began in her adolescence, she unconsciously thought, "I have no control over what's happening in this house. But I can and will control what's happening in my body." Now, as an adult, she has gained more insight into her unconscious thinking, but she still tends to be affected by a belief that "since I have no control over what I feel, I will control what I do [what I eat and how I get rid of what I eat]." This is the crux of perfectionism—to control what we *feel* by attempting to control what we (and people around us) *do*.

Community dynamics

In many ways and on a daily basis, we are all encouraged to aim toward a (more) perfect life. To some extent, that kind of encouragement is intended good-heartedly to point us in worthwhile directions, for it encourages responsible behavior, both socially and individually. But that encouragement can easily be misinterpreted—by both giver and receiver—for there is quite a distinction between excellence (striving with great effort for superior results) and perfection (striving with inhuman effort for impossible results).

This confusion between *literal perfection* and either *thoroughness* or *excellence* is often promoted by our misunderstanding the meaning of such concepts as "aiming high" or "doing our best." The problem is that "perfection" refers to being *completely without defect*. It is an absolute term that requires an absolute attitude. *Excellence* and *thoroughness*, on the other hand, are relative terms that are associated with achieving the highest quality possible.

Relative concepts relate and absolute concepts separate. When we're thorough and we drive toward excellence, we can be inclusive of other people and of the natural disappointments and false steps that life brings. When we're perfectionistically driven, there's no room for error and therefore no room for a realistic sense of our own humanity, individually or collectively.

Personal loss

The impossibility of fulfilling a perfectionistic intent cripples your ability to function at your legitimate best, at the same time robbing you of the opportunity to experience satisfaction for a job that's (merely) *very* well done.

Resource acquired

Perfectionism, within appropriate limits, can teach you about the importance and value of excellence.

Relative concepts relate—
absolute concepts separate

CHAPTER 4

YESTERDAY'S TALES

Flashback: The way we thought we were

In my years of clinical practice, I have come to realize that most of our defense-based problems as well as our complaints about those problems are developments of the five themes I previously mentioned: *abandonment, punishment (experiences of both physical and emotional punishment), body-image shame, sex,* and *relationship*. One or another of these themes usually turns out to be behind the song we sing and the story we tell.

These themes are more than just personal, since every problem we have as individuals is also reflected in and by society, and every problem of society is thus a reflection of us as individuals. Because seeing this mutual reflection gives us a larger appreciation of the powerful way in which defenses weave into our daily lives, I will examine both in this chapter.

IN SOCIETY looks at how we are *collectively* stuck in our stories (how a particular theme has come to be of such widespread concern);

PERSONALLY investigates ways we as individuals are likely to claim one of these collective themes as our particular story;

FEARS will also be part of our discussion, plus some—

SYMPTOMS of those fears, along with the—

PRIVATE THOUGHTS those fears inspire.

The personal accounts I have presented throughout these pages*— which I briefly review below as a reminder of the defenses they illustrate—show how five general themes tend to lurk at the core of stories that individuals hold onto and regard as the cause and center of their difficulties. And in a way they are *both* cause and center—not necessarily because they *created* the difficulties, but because they are the sticking points on which the individual storytellers have based so much of their daily lives.

You think you cannot trust yourself and you think you cannot trust others

You should note what's common to these five themes, which is that each reflects two basic and usually unconscious implicit assumptions related to *trust*: we think **we cannot trust ourselves** and we think **we cannot trust others**. In different degrees, these two assumptions tend to wind their ways through our entire lives, manifesting as unsatisfying relationships, career struggles, money problems, physical trauma, and/or a lack of action-taking behavior. This mistrust of ourselves and of other people will dominate what we think, feel, and do. It's reflected in particular fears and often evokes in us a sense of emptiness and a lack of

* This refers to the *client* stories (announced throughout by the "storybook" icon for easy identification). My *personal* stories have already been discussed in detail and are therefore not reiterated in this chapter.

fulfillment, which frequently shows up as a kind of general complaining and dissatisfaction.

When you combine the meanings embodied in these themes with other ever-present influences, such as environmental modeling (attitudes and actions toward race, gender, ethnicity, physical appearance, intelligence and other characteristics), birth order (the oldest child has a notably different experience than the youngest), and peer-member influence (the effects of friendships), the possibilities for diverse responses multiply significantly. I trust that this brief survey will be both useful and provocative. I also hope that you, the reader, will find your-self somewhere in the material. In order to do so, try writing down the stories (from childhood) you most often tell or think about. Notice which category they're in and try to determine your own fears, symptoms, and private thoughts.

————◦✄◦————

The ABANDONMENT Theme

Abandonment: In Society

The catch-all theme these days, the reigning queen of complaints, inevitably features some use of the word *Abandonment*. Actually, any condition or circumstance that seems lonely, alienating, or rejecting tends to be identified somehow as abandonment and gets shoved into this category. This is to say that "abandoned" is the word I hear most often describing what many people feel much of the time.

Life-threatening abandonment (being left alone without *any* means or capacity for survival) is, in actuality, an extremely rare circumstance for adults. More "commonly" then, the word has often come to mean an ongoing (personal) sense that *true supportive nurturing* has been, is, and always will be absent.

Collectively, we seem to *feel* this kind of non-nurturing more and more. Perhaps that feeling is exaggerated by persistent stories and news photos of ongoing tragedy, including starving and abandoned children, homeless people who are unseen and unacknowledged by society, and ordinary citizens who feel that collective safety systems have failed them (via curtailed welfare, social security that seems insecure, tax increases, and incomprehensible governmental spending, to say nothing of the shocking, unpredictable physical violence of such events as those of 9/11/01 and the daily, widespread experiences of apparently unstoppable endangerment). Thus, whether we've actually been "abandoned" or not, we certainly often feel that way. The result has been an overall attitude of helplessness (leading to blaming and shaming behaviors)—a collective helplessness that (vaguely and subtly) underscores our personal discomfort and therefore undermines our (individual) potential success in both work and in relationships.

Abandonment: Personally

Even in ordinary, healthy circumstances, we face what is or what seems like abandonment. In growing up, when we move from being fed by our (loving, caring, attentive) mother to feeding ourselves, we endure a loss of Mother's complete attention, which can leave us, in some subtle ways, feeling forsaken. We may feel abandoned by Dad when he gets irritated and corrects us—as if he's taken away his love. And when we go to school for the first time, we may feel hurt—like we're being booted out of the house. *These are normal, predictable experiences— natural woundings—and must occur as a necessary part of our maturing process.* Their ultimate effect is generally minimal, because they are counterbalanced by the positive and beneficial effects they produce.

Some "abandonment" is actually normal and even necessary!

Thus, when you learn to feed yourself you gain autonomy; Dad's admonishment teaches you important and helpful behavioral boundaries; and school is, among other things, an initiation into the lifelong process of socialization.

But certain experiences are *not* part of "natural" healthy development. Certain horrible, self-esteem-diminishing incidents and encounters are likely to leave us feeling—and from then on expecting to feel—unsupported, unloved, and unworthy. These could be called <u>*unnatural woundings,*</u> and they include such things as abuse, shaming, and neglect. These kinds of suffering are <u>*not spontaneously or automatically repaired*</u> by compensatory counterbalancing benefits. For life-affirming balance and well-being to be restored, they require that, at some time in our lives, we give them particular (and usually ongoing) healing attention.

The unnatural "abandonment" wounds take four forms, all of which involve action by a caretaker (real or perceived) or a loved one. The first three are:

❖ *Actual departure* (which includes desertion, divorce, or death);

❖*Threatened departure*; and

❖ *Neglect* (without actual or threatened departure), which can result from such causes as alcoholism, workaholism, or parental self-centeredness. Obviously, these three can also occur in any combination (as in, first you are threatened with departure, then Dad leaves for a while but when he returns he ignores you anyway). The fourth wounding, which is often overlooked because it sounds unlike conventional abandonment, is called—

❖ *Suffocation.* Typically, we might be able to recognize childhood (or youthful) suffocation when we see an overbearing, over-involved, over-controlling mother or father. This form of abandonment may be difficult to spot, however, because such a parent often *looks* (to the casual eye) like someone who is just extremely concerned, constantly

Suffocation
is also
a form of
abandonment!

attentive, and exceedingly helpful. An example from my clinical experience is the mother who (in a supposed effort to maintain a constant protective vigilance) kept her daughter Felicity sleeping in bed with her until age fifteen, while Dad slept in a separate room. What Felicity experienced was *emotional incest*—here defined as inappropriate psychic, psychological, emotional, and physical intrusion (the problems between Mom and Dad are yet another story). Felicity, now forty years old, has never married and still lives within a mile of her mother—continuing to report in, through daily phone calls, about her friends, activities, whereabouts, and general safety.

Suffocation registers as abandonment because it's experienced as impersonal. *Our* actual wants and needs are overwhelmed by the suffocater's desires, and we feel neither included nor considered. Finally, we become convinced that we've had no real attention at all.

As always, however, there is good news, which is that *all* woundings, natural or not—obvious or subtle—can help us develop resources that, sooner or later, support the way we (effectively) deal with life.

Abandonment: Its Fears

You
expect
loss

The *experience* of abandonment can lead to the *expectation* of loss. That expectation anticipates loss to take form in either of two ways: **loss of other** or **loss of self**.

Abandonment: Its Symptoms

These expectations of loss are expressed in a number of symptoms, such as fear of commitment, over-dependence, neediness, phobias focusing on death, and rebellion.

Abandonment: Private Thoughts

"I cannot stand another loss. To avoid the deadly pain I will never commit to a relationship," or "I will find others who are unavailable and cannot commit," or "I will look as though I have committed, but I will always keep one foot out the door," or "I will find someone who is certain to leave me," or "I will stay vigilant, looking for deal-breakers and intolerable flaws."

Abandonment Story #1. Marty: Fight Nights (full details on page 66). Marty both "hits" and "runs." Actually, he has a natural yearning for relationship that keeps urging him toward new partnerships. At the same time, however, Marty holds a (mostly unconscious) belief that because all relationships are likely to turn out like the angry, hurtful, violent, abandoning relationship his parents had, he'd best avoid long-term commitment. He blames, judges, and compares . . . then, feeling disappointed and victimized by what he thinks is happening "to him" *again*, he flees the scene.

Marty leaves (abandons!) most of these situations confused, disheartened, and feeling abandoned by everything and everyone, including God. His private thoughts are, "Why me? What's wrong with me? Why can't I find the love of my life? Why doesn't God give me what I need? I really want a lasting love, but something always goes wrong. I don't understand."

Abandonment Story #2. Rachel: The Threat (full details on page 94). Rachel is a "hitter" who, through her primary defense of codependence, is desperately trying to prove she's a good girl—good enough to avoid abandonment. She stays stuck in her original story by, over and over again, finding partners who confirm her worst fears about herself, and who do actually constantly abandon her (either literally by leaving or symbolically through the constant criticism that makes her feel alone). Her private thoughts are, "No matter how hard I try, I'll lose. No one can stand me. I'm bad. I need to try harder."

Abandonment Story #3. Mary: Choosing Sides (*full details on page 207*). Mary is certain that everything is her fault and her responsibility. A "*runner*," she's perfectionistic, counter-dependent (rejecting help and thinking the responsibility to get *any* job done is all hers), and simultaneously codependent (exerting control through caretaking). She stays stuck in her original story by maintaining a skeptical perspective—that is, she doesn't believe she's supported by Life itself or by the people who are in that Life with her. She frequently dissociates so she won't have to feel the fear of abandonment that drives her. Her private thoughts are, "Expect the worst. Everyone's more important than me. I'll always be torn and in the middle."

The PUNISHMENT Theme

Punishment: In Society

Figuring out the rules for punishing right and wrong—or even figuring out what *is* right and wrong—is often difficult and confusing. Society is in a state of transition and doesn't seem to know which way to go. Interest in this area is certainly high, though, which is reflected daily in the media. We see a proliferation of television shows and movies (reality-based and fictional) about extreme violence, amoral characters, crime in general, and drug trafficking in particular, along with tales of police, prisons, and lawyers—particularly in dramatic fiction that is not necessarily based in traditional concepts of right and wrong. Nowadays, telling the good guys from the bad is often hard, which is a tip-off that society itself is anxiously trying to develop new standards.

Nowhere is this more evident than in the American passion for safeguarding personal rights. Unfortunately, that passion often leads to gross misconduct, and before long we've created a society where individuals move easily, often inexplicably, from simple rudeness to treacherous violence. Has more personal freedom somehow led, over time, to public chaos? Now we have trouble figuring out how or when to punish people. We don't know where to look for help. Many people turn to general complaining, engaging in endless conversations about the soundness or sickness of capital punishment, prison reform, welfare, street violence, the war on drugs, sexual harassment, pornography, and other assorted social ills. In many instances, this is not the kind of discussion that leads to more understanding, but rather the sort that exacerbates a general state of discontent. We end up feeling not only as though *we* have no answers, but also as though *no one* has any answers. We are hanging out on a boundariless limb, and we are afraid.

Punishment: Personally

While growing up, nearly all of us get punished somehow. How, when, where, and for what we get punished is the real issue.

Punishment can range from mild lectures to gross violence, and you might logically assume that the harsher the punishment, the more severe the resultant problems and the more difficult the adult life that follows. This, however, is not always true, for it turns out that problems most often spring not from the nature of the punishment itself but rather from how consistently or inconsistently that punishment is administered. (For instance when breaking curfew is ignored on one occasion and met with

Children
take erratic
behavior
personally

beatings the next, a child is likely to have some kind of extreme reaction.) Why? For two reasons. Because children take erratic behavior personally, thinking they are causing it, which confuses them and undermines their confidence, so they begin to think something terrible is wrong with *them*. And also because a sufficient dose of this inconsistent or extreme punishment leaves children feeling that something is not only wrong with them, but also with the world in general.

Punishment usually occurs in one of three ways: *too much, indirect,* or *too little.*

❖ *Too much* punishment involves severe abuse, which is often physical but can also be emotional or verbal.

❖ *Indirect* punishment is more subtle—perhaps involving shaming, neglect, or the withdrawal of loving contact. Surprisingly, these forms can be even more difficult to overcome in later life, because a person may minimize the impact of the experience—especially when it is compared to punishment that is more violent and abusive.

❖ *Too little* punishment has its own problems. Joan, for example, was regularly arrested for smoking and possession of marijuana. Just as regularly, her parents bailed her out of jail, picked her up, and took her to dinner, with never a word about the arrest. She came to a simple conclusion: *Get arrested, go to jail, get a meal!* The result: a boundariless, compulsive adult often tending towards irresponsibility; or, alternatively in some cases, an extremely rigid adult who tries to create the rules (of safety) he or she never felt growing up.

Punishment: Its Fears

The *fear* of punishment usually shows up either as *fear that we will always disappoint other people* or *fear that other people will always disappoint us*.

Punishment: Its Symptoms

These fears are expressed in such symptoms as people-pleasing, isolation, neediness, rejection of relationship, abuse (of self and/or others), and negativity.

Punishment: Private Thoughts

Punishment-related behaviors are accompanied by such thoughts as "Don't get too close. Trust no one. I'll always live under a cloud. The world is not a safe place. I'm bad."

Punishment Story #1. James: The Swim Class (full details on page 62). James is a "hitter," who, in the wake of his history, expects that he will always disappoint others and that others will always disappoint him. He uses the defense of contempt to keep other people away, because he's constantly terrified of getting his sweet, small-boy heart broken. He stays stuck in his original story by (unconsciously) assuming everyone is as mean as his father was, that the rug will always be pulled out from under him, and that he must live in shame. His private thoughts are, "I can't count on anyone. I'm a loser, and I'll never be good enough. Screw 'em all."

Punishment Story #2. Betty: The Silent Treatment (full details on page 26). Like James, Betty expects to disappoint other people, but as a "runner," she chooses the kind of silent withdrawal and withholding her mother taught her. She stays stuck in her original story by refusing to confront her fears—preferring the self-contempt she's so accustomed to. As an adult, she can neither request, nor can she even define, appropriate limits for herself. Her private thoughts are, "Saying nothing is better than

saying the wrong thing. Relationship is a trap. When people ignore me it means I'm a bad person. Speaking my mind will only get me into trouble."

The BODY-IMAGE SHAME Theme

Body-Image Shame: In Society

We are constantly broadsided with images describing how we *should* look, feel, and be—the exemplars usually being skinny models dressed in impractical clothing; perfect-complexioned, forever-young movie stars; and quirky television personalities revered rather than reviled for oddities most of us would try to overcome rather than flaunt. Although little of this reflects real life, many impressionable people do yearn to match these pictures and perceptions. Young girls struggle with anorexia trying to imitate heroin chic, while women (and now men) over forty renounce themselves as used-up and useless. The societal reflections of our body-image shame (revulsion about aging and a distorted reverence for youth) and the businesses that body-image shame supports (the diet industry, the exercise industry, the cosmetics industry, the plastic surgery industry) show again how society simultaneously reflects and also perpetuates our individual focus.

We're told over and over how we should look, feel, and be

Body-Image Shame: Personally

Generally, body-image shame is the symptomatic reflection of apparently unrelated personal feelings—like powerlessness, (worldly) impotence, loneliness, self-doubt, and fear of relationship. The focus thus shifts from the psyche to the body, which appears to be an area we can actually affect. If we're fat we can get thin; if we're ill-groomed we can clean up, if we're flabby we can shape up. Unfortunately, because the psychological issues that support the symptoms (the unwanted physical manifestations) are so deeply rooted, change becomes difficult.

Getting sidetracked is easy, and instead of attacking the *real* emotional concerns (powerlessness, fear, loneliness, etc.), we can focus on tangential issues. Perhaps, for instance, we complain that we don't feel loved for who we are ("People always judge a book by its cover"); or that we *want* to look different but no matter how hard we try we (mysteriously) can't achieve the desired results ("My metabolism is just lousy"); or that we're just too overwhelmed with the rest of life to pay attention ("Hey, I just don't have the luxury of spending twenty hours a day in the gym like some people").

As you read, and if you've struggled constantly and for years against body-image problems, you might be feeling righteously angry at this point. After all, you insist, having spent a lifetime grappling with "the problem," you're absolutely convinced it's your genes or your glands and—well, no matter what it is, it *isn't* your fault.

However, even if you do have a terrible metabolism, a busy life, and live in an image-conscious world, your body-image shame and the symptoms of that shame are, in virtually every case, still reflections of deeper concerns. If you can discover what you're *really* getting from what you're doing to yourself, you might finally and gratefully be able to free yourself from your self-defeating attitude.

The question to be asking here is: *What is the payoff of my self-defeating behavior?* I remember the overweight woman who complained that she could not leave her home to be with friends because she was so gross-looking. This gave her a great reason not to risk having new relationships, for she had "suffered" a difficult divorce following a long marriage. Her body shame kept her safely isolated. The pain she knew seemed better than the pain she anticipated. To discover the payoff of your own behavior, look at the *actual results* of that behavior.

Body shame is a symptom not a problem

The pain you know seems better than the pain you anticipate

Discover the payoff of your behavior by noting the actual results of that behavior

Body-Image Shame: Its Fears

The fears associated with body-image shame are simple enough: *fear of rejection* and/or *fear of connection*.

Body-Image Shame: Its Symptoms

These fears are expressed in such symptoms as an inability to connect with others, self-contempt, clinging, lack of sexual desire, erratic eating habits, and self-centeredness.

Body-Image Shame: Private Thoughts

They are accompanied by such thoughts as "I'm ugly. No one will ever want me. I'd better make sure I can wow them another way. People are always noticing my flaws."

Body-Image Shame Story #1. Susan: The Birthday Party (full details on page 178). Susan is a fine example of both a "hitter" and a "runner." She is explosively Angry, full of Contempt, and sees the world as a battlefield peopled by enemies. She runs around on that battlefield creating Chaos for herself and others—behaving Compulsively (with both food and with the hungry, needy way she treats people). She uses the defense of Paranoia—ever-vigilant for the enemy who will Victimize her next. She's certain she will never be safe and thinks that everything everyone does is about her and, in fact, against her. She stays stuck in her original story by spending much of her time with people who prove her worst expectations to be correct. Her private thoughts are, "It's not my fault. I'm fat because I never had love. Anyway, people should be able to see past what I look like and love me for who I am inside. They don't and can't because something's wrong with them. They just don't understand how hard my life has been."

Another example of this theme can be seen in the following account: Body-Image Shame Story #2.

RON AND THE MOTHER KINSHIP
Body-Image Shame
The Pie

I remember one evening in 1967 when I was seven. We were having company over for dinner. It was going to be me, my sister, my stepmother and two lady friends of my stepmother. When the lady friends arrived, I introduced myself to them and brought them into the den, as my stepmother was still showering. The women seemed nice. At one point in the conversation, one of the women said she had brought a cherry pie for desert. I was very excited, because my stepmother was always on some new health kick and I was seldom allowed to eat sugar.

I was exclaiming my excitement when I heard my name called. I went to the bathroom with a sense of fear and dread. As I got there, my stepmother—wrapped in a towel—suddenly grabbed me by the short hair above my ear and snarled, "So you think you're gonna have pie?" She was obviously tense, and her angry movements resulted in her towel falling away. She told me to go out and tell the ladies I had made a mistake, that I *would not be eating pie.*

I went out, with my face all red and my hair askew. Right away everyone knew something was wrong, and they asked me if I had been crying. I said no and pretended like nothing had happened. For about fifteen years, I could never eat pie.

Ron is now a furious forty-year-old man who uses his rage, control, and judgment to "hit" his way through his life and his continuing compulsivity with food to "run" from that life. He attempts to override both the rage and the judgment with his wonderful sense of humor and his expert ability at masking (he's the ever-affable life of the party). He stays stuck in his original story by using his (considerable) weight as an excuse to stay out of relationships—which he always expects will be disappointing anyway. Thus, he has carefully avoided them altogether. His private thoughts are, "I wish I could have a relationship, but who would want me looking the way I do? Fuck it! I'll eat what I want to and put all my energy into my work. After all, life is no pie of cherries. Ha!" His unconscious driving ideas are: "Expect disappointment, but always pretend nothing is wrong."

The SEX Theme

Sex: In Society

Today, sex is splashed across screens of every variety. We see it in the movies and on television and can even view hard-core pornography on the Internet. And it is relentlessly chronicled in tabloid newspapers, frequently pictured in magazines, and constantly written about in books. The public thirst for sex-related information, images, and references is unquenchable.

But what is really fanning the flames of our apparent desire? The media tell us they only report the sordid details of the lives of the rich and famous because the public demands it, while the public rails and protests against what's considered by some to be sexploitation. The truth is that *sex sells*—because it is at least interesting and even compelling to just about everyone. It also sells because it revives even as it reviles us—reflecting our secret wishes and at the same time exposing our worst fears.

The decades of the sixties, seventies, and eighties thus found us tired of being "good"—and ready to express ourselves outright in sexual ways. We no longer wanted to be stuck in a morality with which we (secretly) did not concur. What happened next was called the sexual revolution—an eruption of repressed desires. And now, following that initial eruption, many people find that it's difficult to un-ring the bell!

This societal emphasis on sex and sexiness adds fuel to whatever personal hesitation, self-consciousness, compulsivity, and inadequacy exists within us. In the wake of this combination of personal inclination and public approbation, we tend more and more to use outside models to judge our own attitudes and actions. We compare ourselves to, contrast ourselves with, and outright emulate or even mimic what and who we see everywhere around us.

Sex: Personally

For most people sex is an ongoing mystery play—puzzling, urgent, even mandatory—at times exhilarating, at other times frightening. In our pubescent years, sex is usually at the very center of our lives. It's what we and most of our peers talk about (or avoid talking about), try to experience (or to avoid experiencing), and in some form or another regularly think about: "Am I going to get it or not?" "What do I need to do to get to first base?" "How can I say no and still be liked?" "Do I look sexy?" "Oh, he's so sexy!" "She's so fine!" "Nobody thinks I'm cute," and so forth.

The erotic urge drives most of us when we are young (especially when we are adolescents, but for many people it begins even when they are tots). How easily and clearly we express this normal craving will

The way
you deal
with sex
depends on how
what you're told
and
what you've
experienced
collide
with
your nature

depend greatly on the *information* we are given (who talks to us about it, what we're told, and how clear is it), our actual *experiences* (what happens and what we're told about what happens), and our basic nature (whether we're naturally shy or bold, innately passionate or inhibited). Because our desire to discover the various dimensions of sexuality (and/or to "get some") could easily have overcome our good sense, we might at times have found ourselves in offensive or unmanageable circumstances.

For the rest of our lives, sex remains—among other more obvious things like a way to have fun, to get and give pleasure, and to show how powerful, terrific, important, or thoughtful we are—both a reflection and a revelation of our fears, fantasies, and areas of greatest vulnerability (vulnerabilities like "Am I good enough, attractive enough, lovable enough?"). These reflections and revelations are expressed through responses like self-consciousness, self-contempt, increasing or decreasing sexual desire, compulsive sexuality, obsessive involvement with pornography, and extramarital affairs.

Remember that if sex ceases to be mostly an expression of pleasure given and pleasure received, and if it begins instead to be a source of trouble in our lives, the hesitations, revulsions, fears, rejections, doubts, and driving needs that start coming into sharp relief at such a time *were already present in our personality*. For example, our terror that we are being unlovable turns into a fear of being sexually undesirable, or our experience of financial impotence or career failure reveals itself as sexual apathy. Or we have an intense unconscious fear of connection that shows up in frequent sexual dissatisfaction that we blame on "inadequate" partners or our own exhaustion.

Thus, basic sex often acts as a barometer of how we feel about ourselves and/or about our relationships. Its quantity and quality can be

Troublesome sex
reflects
already present
seemingly
unrelated
needs & wants

tracked straightforwardly through questions about "how often" and "how good."

But that "barometer" is actually inefficient. Why? Because physical sex itself—the biological action—is not the real issue here. If it were, we could just as easily experience it as cats do: quickly, efficiently, and to the sole, immediate purpose of reproducing our kind. However, it turns out that what actually moves us toward (or drives us away from) sexual interaction is seldom simply biology, but rather includes an impulse to *partnership*.

Partnership reveals a whole new range of factors called *nonsexual* gratifications. Among them are feelings such as power/powerlessness, approval/disapproval, importance/unimportance, or physical beauty/shame.

Try identifying the kinds of nonsexual gratifications that are important to you when you evaluate a potential or existing partnership. List the needs and responses you think drive you toward or away from sexual *engagement* (as opposed to intercourse).

Sex: Its Fears

Fear of sexual intimacy is complicated to analyze. Overall, what we're probably most afraid of is either that *we will be consumed* and lose ourselves or that *we will be abandoned* because, we think, we are not sufficiently worthwhile. In the wake of these fears, some people cling, some run, others go numb. That is, some are driven away from sex, while others are driven toward it.

Sex: Its Symptoms

Running away from (or avoiding) sex often looks like simple *rejection* (of ourselves or others). We will frequently offer seemingly "good reasons" for saying no (exhaustion, illness, irritation, overwork, kids, time constraints). Symptoms of running away include fear of sexual intimacy, denial of desire, embarrassment, self-contempt, sexual disgust (or prudishness), judgment about ourselves or our partners, and anger about other issues in the relationship.

Symptoms of running toward sexuality often look like a *compulsivity* that might include promiscuity, over-involvement with pornography, anonymous sex, multiple-partner sex, excessive masturbation, and preoccupation with sexual fantasies.

Either way, whether you run toward or away from sexual intimacy and sexuality itself, if you wish to heal in this area, you will need to look deeply within yourself for the **true** source of your response.

Sex: Private Thoughts

Thoughts that accompany running away from sexuality include, "I can't count on anyone to be there for me. I get too involved when I have sex. He just wants me for sex. Companionship is the important thing and this emphasis on sex is ridiculous. She never seems satisfied anyway, so why bother?"

Thoughts that accompany running toward sexuality include, "I've got to have it. Who am I hurting anyway? It's fun. It eases my tension. I just need it a lot. It's just the way I am."

Sex Story #1. Anne: Daddy's Hands (full details on page 113). Anne both "hits" and "runs." She hits mainly through Projection (imagining that people think as little of her as she thinks of herself), Judgment (seeing nearly all men as sleazy jerks), and Masking (pretending to like many people when in actuality she dislikes more than she likes). She runs through Withdrawal (in the form of isolation) and Denial (no matter what the evidence, she continues to forgive her husband's lies). She has stayed stuck in her original story by marrying a man who almost exactly replicates her father. Anne's private thoughts are, "I know people are looking at me as if something's wrong with me. I'll be really nice, and maybe they'll leave me alone. I must learn to trust my husband."

Another example of how the groundwork for adult sexual shame can be prepared in childhood is seen in the following account: Sex Story #2.

MICHAEL & THE MOTHER KINSHIP
Sex
The Camping Trip

I always knew I was different from others, that I was gay.* What I did not always know was how to act or what to say. My mom caught me with my pants down when I was about 5 or 6 playing with Patrick in the backyard. She spanked me and carried me into my room—still with my pants down—while my brother and sister laughed. From that point on, I knew I had to keep my desires to myself.

When I was 13 my family and I went camping. Mom started talking about a friend of mine being in the girl-crazy stage. Then she said my friend's dad thought I was gay because I was such a little sissy. I was embarrassed and frightened. How could they know! I said something to

---

* Psychiatrists diagnose homosexuality as a problem only if it's a problem for the homosexual individual. However, my experience has been that even the most well-adjusted, happy homosexual endures an early discovery period that includes actual or perceived alienation, concern about parental and societal response, and an anticipation of ridicule. The most common response to these experiences is shame.

cover like, "Well, my friend is just trying to get girls to impress me!" I was not even sure what I meant. I realized that I should just say nothing, rather than risk saying the wrong thing!

Michael is a "runner," whose defenses of Self-contempt and Shame only serve to support his Withdrawal (which shows up in silence), his Withholding (which shows up in isolation and emotional unavailability), and his extensive Fantasy life (which reveals itself in his excessive involvement with pornography). He really believes that hiding out is the best defense against a cruel, judgmental world. His private thoughts are, "Life is tough and then you die," "Keep it to yourself," and "At least on the Internet, I do what I want when I want to do it." His unconscious driving ideas are: "It's better to say nothing rather than to risk a mistake. Being gay is shameful."

The RELATIONSHIP Theme

Relationship: In Society

Why most people falter or fail in their relationships is hardly a mystery. We need simply to notice our own circumstances: the negative, confusing messages we got early in life, the way we form our connections today, and where we learned the rules we follow—if indeed we follow any in the first place. And what about role models? Since role models often include scuzzy politicians and flagrant movie stars as well as terrible family examples, it's amazing that anyone is able to have halfway decent relationships at all.

Society's standards for relationship often depend on which side we choose, are born on, or are indoctrinated into. On one extreme, we are pummeled with family-values teachings (relationships must support "tradition," whatever that is; it includes no premarital sex, sex for procreation only, no abortion, and Mom must always be at home, etc.). The other extreme, which tends to have little regard for tradition, often cynically recommends that we trash convention and make our own rules (marriage is just a piece of paper—don't bother; people aren't meant to live monogamously; so-called family values are a plot to keep women down, etc.). The majority of us are somewhere in between, attempting to blend the best of traditional social values with innovative approaches that are worthwhile and useful.

Relationship: Personally

Most people quickly discover that creating functional, supportive, healthy relationships is an arduous process. Why is that so?

First, we often find little or no guidance in society about how to have a good relationship, so we're left to our own devices to create satisfactory ways of being with others. In effect, we are charged with inventing a cultural model on our own.

Second, we tend to follow in the clumsy footsteps of family credos that include everything from "relationships never work" or "relationships are just something you must have [like a car!] to get around" to "there is a perfectly right prince/princess who will inevitably come to you." So we become negatively predisposed and unenthusiastic, or we live in an unrealistic fantasy world that promises the moon and the stars but frequently brings just darkness and disappointment.

Relationship brings you face-to-face with yourself!

Third, most relationships, particularly intimate relationships, are inherently difficult because our natural urge to heal our problems keeps drawing us to people who bring with them exactly the problems we most need to face—and least enjoy. Usually these are also the very problems about which we have the least information when it comes to how to do things differently.

Luckily, a number of teachers are now offering examples of healthy relationships (for example, John Gray in *Men Are from Mars, Women Are from Venus* and Thomas Moore in *Soul Mates*), but such good advice is often counteracted by showmen like Jerry Springer and books like *The Rules*, which stamp relationship with either the mark of vileness and violence or paint it in the pretty colors of a simplistically played game.

Relationship: Its Fears

Fear of real relationship results in *a hesitation to commit* or *an inappropriate rush to commitment*.

Relationship: Its Symptoms

The symptoms of *hesitation to commit* include excessive criticism of partners, reluctance to progress to a new stage of relationship, and a feeling that the grass is always greener on the other side of the street.

The symptoms of a *rush to commitment*, though not as easy to recognize and understand as the symptoms of a hesitation to commit, are equally indicative of our fear to have relationship—and just as common. They include an extensive fantasy life, over-eagerness to proclaim affection, excessive anxiety about outcomes, and a tendency, initially, to put the partner on a pedestal, only—inevitably—to move to disappointment (about the partner's imperfection), followed by criticism, punishment, and rejection.

Relationship: Private Thoughts

Thoughts accompanying the hesitation to commit are, "I just don't want to make a mistake. I need to be sure. I'm not ready to settle down. How do I know that he [she] is the right one for me? What if there's someone better out there for me?"

The thoughts that often accompany the rush to commitment are, "He's *it!* She's the *one* I've been waiting for! Better strike while the iron is hot. This is perfect. He's the man of my dreams. I'm in love! Why wait?"

Relationship Story #1. Karla: Alone in the Dark (full details on page 59). Because of her nature, Karla, as a "runner," turned inward. She clings anxiously to her memories of how her mother had more important things to do, didn't rescue her, and didn't listen. By maintaining her sense of aloneness, Karla stays stuck in her original story. She does so through the defenses of Isolation (privately thinking, "No one hears me"), by Comparing herself to others (privately thinking, "Other people are more important than me"), and by staying silent instead of communicating her needs, wants, and feelings (privately thinking, "I have no hope, so why should I bother asking for things I'll never get?"). Further, she's married to a man who speaks very little (and never about his feelings). Even with her close friends she's hesitant to speak up for herself.

Relationship Story #2. Tommy: The Taunting (full details page 137). Tommy is a "runner" who disconnects primarily through Shame and Withdrawal. He believes he's (Terminally) Unique and that the differences that make him "unique" mean something's wrong with him—although he's not sure what that is. Tommy believes success would bring visibility, which would mean attack from others, so he chooses to sabotage his potential for success (through procrastination and depression). He stays stuck in his original story by remaining as quietly invisible as possible. His private thoughts are, "No one wants to hear what I have to say. I'm different and I don't fit in. If people could see how mad I am, they'd hate me even more."

CHAPTER 6

A NEW VIEW

Identifying patterns

By now in your journey, you have remembered your early stories, traced your defensive reactions to those stories, and learned to recognize the present-day repercussions of the thinking, feeling, and behavior that developed as a result of your defensive reactions. In other words, you've begun to identify the patterns that keep you stuck.

Still, many people are tempted to get bogged down in remembered circumstances and in the question *Why?* It goes on and on. *Why* did my father beat me? . . . *Why* was I molested and exactly who did what when? . . . *Why* am I morbidly obese? . . . *Why* am I afraid of intimacy? However—*stop getting bogged down by those questions!* Not only will any answers you figure out not relieve you of feeling the effects of those early-life experiences, but every time you pose those questions, you also divert your attention from more helpful, useful concerns. The questions to focus on now are: *When* did your patterns begin? *How* did you

Don't get bogged down by *why* questions

Focus on:
When
How
What
Where

perpetuate those patterns? *What* can you do differently now? And *where* are you headed?

Step-by-step ways in which you can confront your old ideas and then establish new behaviors that will actually *change your life* are clearly developed in the companion to this book, the *Stuck No More Workbook*. You're able to go on now because you know that the way things *were* is not the way they *must* be, and because you have come to realize that you don't need to stay stuck in your stories—not at home, not at work, not at play. Work the fifteen "Defense Busting" steps and eventually you can and will see that, incidents of childhood notwithstanding, nearly everything that happens in your life now, or at least how you *react* to nearly everything that happens in your life now, is up to *you*. Release yourself from outdated perspectives. Take your life back. You have the power.

"To Change Or Not To Change... That Is The Question!"

Step 15 in defense busting:
Realize that change is a matter of choice.

At the end

I have included various tales from my personal life to let you, the reader, know that I understand these struggles—not only as a professional but also as a person who has needed to free herself from a lifetime of stuckness. I will end as I began—with a mother story—this time a story of resolution and hope.

Forty-nine years went by. Mother and I had gone at it from the East Coast to the West Coast—in restaurants and apartments, in person and on the phone, with vehemence and with restraint. In fact, over the years I had tried everything to change her . . . *to get her to see what she had done to me!* I had shouted, insisted, begged, blamed, accused, analyzed, and forgiven—then recanted the forgiveness. Over and over I had reminded her about the lonely hotel rooms of my childhood; the eleven years of boarding school with their accompanying feelings of abandonment; the drunken years; the verbal violence; the lost father; the critical, emotionally incestuous stepfather; and the neglect. Never in all that time had my mother budged an inch from her survival-of-the-fittest position or from her convenient "Oh, things weren't that bad!" revisionist memory.

Then one day after yet another three-year silence between us, I heard through the family grapevine that Mom was experiencing heart trouble and I called to inquire after her health. She told me she was fine, spoke of an intended upcoming trip to California where I live, and wondered if I would be willing to have dinner with her. I said yes.

By then I had attended to understanding my personal (mother/father/child) kinships for many years. I had wept, prayed, written, analyzed, ritualized, re-membered, and re-viewed. Finally, I had ceased focusing on what my parents did to me and started paying attention both to the impact of my experiences and to my reactions to events past and present. At last I stopped trying to change my mother and concentrated on changing myself.

I was amazingly unperturbed as I drove to my aunt's house to retrieve my mother—my seventy-four-year-old mother—after the long, dry lifetime of my discontent. That night, for the first time in memory and for reasons unknown to me, Mother did not drink. I was interested and honored.

When she spoke, however, I realized that little else had changed. As usual, she chattered on self-centeredly about her business, who she was currently suing, and how her sex life was going. During this dinner I noticed how amusing I found even her most noxious meanderings to be. I was fascinated to observe the way comments that would ordinarily have infuriated me bothered me not at all. And I recognized that for the first time in my life I was truly free of the desire to inform, fix, or change my mother!

This news washed over me like a welcome shower after a blazing heat wave. I felt exhilarated, relieved, and nourished. And in that moment I knew absolutely that a thorough, profound, and lasting shift had occurred within me. I was done with my mother dance!

Our conversation went on for about an hour, while I made no attempt to share what could not be received. When it was over, we stood up and I put my arm around her shoulders as we left the restaurant.

Then outside, a most astonishing thing happened. Suddenly and without either warning or explanation, my mother nuzzled her head in the crook of my neck and whimpered a high-pitched series of soft little cries, like a young pup. Time stood still as a wave of sweet gratitude went through me. It was the dearest moment my mother and I had *ever* shared.

The mother story was ended . . .

. . . and so was my stuckness.

Appendix
FIFTEEN STEPS IN DEFENSE BUSTING

Step 1

Identify the childhood patterns that still color your life.

Step 2

Recognize and appreciate your own particular, natural style.

Step 3

Understand that what you have is what you (unconsciously) want.

Step 4

Realize that *all* behavior has a payoff.

Step 5

Realize that feeling safe is an inside job.

Step 6

Notice the way yesterday's ideas are affecting today's happiness.

Step 7

Realize that the *defense itself* is not the actual problem. The actual problem is that you have made an *inner connection* between the defense and the pain-filled fears that originally called the defense into play.

Step 8

Uncover the basic *stories* in which you are stuck. To do this, look at your relationship with your father, with your mother, and with yourself as a child.

Step 9

Realize: the bigger your reaction, the older the memory inspiring that reaction.

Step 10

Dig deep. Figure out which defenses you use most, recognize the origin of the defenses, and notice how they are now appearing in your life.

Step 11

Are you chained to old ideas? Wrapped up in false self-concepts? Discover the specific ways you keep yourself attached to the past.

Step 12

Take the work of growth and discovery seriously, and take yourself lightly!

Step 13

Realize that all conscious feeling and thinking themes are inevitably balanced by equal and opposite *unconscious* feeling and thinking themes. Look for the opposites in yourself

Step 14

Notice how expectation leads to manifestation. In other words, what you expect, you get. So if you're watching every step you take because you expect to fall—you can expect to fall!

Step 15

Realize that change is a matter of choice.

AN INVITATION FROM THE AUTHOR

The forty-one defenses at the core of *Stuck in the Story No More* offer a thorough look at some common psychological protections. But I have no illusions that this list is exhaustive or that it includes every possible defense. I no doubt missed a few. Perhaps I was not alert to certain issues that are very familiar to particular individuals or groups of readers. Or maybe new types and variations of defenses will show up in the psychological whirlwind of modern life. Who knows?

For these reason, I invite you, my readers, to send me brief written summaries of any defenses you believe deserve to be added to my list of forty-one and included in a future edition of this book.

Please keep in mind that determining whether a certain pattern of thinking, feeling, or doing is an actual defense is sometimes tricky. For instance, what seems like a separate defense often turns out to be best understood as a subset of another defense. (People-pleasing is clearly a defense, but it's actually part of the larger defense of Codependency.)

I thank you in advance, and I ask that you address your correspondence to:

Dr. Nicki J. Monti
269 South Beverly Drive, Suite 430
Beverly Hills, CA 90212